"From the beginnings of our Order, Cistercian monks and nuns have expressed their desire for—and sometimes their insistence on—seeing God in the here and now *'sicuti est'* ('as he is,' 1 Jn 3:2), and none more than Bernard of Clairvaux. In this clear and illuminating study, Slater demonstrates to what extent Bernard considered this contemplative knowledge possible in this life, to what extent he accepted it as impossible, and how, by the transformation of desire, men and women could be brought closer to the impossible. Reading Slater's book, we are renewed in the willingness to allow the Word to work on who we are interiorly in the unrelinquishable hope of coming to knowing him for who he is."

— Bernard Bonowitz, OCSO, author of
*Saint Bernard's Three-Course Banquet:
Humility, Charity and Contemplation in the* De Gradibus

"Slater's innovative work is unique in taking into account both the theological as well as the artistic dimensions of Bernard's writings. Attending to Bernard's insights into the role of the imagination and desire in spiritual transformation, *Beyond Measure* resonates with current concern about the true self and an accurate perception of the world and shows how the divine works through distortions and turns all things to good. It sheds new light on topics such as art, experience, and freedom in Bernard's corpus."

— Raymond Studzinski, OSB
The Catholic University of America

CISTERCIAN STUDIES SERIES:
NUMBER TWO HUNDRED SEVENTY-NINE

# Beyond Measure

The Poetics of the Image in
Bernard of Clairvaux

*Isaac Slater, OCSO*

## α

Cistercian Publications
www.cistercianpublications.org

**LITURGICAL PRESS**
Collegeville, Minnesota
www.litpress.org

A Cistercian Publications title published by Liturgical Press

**Cistercian Publications**
Editorial Offices
161 Grosvenor Street
Athens, Ohio 45701
www.cistercianpublications.org

Biblical citations are based for the most part on New Revised Standard Version Bible © 1989 National Council of the Churches of Christ in the United States of America; and on the ESV® Bible (The Holy Bible, English Standard Version® © 2001 by Crossway, a publishing ministry of Good News Publishers). All rights reserved.

© 2020 by Isaac Slater, OCSO
Published by Liturgical Press, Collegeville, Minnesota. All rights reserved. No part of this book may be used or reproduced in any manner whatsoever, except brief quotations in reviews, without written permission of Liturgical Press, Saint John's Abbey, PO Box 7500, Collegeville, MN 56321-7500. Printed in the United States of America.

**Library of Congress Cataloging-in-Publication Data**

Names: Slater, Isaac, 1974– author.
Title: Beyond measure : the poetics of the image in Bernard of Clairvaux / Isaac Slater, OCSO.
Description: Collegeville : Cistercian Publications, 2020. | Series: Cistercian studies series; number two hundred seventy-nine | Includes bibliographical references. | Summary: "A study of the literary, philosophical, and theological strands densely interwoven through the writings of Bernard of Clairvaux. His apparent iconoclasm with respect to art, affectivity, and the humanity of Jesus is revealed as an alternative mystical aesthetic, congruent with his program for monastic reform"— Provided by publisher.
Identifiers: LCCN 2019034044 (print) | LCCN 2019034045 (ebook) | ISBN 9780879072797 (paperback) | ISBN 9780879071790 (pdf) | ISBN 9780879071790 (epub) | ISBN 9780879071790 (mobi)
Subjects: LCSH: Bernard, of Clairvaux, Saint, 1090 or 1091–1153.
Classification: LCC BX4700.B5 S53 2020 (print) | LCC BX4700.B5 (ebook) | DDC 230/.2092—dc23
LC record available at https://lccn.loc.gov/2019034044
LC ebook record available at https://lccn.loc.gov/2019034045

*To my father with gratitude: for kindling in me both the love of learning and the desire for God.*

# Contents

Acknowledgments ix

Abbreviations xi

Introduction 1

Chapter 1     In the Image    7

Chapter 2     Real Shadows    20

Chapter 3     Beyond Measure: The Human Imagination of God    38

Chapter 4     *Amor Carnalis*    61

Chapter 5     "Black but Beautiful": Bernard's Incarnational Poetics    83

Chapter 6     The Poetics of *Apology*    98

Chapter 7     "Mysticism Turned Inside Out": Julia Kristeva on Bernard of Clairvaux    124

Chapter 8     "Love Itself Is Knowledge": Jean-Luc Marion and Bernard of Clairvaux    156

Appendix 1    187

Appendix 2    204

Appendix 3    210

Bibliography    213

Scripture Index 224

Author Index 225

Subject Index 227

# Acknowledgments

Earlier versions of two of this book's chapters appeared as articles:

" 'Mysticism Turned Inside Out': Julia Kristeva on Bernard of Clairvaux." *Cistercian Studies Quarterly* 46, no. 2 (May 2011): 143–70.

"The Poetics of Bernard's Apology." *Cîteaux: Commentarii cistercienses* 64, nos. 1–2 (2013): 245–63.

---

Jean-Luc Marion, *The Idol and Distance: Five Studies* © Fordham University Press, 2001, via Copyright Clearance Center.

Jean-Luc Marion, *Le phénomène érotique* © Editions Grasset & Fasquelle, 2003.

Paul Mommaers, *The Riddle of Christian Mystical Experience: The Role of the Humanity of Jesus*, Louvain Theological and Pastoral Monographs no. 29 © Peeters Press, 2003.

---

Quotations from translated works of Bernard of Clairvaux used by permission of Liturgical Press, Collegeville, Minnesota.

# Abbreviations

| | |
|---|---|
| ABR | *American Benedictine Review* |
| ASOC | *Analecta Sacri Ordinis Cisterciensis / Analecta Cisterciensia.* Rome, 1945– . |
| CF | Cistercian Fathers series. Spencer, MA; Washington, DC; Kalamazoo: Cistercian, 1970– . |
| Cîteaux | *Cîteaux: Commentarii cistercienses; Cîteaux in de Nederlanden* |
| Coll | *Collectanea Cisterciensia* |
| CS | Cistercian Studies series. Spencer, MA; Washington, DC; Kalamazoo: Cistercian, 1966– . |
| CSQ | *Cistercian Studies Quarterly; Cistercian Studies* (periodical) |
| RBen | *Revue bénédictine.* Maredsous, Belgium, 1884– . |
| SBOp | Sancti Bernardi opera. Ed. J. Leclercq, H. M. Rochais, C. H. Talbot. Rome: Cistercienses, 1957–1977. |
| SCh | Sources chrétiennes series. Paris: Les Éditions du Cerf, 1941– . |
| Spec car | Aelred of Rievaulx, *Speculum caritatis.* |
| TS | *Theological Studies.* New York; Woodstock, MD; Baltimore, 1940– . |

## Works of Bernard

| | |
|---|---|
| Apo | *Apologia ad Guillelmum abbatem* |
| Asc | Sermo in ascensione domini |

| | |
|---|---|
| Conv | Sermo de conversione ad clericos |
| Csi | *De consideratione* |
| Ded | Sermo in dedicatione ecclesiæ |
| Dil | *Liber de diligendo Deo* |
| Div | Sermo de diversis |
| Gra | *Liber de gratia et libero arbitrio* |
| Hum | *Liber de gradibus humilitatis et superbiæ* |
| Nat | Sermo in nativitate domini |
| Nat BVM | Sermo in nativitate B.V.M. |
| 1 Nov | Sermo in dominica I novembris |
| OS | Sermo in festivitate omnium sanctorum |
| Par | *Parabolæ* |
| Pent | Sermo in die sancto pentecostes |
| QH | Sermo super psalmum "Qui habitat": SBOp 4 (1966), 458–62 |
| SC | *Sermo super Cantica canticorum* |
| Sent | *Sententiae* |

# Introduction

This study began with my surprise at how often Bernard stressed the way the quality of a person's desire limits and colors his or her imagination of God.[1] That Bernard should employ this basic idea is not surprising: it was ubiquitous in the classical and medieval world, from Plato through Origen and onward. Truth and goodness were considered to be co-inherent. Only the virtuous person was disposed to perceive truth. In Christian language, only the pure of heart see God. Likewise, in the monastic tradition John Cassian began his *Conferences* by arguing that monastic ascesis ought to focus on cultivating purity of heart in order that a monk might receive the free gift of contemplation. Tracking the different articulations of this classical idea in Bernard, I began to advert to the various ways he modified and adapted it in different settings, towards different rhetorical ends. Often the notion was accompanied by a particular cluster of scriptural texts, associated ideas, and images that he subtly adjusted and refined across a range of contexts.

One measure of how important it was to Bernard to stress that the quality of desire shapes knowledge is the fact that he

---

[1] Later I was confirmed in this perception when I came across a similar observation by Jacques Blanpain: *"Il est frappant de constater que Bernard est très conscient du fait que notre conception de Dieu naît de nos désirs et de nos dispositions et aspirations"* ("It is striking to note that Bernard is keenly aware of how our conception of God is born from our desires, from our attitudes and aspirations.") (Jacques Blanpain, "Langage mystique, expression du désir," *Collectanea Cisterciensia* 36, no. 1 [1974]: 56).

began his masterpiece *On the Song of Songs* by underlining this very point. He entices readers who overhear his imagined discourse to an elite in-group of cloistered monks with the promise of "solid food" instead of milk.[2] He portrays different books of the Bible as suitable for different levels of attainment in the spiritual life, with the Song of Songs at the summit: its inner meaning is available only to those with personal experience, or at least with the ardent desire for such experience.[3]

Tracking the different ways Bernard made use of this notion brought to light connections among multiple key strands in his thought, all centering on his understanding of mediation: how revelation is mediated to humanity by the incarnation of the Word, and how the humanity of Jesus, along with other created realities, is perceived differently by human beings depending on their own degree of likeness to him. Bernard's alleged iconoclasm with regard to art, the body, creation, his attitudes toward affectivity, the humanity of Jesus, and the interpretation of Scripture becomes clear with the recognition that he presents all of these realities as ambiguous not because they are in themselves suspect but because human desire, which is in fact ambiguous, mediates their perception.

In the Coda to his study of Plato's *Republic*, D. S. Schindler describes a dynamic closely akin to what we find in Bernard. Commenting on the seeming contradiction of Plato's disparaging literary forms and images while making expert use of them, Schindler reads the famous allegory of the cave to mean that images mean one thing to philosophers and another to those who have never seen the sun. When one has throughout one's life taken flickering shadows on a stone wall for reality, the

---

[2] Bernard, SC 1.1 (SBOp 1:3; *On the Song of Songs I*, trans. Kilian Walsh, CF 4 [Kalamazoo, MI: Cistercian Publications, 1971], 1). Citations to Bernard's works here and below refer to the critical editions and translations listed in the Table of Abbreviations. I follow the translations as cited, with occasional minor adjustments.

[3] Bernard, SC 1.2, 11 (SBOp 1:3, 7; CF 4:1, 6).

shadows are opaque, objects of idolatrous attachment. But the philosopher who has known the sun on her face and seen the realities of which the images are merely shadows can see the images as transparent; she can make use of them to steer others toward the light.[4] Bernard's attitude towards "images" (the humanity of Jesus, art, affectivity, creation, Scripture) is much the same. At a certain point the opaque becomes transparent, the idol becomes an icon—not because of any change in the perceived but because of a change in the perceiver.

Bernard and other Cistercian writers like William of Saint-Thierry and Aelred of Rievaulx describe such a pivotal moment in the spiritual life, often in terms of a movement from the carnal to the spiritual. The various arrangements of steps Bernard describes in the spiritual life frequently have the same basic structure: after an initial, highly emotive, consolation-based attachment to the humanity of Jesus, a person moves to a more rational, less heated phase characterized by zeal for virtue. A third stage sees the recapitulation of affectivity, made spiritual and transparent by the grace of mystical contact. The spiritual level lights up everything on the plane of the soul (*psyche*) in such a way that what could once have been an idol has become an icon. A taste of the divine radically relativizes all lesser realities, setting them free to reach their fullest meaning. In a striking passage, Bernard places on the lips of such a person the words of Jesus: "When I am lifted up from the earth, I shall draw all things to myself."[5] So he shows that the recapitulation that occurs on a cosmic scale in Christ the Image is replicated in the lives of human beings "in the Image."

One of the rewards of material renunciation, Bernard says, is to receive the gift of right relation to all things. Of those who

---

[4] D. S. Schindler, *Plato's Critique of Impure Reason: On Goodness and Truth in the* Republic (Washington, DC: Catholic University of America, 2008).

[5] Bernard, SC 21.7 (SBOp 1:126; Bernard of Clairvaux, *Sermons on the Song of Songs II*, trans. Irene Edmonds, CF 7 [Kalamazoo, MI: Cistercian Publications, 1979], 9).

practice such renunciation he writes, "They do possess earthly things, but with the spirit of men who possess nothing; in reality they possess all things, not like unhappy beggars who get what they beg for, but as masters, masters in the best sense because devoid of avarice. To the man of faith the whole world is a treasure-house of riches: the whole world, because all things, whether adverse or favorable, are of service to him; they all contribute to his good."[6]

Bernard shows creation as intrinsically good, at the level of being. But he speaks from the perspective of desire and experience, where created realities appear ambiguous because desire is ambiguous. Frequently confusion arises when these levels are confused, and a reader may take Bernard to be speaking categorically about the intrinsic worth of one or another reality when in fact he is speaking about the way it is experienced. Likewise Bernard addresses an audience composed of hearers or readers at different stages in the spiritual journey and at times modulates his presentation accordingly, trying somehow to reach them all at once. Bernard's creative appropriation of Origen, for instance, makes a metaphysical model into a kind of poetic hermeneutics. More radically, it may be that for Bernard being itself is figural, and that metaphysics and poetics are one. Then the whole creation, bearing traces of the Word, the Image of the invisible, is not a static, conceptual reality best captured by the language of classical metaphysics, but divine rhetoric, a sacred text whose inner meaning lies open only to lovers, since in this view "love itself is knowledge."

So Bernard not only returns frequently to the classical idea that virtue and right desire are requisite to knowing truth—he develops and applies this idea in multiple ways. Adapting a medieval epitaph, Henri de Lubac once aptly described Bernard as not only the last of the fathers but also "the first of the great

---

[6] Bernard, SC 21.7 (SBOp 1:126; CF 7:9).

moderns."[7] His writings uniquely and exquisitely balance intense spirituality and the longing for heaven with a keen sensitivity for experience, an awareness of the Word beyond thought and images and the dignity and goodness of the human Jesus. This balance can be seen in the way he adapts classical epistemology, underlining the role of the self, experience, affectivity, and freedom in ways that have made him attractive to several important contemporary thinkers from Maurice Blondel, at the end of the nineteenth century, through the recent work of Emmanuel Falque. In fact, modernity and the advent of critical thought are characterized by a heightened perception of the very thing Bernard so emphasized: the status of the viewer shapes what is seen. In perspectives beyond those available to Bernard, contemporary thought has taken account of the ways class, gender, race, and a range of social, psychological, and historical factors shape how an individual sees the world. Even the hard sciences report the phenomenon of observer interference.

Along with modern sensitivity to ways that social programming limits and colors perceptions comes anxiety about whether one can really know another, any other, as he or she is, without reducing them to one's own horizon. While Bernard lacked the critical distance of modern thought, he stressed the way that at a deeper level, right desire and the practice of virtue open the way to a more accurate perception of other persons and especially of God in his otherness. That is, he recognized a mechanism akin to what we speak of today as projection, but he held that the images one generates can be more or less accurate, that it is possible to reach an other on the far side of images that become more transparent as a person's own likeness to God increases. Such images can be recognized as images, not as God as he is in himself. At the same time they can serve to educate right desire towards real contact with a reality

---

[7] Henri de Lubac, *Medieval Exegesis, Vol. 2: The Four Senses of Scripture*, trans. E. M. Macierowski (Grand Rapids, MI: Eerdmans, 2000), 153.

beyond what can be imagined. For Bernard it is freedom that constitutes the likeness between God and human beings, a freedom realized most perfectly in love. Love alone provides a way to know something of another in that person's otherness. Love, that is, freedom, cast toward the far horizon of the divine Other makes created realities appear in right perspective.

A fresh look at how Bernard understands mediation lights up every major facet of his thought: his theology, his Christology, including the vexed questions around the humanity of Jesus, and his anthropology; his understanding of freedom, affectivity, the nature of the self, and the relation of these concepts to exegesis, as well as his account of the move from the carnal to the spiritual and its implications for what Luke Anderson has described as Bernard's "rhetorical epistemology."[8] Bernard's sensitivity to the manner in which "love itself is knowledge" holds an important insight for contemporary thought in its struggle to know others without reducing them to the familiar. His description of deep, instinctive affectivity recapitulated on the far side of the struggle for virtue restores a place for religious feeling beyond the merely sentimental. Bernard also provides a way to see union with God in heaven not as a betrayal of life in time but its culmination.

---

[8] Luke Anderson, "The Rhetorical Epistemology in Saint Bernard's *Super Cantica*," in *Bernardus Magister: Papers Celebrating the Nonacentenary of the Birth of Bernard of Clairvaux*, ed. John R. Sommerfeldt, CS 135 (Kalamazoo, MI: Cistercian Publications, 1992), 95–128.

## 1. In the Image

In his works Bernard develops a distinction made by Augustine between two ways of speaking about God. He makes certain statements of God as he is ("God is unchanging"), while others pertain to God in relation to his creatures ("The Lord is my shepherd"). He distinguishes between the language of revelation, the doctrinal formulations carefully carved out by tradition through the centuries, and the more fluid and imaginative, metaphorical language of God as encountered in the world of human experience.[1] God is his attributes, while human beings simply share in them. The Son of God is the *imago dei*, while his human nature and the nature of every human being is in the image, *ad imaginem*. By his incarnation the Son bridges the two spheres and makes it possible for images in the shifting realm of human experience effectively to signify divine realities. The transparency or opacity of such images as creation and figures in Scripture depends on the degree to which people have realized their own likeness to the image.

The fields of faith and experience are hardly airtight, however. They overlap and interpenetrate. People may find that they have faith in what is beyond experience, and that their

---

[1] As Kilian McDonnell explains, "Faith gives birth to experience; faith norms experience. But experience gives another dimension of actuality and firmness to faith. Experience is another way of knowing. What is given to experience is not taken away from faith, because experience exists only in faith" ("Spirit and Experience in Bernard of Clairvaux," *Theological Studies* 58 [1997]: 16).

faith is alternately challenged and supported by what they experience. Truths revealed by God once for all are sifted and assimilated in human terms through the centuries by tradition. In this way truths like the triunity of God or the hypostatic union come to be clarified. Bernard is not inclined to innovate at this level of theological discourse. Instead he is concerned with the human experience of the divine in the ups and downs of spiritual life, the encounter with God not "as he is"—which apart from the signposts provided by dogma cannot be known in this life—but as he appears.

While God *is* his attributes—he is unchanging, for instance—he is *like* a teacher, a bridegroom, a warrior. The notion that the quality of one's desire colors one's imagination of God pertains to this second kind of language. Desire would seem to affect the first kind of language as well, however: one can relate to a dogmatic truth ideologically and restrict its resonance. Bernard himself, having distinguished two ways of speaking about God, appears deliberately to merge and confuse them. There remains for him a way of relating to language by right desire, which allows it to become transparent to what is beyond language, and he cultivates this desire.

## *De Trinitate*

Augustine begins Book V of *De Trinitate* by stating that God is Being and that what distinguishes the Being of God is that he alone is unchanging: "The substance or being that is God is alone unchangeable, and therefore it pertains to it most truly and supremely to be, from which comes the name 'being.' . . . only that which not only does not but also absolutely cannot change deserves without qualification to be said really and truly to be."[2]

---

[2] Sancti Aurelii Augustini, *De Trinitate*, Libri I–XII, ed. W. J. Mountain, Series Latina Libri XV (Turnhout: Brepols, 1968), 5.1.3; Augustine of Hippo, *The Trinity (De Trinitate)*, trans. Edmund Hill (New York: New City Press, 1991), 190.

Augustine observes that certain things are said of God as "substance" and others with respect to one of the three persons: the Son is so called only in relation to the Father and vice versa. Whatever is attributed to God is said of his being in the singular ("God is great") as well as of each of the three persons ("The Father is great, the Son is great, the Spirit is great").[3] God is his attributes: "As it is not one thing for God to be and another for him to be great, but being is for him the same as being great, for that reason we do not say three greatnesses any more than we say three beings, but one being and one greatness."[4] God does not, like creatures, "participate" in qualities like greatness; rather, "he is great with a greatness by which he is himself this same greatness . . . he is his own greatness."[5] This principle applies to "absolutely all" that can be predicated of God, Augustine says, "because it is all said with reference to himself, and not metaphorically or in simile but properly."[6]

Immediately after this, at the outset of Chapter 3, Augustine notes that what can be said of each of the persons uniquely (for example, the Son is "begotten") is said "with reference to each other or to creation," by relationship, not substance. Augustine mentions in passing that the being of God (as opposed to the first person of the Trinity) could not be called Father "except perhaps metaphorically" insofar as the triune God creates humanity and regenerates it by grace.[7] Later he uses the example of a coin that remains substantially the same whatever changing values are assigned to it. Theological language that speaks of God with reference to creation likewise implies no change in his being but rather in that of the creature. Nothing new occurs in God when human beings become his "offspring," but rather they are themselves changed, and related

---

[3] Augustine, *The Trinity*, 5.2.9 (Hill, trans., *The Trinity*, 195).
[4] Augustine, *De Trinitate* 5.2.9 (Hill, trans., *The Trinity*, 195–96).
[5] Augustine, *De Trinitate* 5.2.10 (Hill, trans., *The Trinity*, 196).
[6] Augustine, *De Trinitate* 5.2.10 (Hill, trans., *The Trinity*, 196).
[7] Augustine, *De Trinitate* 5.3.12 (Hill, trans., *The Trinity*, 197). Some metaphors are excluded; there is no accurate metaphorical sense in which, for example, the divine nature could be spoken of as humanity's "Son."

to God in a new way. Scripture and tradition speak of God in this way that he may be "grasped by human feeling": "So too when he is said to be angry with the wicked and pleased with the good, they change, not he; just as light is harsh to weak eyes, pleasant to strong; but it is the eyes, not the light, that change."[8]

The language of Father, Son, and Spirit, while in one sense metaphorical and a concession to the weakness of human understanding, designates the relations between the persons within the Trinity, relations that do not change, rather than relations between human beings and God. In regard to human beings, however, the field is open for a variety of metaphors. Here the vast array of images from Scripture (God as rock, mother, helper, teacher, lord, and so on) comes into play. It is principally at this level that the soul's spiritual state affects the way one imagines God.

Bernard employs Augustine's conception of unchanging being at the beginning of his Sermon 31 on the Song of Songs: "That alone truly is, which is neither altered from its past mode of being nor blotted out by a future mode, but 'is' alone is predicated of it impregnably and unchangeably, and it remains what it is." This statement introduces a comparison of two kinds of "vision" of God: the unchanging vision of God in heaven, and the experiences of God enjoyed in this present life, where the Word "often makes himself known under more than one form."[9] The sermon returns like a refrain to the idea that in this life God is encountered in the mode in which he chooses to present himself, not as he is (*non sicuti est*). Bernard appears to be directly following Augustine's text. For instance, he uses the same example of the attribute "greatness" in his

---

[8] Augustine, *De Trinitate* 5.4.17 (Hill, trans., *The Trinity*, 201).
[9] Bernard, SC 31.1 (*Sermones super Cantica Canticorum* 1–35, ed. Jean Leclercq et al., SBOp 1 [Rome: Editiones Cistercienses, 1957], 219; Bernard of Clairvaux, *On the Song of Songs II*, trans. Kilian Walsh, CF 7 [Kalamazoo, MI: Cistercian Publications, 1976], 124). This thought is developed in chapter 2 below.

discussion of the likeness and unlikeness of human being and God. He also employs and develops Augustine's image of the eye and light. He explains that people see not the sun itself but the sun as it lights the air and reflects off surfaces; they see it by means of the eye, which bears a likeness to that which it beholds: "Even the eye itself, when troubled, cannot approach the light, because it has lost that likeness. Just as the troubled eye, then, cannot gaze on the peaceful sun because of its unlikeness, so the peaceful eye can behold it with some efficacy because of a certain likeness. If indeed it were wholly equal to it in purity, with a completely clear vision, it would see it *as it is*, because of the complete likeness."[10] So in heaven Bernard anticipates a folding together of being and experience.

### The Kiss: SC 8

Bernard gives particular attention to the likeness between the human soul and the divine Word in Sermon 8, and he revisits the theme twenty years later in Sermon 80 *On the Song of Songs*. Both the trinitarian framing of this material and the distinction between metaphorical and ontological ways to speak of God are creative developments of ideas drawn from Augustine. In the course of commenting on the first verse of the Song of Songs, "Let him kiss me with the kiss of his mouth," Bernard distinguishes the kiss of the mouth from a direct kiss mouth to mouth. The mediated kiss, the kiss of the mouth, is that enjoyed by human beings in mystical experience, whereas the more direct experience is that enjoyed by the Father and Son alone. Citing Matthew 11:27, "No one knows the Son except the Father," Bernard explains that unique relationship: "For the Father loves the Son whom he embraces with a love

---

[10] Bernard, SC 31.2 (SBOp 1:220; CF 14:126). See Augustine, *De Doctrina Christiana* 2.9, for a related use of the eye image.

that is unique; he who is infinite embraces his equal, who is eternal, his co-eternal, the sole God, his only-begotten."[11]

While the human, mystical experience of the kiss is a theme, he says, that is "sweet to the spirit above all other," "rare" and "difficult to understand," Bernard finds it expedient to delineate the sphere of the intimacy enjoyed by the Son alone, "a kiss past comprehension, beyond the experience of any mere creature." The mutual love between the Father and the Son is "a kiss that is utterly sweet but utterly a mystery as well."[12] He goes on: "If, as is properly understood, the Father is he who kisses, the Son he who is kissed, then it cannot be wrong to see in the kiss the Holy Spirit, for he is the imperturbable peace of the Father and the Son, their unshakeable bond, their undivided love, their indivisible unity."[13]

Within the Trinity, the Spirit relays the mutual knowledge and love of the Father and Son. He is the fruit of this mutual exchange, and he brings a gift of both love and knowledge,[14] truth and devotion, to the bride.[15] In this twofold knowledge it cannot be the case that, as some suggested in Bernard's day, the divine attributes lined up with different persons in the Trinity (Father-omnipotence, Son-wisdom, and Spirit-love), for the Father and Son both know and love one another, mutually, and the Spirit communicates not only love but love and knowledge. He is implied in the love-knowledge that human beings can have of the Father and Son: "The Holy Spirit indeed is nothing else but the love and benign goodness of them both."[16]

---

[11] Bernard, SC 8.1 (SBOp 1:36; CF 4:45).
[12] Bernard, SC 8.1 (SBOp 1:36; CF 4:45).
[13] Bernard, SC 8.2 (SBOp 1:37; CF 4:46).
[14] "For the favor of the kiss bears with it a twofold gift, the light of knowledge and the fervor of devotion" (SC 8.8 [SBOp 1:41; CF 4:49]).
[15] Bernard, SC 6.3 (SBOp 1:27; CF 4:50).
[16] Bernard, SC 8.4 (SBOp 1:38; CF 4:47). Bernard speaks in SC 8.5 of a *threefold* knowledge when the bride asks for the kiss.

The Son, Bernard goes on, reveals himself and the Father through the Spirit:[17] "giving, he reveals, and revealing, gives" (*dando revelat et revelando dat*).[18] The gift, again, "not only conveys the light of knowledge but also lights the fire of love."[19] The Father "is never fully known until he is perfectly loved" (*nequaquam plene cognoscitur, nisi cum perfecte diligitur*).[20] For Bernard, pagan philosophers knew God through creation, but their knowledge was imperfect because they did not love. They could perceive something of divine majesty through creation but, in Bernard's judgment, were "content with the knowledge that gives self-importance" and so were unable to appreciate the gentleness and humility of God revealed in the incarnation. Bernard insists here on the likeness between knower and known. Those who seek knowledge for the sake of prestige can see only the God of Power, a real knowledge to some degree but reflecting and distorted by their own desire for honor. To receive the much fuller revelation of himself God makes in his incarnation, they would need, like the God revealed, to be humble.[21] Bernard goes on to counsel his reader to seek God in love rather than curiosity, stating that neither those who have knowledge without love nor those who love without knowledge have received the kiss of the Spirit, a kiss placed on the two lips (reason and will) of the bride.

Elsewhere Bernard uses the image of the kiss not for the unity between the Father and the Son that is the Holy Spirit but for that of the two natures of the Incarnate Word: "The mouth that kisses signifies the Word who assumes human nature; the nature assumed receives the kiss."[22] Bernard depicts

---

[17] Bernard, SC 8.5 (SBOp 1:38; CF 4:47).
[18] Bernard, SC 8.5 (SBOp 1:38; CF 4:47). My translation.
[19] Bernard, SC 8.5 (SBOp 1:39; CF 4:48).
[20] Bernard, SC 8.9 (SBOp 1:41; CF 4:52).
[21] "They in their presumption of spirit—their own spirit, not God's—studied his attributes of sublimity and majesty" (SC 8.5 [SBOp 1:39; CF 4:48]).
[22] Bernard, SC 2.3 (SBOp 1:9–10; CF 4:10).

the Son as the true Image of the Father, an image in all ways equal to its exemplar. The Son receives the kiss as an equal, whereas the Christian "must abide content within the limits of his capacity."[23] For Christ, he says, "the kiss meant a totality, for Paul only a participation."[24] Bernard implies that Paul (whose experience is an example of the heights a human being can attain) was "kissed by the kiss." Human nature, he writes, is *ad imaginem*. The human nature of Christ agrees perfectly with the Image that is the divine nature of the Word. The union of the two natures in Christ in turn sets up the possibility of human beings growing to be more like God, realizing their imagehood: "For what is made in the image should become like the image, and not merely share the empty name of image—as the image [of God] himself is not merely called by the empty name of image."[25]

Although Bernard generally presents mystical contact as between the soul and the Word of God, with God the Word assuming the various guises and appearances (teacher, bridegroom, and so on) suitable to the soul at the different stages in her development, the conclusion of SC 8 is marked by more directly trinitarian mysticism. It fuses the two vocabularies. With the Son the soul is daughter of the Father. In sharing a Father she is sister to the Son, and in sharing his Spirit she is his bride: "For if marriage according to the flesh constitutes two in one body, why should not a spiritual union be even more efficacious in joining two in one spirit?"[26]

---

[23] Bernard, SC 8.8 (SBOp 1:41; CF 4:51).

[24] Bernard, SC 8.8 (SBOp 1:41; CF 4:52).

[25] Bernard, SC 80.2 (SBOp 2:278; Bernard of Clairvaux, *On the Song of Songs IV*, trans. Irene M. Edmonds, CF 40 [Kalamazoo, MI: Cistercian Publications, 1980], 147).

[26] Bernard, SC 8.9 (SBOp 1:41; CF 4:52). For a fine study of the Trinity in Bernard, see Anne Morris, "The Trinity in Bernard's Sermons on the Song of Songs," CSQ 30, no. 1 (1995): 35–50.

## SC 80

When two decades later Bernard revisited the relationship between the Word and the soul, he again sprang from the topic into a discussion of the Trinity. Distinguishing souls made in the Image of God from the Word who is the Image itself, he segues into a critique of views attributed to Gilbert of Poitiers by means of the Augustinian position that God is identical with his attributes. Bernard's poetics, his understanding of how human beings imagine God, is interwoven with his account of how ontologically they are made *ad imaginem*. This anthropological perspective in turn gels with his presentation of the Trinity. Bernard extends the Augustinian insight that God, unlike human beings, is his attributes into a portrayal of the Word as the Image while human beings only share in it. By means of the real affinity human beings have with the Word, and depending on the degree of likeness they have realized ontologically, they imagine God by means of more or less accurate likenesses.

From the outset of Sermon 80 Bernard places the discussion of the likeness between Word and soul in a trinitarian context. He identifies a "natural kinship" between the Image and those made in that image and holds that "their resemblance argues some affinity [*similitude*]."[27] Refining his distinction between *imago* and *ad imaginem*, Bernard accents the dignity of human beings, who while not themselves the image, remain like it. He correlates image with "greatness" and likeness with "longing":

> The word is truth, it is wisdom and righteousness. These constitute the Image. The image of what? Of righteousness, wisdom, and truth. For the image, the Word, is righteousness from righteousness, wisdom from wisdom, truth from truth, as he is light and God from God. The

---

[27] Bernard, SC 80.2 (SBOp 2:277; CF 40:146).

soul is none of these things, since it is not the image. Yet it is capable of them and yearns for them; that perhaps is why it is said to be in the image. It is a lofty creature in its capacity for greatness [image], and in its longing we see a token of its uprightness [likeness].[28]

The chiastic reversal of word order in the list "truth, wisdom, righteousness" suggests a mirror. The Nicene language ("God from God") invokes the trinitarian horizon and states at once the equality of the Son and the identity of attributes in the divine simplicity. The soul is not these attributes but is capable of them and by right desire grows like the image in which it is made. The Word is the image of God; when incarnate, "what is made in the image [his human nature] agrees with the image." So human likeness to God is through him who is the image of God.[29]

Where the soul is endowed with greatness and uprightness "according to its capacity," the image by contrast "receives in equal measure with God . . . receives them by God's begetting." Building on the distinction between substantial and accidental attributes, Bernard further distinguishes the *imago* from the *ad imaginem*: "Although man received his gifts from God's hands [*a Deo*], the image received them from God's being [*de Deo*], that is, from his very substance. For the image of God is of the same substance as God, and everything that he seems to share with his image is part of the substance of both and not accident."[30] Bernard provides a simultaneous affirmation of both the Son's equality with the Father and the identity of the persons of God with their attributes. He thereby insists that attributes pertain to the substance of God and are not acci-

---

[28] Bernard, SC 80.2 (SBOp 2:278; CF 40:146).
[29] Bernard, SC 80.2 (SBOp 2:278; CF 40:147). SC 81 goes on to discuss the similarities and differences between the word and the soul in terms of liberty, immortality, and simplicity.
[30] Bernard, SC 80.3 (SBOp 2:278; CF 40:148).

dents. In the soul the attributes of uprightness and greatness are distinct from the soul and from each other. Although greatness is inseparable from the soul, Bernard writes, "The soul itself does not consist of its greatness any more than a crow consists of its blackness."[31] For Bernard, only the Trinity possesses the "pure and unique simplicity of essence" in which it is its attributes.[32]

At this point Bernard warns his readers against recent views that he presents as rejecting this teaching. He claims that Gilbert of Poitiers has misread Boethius on the Trinity so as to conclude that "God . . . is God by reason of his divinity, but the divinity is not God."[33] In support of this objection to Gilbert, Bernard invokes "Augustine . . . that mighty hammer of heretics" and his doctrine of the identity of attributes. If for Gilbert God is not his divinity, the divinity by which God is God must be greater, equal to, or less than God. It cannot be less, since by it God is God. If equal, then there are two Gods. If it is greater, "it is itself the highest good but it is not God."[34] Similarly Bernard cites Gilbert's gloss on the statement in Boethius that "God, God, God—refers to the substance": "Not what [the substance] is but by which it is what it is." Bernard comments, "God forbid that the Church should give assent to the proposition that there is any substance, or any other thing, by which God is what he is, but which is not God."[35]

---

[31] The illustration is borrowed from Augustine's *De Trinitate* (5.4.5) and effects a shift in the sermon from the Word and the soul to the Trinity.

[32] Bernard, SC 80.5 (SBOp 2:280; CF 40:151): "In the Trinity many diverse qualities are united, so that it does not suffer plurality as a result of multiplicity of elements, nor change as a result of variety."

[33] Bernard, SC 80.6 (SBOp 2:281; CF 40:152).

[34] Bernard, SC 80.6 (SBOp 2:281; CF 40:152).

[35] Gilbert was probably accused unjustly; see N. H. Häring, "The Case of Gilbert de la Porrée, Bishop of Poitiers (1142–1154)," *Mediaeval Studies* 13 (1951): 12–13.

## In a glass darkly . . .

Bernard frequently returns to the idea that the soul's un/likeness to God colors the accuracy of its perception of him. Changes in the quality of one's desire make God himself appear to change:

> We call God by various names: sometimes Father, sometimes Master or Lord. This is not because of any diversity in God's most simple and utterly invariable nature, but rather because of the multiple variations of our affections, according to varied progress or failure of the soul. . . . So God seems to progress with those who progress, to change with those who change.[36]

The passage has in view the language Christians use to speak about God: for instance, father, teacher, or bridegroom. The variety referred to does not imply change in God but reflects speakers' own changing dispositions. Souls form images of God that reflect their own state of being. When Christian tradition speaks of God as great, it refers to his being (in terms of substance), when it speaks of him as "Son" it does so in relation to the Father, but when it speaks of him as "Lord" or Creator it does so in relation to creation. The "variety of names" to which Bernard refers is clearly in this last category.[37] He tends to speak of Father, Son, and Holy Spirit in connection with the God of revelation known by faith. In describing the experience of souls, following the precedent of Scripture, he employs a whole array of names and images that vary with

---

[36] Bernard, Div 8.1 (SBOp 6:111; *Monastic Sermons*, trans. Daniel Griggs, CF 68 [Collegeville, MN: Cistercian Publications, 2016], 49).

[37] The Scriptures speak of God as having hands and feet, but of course, as Bernard declares, "God does not have these members by his nature; they represent certain *modes of our encounter* with him [*habet Deus omnia per effectum, non per naturam*]" (SC 4.4 [SBOp 1:20; CF 4:23]). So metaphors used for God characterize a person's mode of encounter with him rather than speaking about God as he is in himself.

the soul's dispositions. It is chiefly God the Word to whom this variety of names pertains, and it is through growing in likeness to him that the soul knows God more fully and that faith begins to pass into vision.

Through developing in herself virtuous attributes, the soul comes to recognize these qualities in God as well, "recalling his promise, 'with what measure you measure it shall be measured out to you in return. . . .' She knows then without any doubt, from the attributes which have their origin in God, that she who loves is herself loved."[38] The soul participates in the attributes that God is, and by this participation she comes to be like him and so to know him as he is.

Purified desire, transformed affectivity, allows the soul a fleeting glimpse behind the veil, which in turn transforms the soul at the deepest level of its being. Reciprocally, as the soul is likened to God it can be seen by him more clearly, because it *is* more fully: "For when the soul can once perceive the glory of God without a veil, it is compelled by some affinity of nature to be conformed to it, and be transformed to its very image. So God must appear to you as you have appeared to God."[39]

Bernard grounds his presentation of the way human beings *ad imaginem* experience God through the lens of their own imagehood in his account of the triune God, and in his portrayal of the likeness between the soul and the Word. Building with confidence on the Augustinian distinction between language about God in himself and language about God in relation to creatures, he is able both to unite and to distinguish a traditional account of the Trinity known to faith with a richly imaginative expression of human mystical experience.

---

[38] Bernard, SC 69.7 (SBOp 2:206; CF 40:34), citing Matt 7:2.
[39] Bernard, SC 69.7 (SBOp 2:206; CF 40:34).

## 2. Real Shadows

The fact that for Bernard God does not merely possess but is his attributes both secures the possibility of meaningful speech and relativizes every image that would seek to exhaust divine mystery. That the Son as *imago dei* has taken flesh as a human being *ad imaginem* bridges the gap between being and appearance while at the same time screening the beauty of his mystery in the blackness of mortal humanity.[1] Like the humanity of Jesus, the figures and images of Scripture, which Bernard likens to "shadows," possess a real power to communicate a trace of the divine. The limitation and ambiguity of images derives from their mediation by mortal human beings imperfectly in the image of God.

Christine Mohrmann writes of Bernard's understanding of the capacity for mystical experience to be at least partially conveyed in images and its connection to human being *ad imaginem*:

> Considering the image in this way as an essential element of the soul's encounter with the Word of God, Bernard created the possibility of a figurative mystical language. This is combined in him with the spiritual interpretation of scripture, particularly in the meditative Sermons on the Canticle of Canticles. This idea that the mystical experience is partly communicable, and can be concretized in language through images is explained, it seems to me,

---

[1] See Chapter 5, "Black but Beautiful."

by the fundamental ideas of Bernardine theology on the one hand and by certain special features of his personal character on the other. Whoever is acquainted with the important role which the image and likeness plays in the thought of St. Bernard will not be astonished at the role of the image in mystical experience.[2]

That human being itself is (in an analogous) way figural, an image of the Image of God, grounds the potential for scriptural types to portray something of the divine. In the first sermon of his commentary Bernard describes the Song as *aeterni connubii cecinit sacramenta*, and *iucundo composuit elogio, figurato tamen*.[3] The Song, composed of delightful figures, is itself an image of the eternal marriage of Christ and the church, God and the soul.

Bernard insists that these images are incorporeal.[4] Drawing on Origen, as Jean Danielou has shown, he presents a scheme wherein just as the revelation to the Jews before Christ is understood as a shadow of the truth fulfilled in the incarnation, so the mortal humanity of Jesus and, in our own time, the Eucharist, are shadows of a reality whose substance is still to be unveiled:[5] "We therefore who walk by faith live in the shadow of Christ; we are fed with his flesh as the source of our life. *For*

---

[2] Christine Mohrmann, *S. Bernardo: Pubblicazione commemorative nell'VIII centenario della sua morte*, ed. Agostino Gemelli, Soc. Ed. Vita E. Pensiero (Milan: Vita e pensiero, 1954); "The Style of Saint Bernard," in *Berryville Cistercian Studies*, Vol. II, Part I (Berryville, VA, 1961), 12.

[3] Bernard, SC 1.8 (SBOp 1:6; Bernard of Clairvaux, *On the Song of Songs I*, trans. Kilian Walsh, CF 4 [Kalamazoo, MI: Cistercian Publications, 1971], 5).

[4] Bernard, SC 31.6 (SBOp 1:223; Bernard of Clairvaux, *Sermons on the Song of Songs II*, trans. Irene Edmonds, CF 7 [Kalamazoo, MI: Cistercian Publications, 1979], 128–29). This is underscored by the first phrase in the sermon: it is to *studiosis mentibus*, to zealous *minds* that God reveals himself in varied ways (SC 31.1 [SBOp 1:219; CF 7:124]).

[5] Jean Danielou, "Saint Bernard et les Pères Grecs," in *Saint Bernard Theologien: Actes du Congres de Dijon 15–19 Septembre 1953* (Rome: Editiones Cistercienses, 1956), 48–50; SC 31.8 (SBOp 1:224; CF 7:135).

*Christ's flesh is real food.*"[6] Something real of the unchanging and invisible God can be communicated by signs and types. The Eucharist, a singular instance of the sign's bearing what it signifies, grounds and exemplifies the communication of God by types. In a clear eucharistic allusion, the first sermon of the commentary compares interpreting the text of the Song to "the breaking of bread."[7] Like the Eucharist, the shadows, the types of Scripture require faith in order to be rightly interpreted.

The same first sermon *On the Song of Songs* suggests a rich comparison between commentary and the multiplication of loaves. An aspect of the reciprocal imaging of God and the soul in these pages is the likeness between the Word and his preacher. The divine pedagogy by which the Word in the Song appears alternately as shy seducer, kind physician, fellow traveler, father of the house, and king models the roles Bernard assumes rhetorically in the course of commenting on the poem. He too seeks to elicit and shape the desire of his audience. More than once he comments on his responsibility toward those who are weak, and he positions himself as a fellow traveler, along with his hearers, equally in need of grace. It can be said of Bernard too that he "lightens the hardships of the journey by his fascinating conversation. A silver-tongued companion who, by the spell of his words and manners, persuades everyone, as if in a sweet-smelling cloud arising from the ointments, to follow him" (SC 31.7 [SBOp 1:224; CF 7:130]). In Sermon 1 he presents the Song as bread to be broken by the *paterfamilias*, and while he assumes the role of fellow beggar alongside his audience, he simultaneously stands in as the one through whose hands the bread of the Song is broken open. Like the king, Bernard encourages his audience by sharing his insights, "the riches of his wine-presses and storehouse, the produce of his gardens and fields, . . . finally introducing her

---

[6] My emphasis. Bernard, SC 31.10 (SBOp 1:225; CF 7:132).
[7] Bernard, SC 1.4 (SBOp 1:4; CF 4:3); citing Luke 24:35.

into his private apartments," in the accounts of his own spiritual experience. Whether or not Bernard deliberately presents the Word in the image of his own ideal rhetorician, his depiction clearly tells something of how he imagines his role as preacher.

Merging his own rhetorical activity with that of Christ, Bernard effectively incarnates the Word through his writing. Whether in writing or in the human life of Jesus, readers are meant to pass through the shadow to the substance. For Bernard to consider the mortal humanity of Jesus not as a stopping point or end in itself but a way that leads to the divinity of Christ revealed in his risen body does not detract from the value of that humanity. The one is meant to lead on to the other. Moving through the humanity to the divinity means that one has read it correctly. In the same way the Son points to the Father. Mary Carruthers' analysis of the rhetorical *ductus* of a text, the manner in which it leads a reader through itself to a new place, is relevant here. As she writes, "*Ductus* is the way by which a work leads someone through itself: that quality in a work's stylistic patterns which engages an audience and then sets a viewer or auditor or performer in motion within its guiding structures and articulating colours, an experience more like traveling through stages along a route than like perceiving a whole object."[8] Bernard implies a view of the Incarnate Word as just such a structure of divine rhetoric, leading its "readers" beyond itself to another level of awareness and encounter. As with the humanity of Jesus, so with the images in Scripture: faith, the depth of readers' spiritual experience, their degree of likeness to the Word, allow them to pass through the image. Bernard speaks of his object in writing as *desiderior feror non rationes*, to bear along desire, not to give reasons. The Cistercians' attraction to *ductus*, their view of the incarnation, and the nature of the spiritual interpretation of Scripture are then

---

[8] Mary Carruthers, *The Experience of Beauty in the Middle Ages* (Oxford: Oxford University Press, 2013), 54.

closely interwoven. That is, the rhetorical *ductus* in the texts they generated mirror and embody a theology of the incarnation in which the "text" of Jesus' humanity is not a stopping point but a way through to something higher.

That the encounter with the divine is mediated and conducted by images is a positive reality for Bernard. Images not only dim the glory of God to what human beings can bear but educate faith and orient desire: "the faith is shadowy is a blessing, it tempers the light to the eye's weakness and prepares the eye for the light; for it is written, 'He cleansed their hearts by faith.'" The struggle of faith at work as spiritual interpretation purifies the eye of the heart, enabling it to receive the light: "Faith therefore does not quench the light but protects it." Bernard goes on to speak of the mortal humanity of Jesus as a shadow to Mary, and "no mean shadow" at that, a "veil" and "envelope" of divine power. He goes out of his way to emphasize that both the power of Christ's divinity and the shadow of his humanity "put the demons to flight and became a shelter for men: an invigorating shadow surely, a shadow radiating coolness."[9]

### Sicuti Est

Rather than speaking from the perspective of the soul, whose moral standing limits what it can see of God, in Sermon 31 Bernard explores how and why God chooses to reveal himself in various ways (*non sub una specie*) to zealous minds (*studiosis mentibus*).[10] He speaks of God appearing (*apparet*) to these minds. That Bernard intends a kind of ontological empathy, a wholly spiritual mode of perception, is clear from a later passage: "Be careful, however, not to conclude that I see something corporeal or perceptible to the senses in this union between

---

[9] Bernard, SC 31.9 (SBOp 1:225; CF 7:132).
[10] Bernard, SC 31.1 (SBOp 1:219; CF 7:124).

the Word and the soul."[11] In this life, God "appears" in various ways because he cannot be seen as he is (*nondum videtur sicuti est*).[12] Sermon 31 contrasts the vision of heaven and the different kinds of vision by which God is known in this life: through creation philosophers intuit the Creator as cause, through dreams and locutions the prophets grasp something of the living God, through mystical experience the bride enjoys a more intimate contact with the Word.[13]

Bernard anchors the thirty-first sermon in 1 John 3:2.[14] Three of his five uses of this verse in the sermons of *On the Song of Songs* occur in Sermon 31. He suggests that while God is not seen "as he is," nonetheless "he does not reveal himself as altogether different from what he is" (*non omnino aliud hoc modo exhibeat, quam quod est*).[15] Appearance then is not simply deceptive or illusory for Bernard but can accurately communicate something of the divine. In a later sermon—though still commenting on Song 1:6—Bernard underlines the mutuality between knower and known and the imperfect, partial quality of self-knowledge in mortal life. Alluding to 1 John 3:2, he has the bridegroom ask the bride,

> With your beauty still incomplete how can you consider yourself fit to gaze on beauty in its totality? And why should you want to see me in my splendor, while you still do not know yourself? . . . The time will come when I shall reveal myself, and your beauty will be complete, just as my beauty is complete; you will be so like me that you will see me as I am. . . . But for now, though there

---

[11] Bernard, SC 31.6 (SBOp 1:223; CF 7:128–29).
[12] Bernard, SC 31.1 (SBOp 1:219; CF 7:124).
[13] Bernard, SC 31.3–5 (SBOp 1:221–22; CF 7:126–28).
[14] "Beloved, we are God's children now, and what we shall be has not yet appeared; but we know that when he appears we shall be like him because we shall see him as he is." See Appendix 1 for a fuller discussion of 1 John 3:2.
[15] Bernard, SC 31.7 (SBOp 1:223; CF 7:129).

is some resemblance, there is also some want of resemblance, and you must be content with an imperfect knowledge.[16]

As Bernard describes it, the visions of God vary as part of a divine pedagogy, a way to cultivate right desire in the fervent: "For the various desires of the soul it is essential that the taste of God's presence be varied too, and that the infused flavor of divine delight should titillate in manifold ways the palate of the soul that seeks him."[17]

Bernard understands God as the one who alone truly "is"—*increabile, interminabile, invariabile*—and the vision of God is likewise enduring: "When he therefore who exists in this manner—who, furthermore, cannot be one moment in this form, another in that—is seen just as he is, that vision [*visio*] endures . . . since no alteration interrupts it [*nulla eam interpolat vicissitude*]."[18] The vision of God as he is in himself is thus completely satisfying, for as Bernard writes, "if both the ability and will to contemplate are prolonged eternally, what is lacking to total happiness?"[19] He implies the ultimate lack of satisfaction with every image that is less than God himself. This lack is of course, simultaneously dissatisfaction with one's own incompletion, which prevents the clear vision of God. As the refrain of this sermon (*sicuti est*, again alluding to 1 John 3:2) suggests, there is reciprocity, and ultimately identity, between being and seeing. While it is easy, then, to accept that God as experienced now is but a trace of the glorious presence to be revealed and enjoyed to the full in eternity, one's true self is also known in this world "in a glass darkly," is indeed that

---

[16] Bernard, SC 38.5 (SBOp 2:17; CF 7:191).

[17] This likewise applies to the rhetorician who would kindle desire rather than provide reasons, mediating the encounter between the Word and the soul. Bernard faced the constant challenge of speaking to an audience with varied levels of spiritual maturity. See SC 31.7 (SBOp 1:223; CF 7:129–30).

[18] Bernard, SC 31.1 (SBOp 1:219; CF 7:124–25).

[19] Bernard, SC 31.1 (SBOp 1:219; CF 7:125).

very glass: "What we shall be has not yet been revealed. We do know that when it is revealed we shall be like him, for we shall see him as he is."[20] Elsewhere Bernard underlines the mutuality between self-realization and awareness of God when he writes of God experienced "not as he truly is, a thing impossible for any creature, but rather in relation to your power to enjoy," and continues, "Then you will experience as well your own true self."[21] The true self is fully activated when completely caught up in gazing on God and entirely self-forgetful. The self fully activated *is* gazing on God.

Bernard conceives that from the human side vision is limited by mortal bodies, which demand that God, who is spirit, appear in one or another guise. It is limited as well by the soul's degree of likeness to the one it beholds. God is free to appear in whatever image he chooses, "but as he pleases, not as he is."[22] Bernard compares the soul's awareness of God by ontological affinity with the eye, which, so long as it is healthy, can see the sun because of a certain likeness to it. Shifting his comparison from the physical sun to the Sun of Justice, whose gift of light makes one like and so able to see him to a greater or lesser degree, Bernard invokes 2 Corinthians 3:18: *ut revelata facie speculantes gloriam Dei, in eamdem imaginem transformemur de claritate in claritatem, tamquam a Domini Spiritu.*[23] For Bernard then, the revelation of our own face corresponds to seeing/becoming like God.[24] Indeed, after describing the approach to God as a growth in "brightness" (that is, likeness) he provides the striking formulation, "to see him as he is means to be as

---

[20] In Latin Bernard sonically stitches together the concepts of knowing, (future) being, likeness, and vision, with a repeated *im*: *Sc*im*us quia, cum ap-paruerit, s*im*iles ei er*im*us, quia videb*im*us eum sicuti est.*

[21] Bernard, SC 50.6 (SBOp 2:82; *On the Song of Songs III*, trans. Kilian Walsh and Irene M. Edmonds, CF 31 [Kalamazoo: Cistercian Publications, 1979], 35).

[22] Bernard, SC 31.2 (SBOp 1:220; CF 7:125).

[23] Bernard, SC 31.2 (SBOp 1:220; CF 7:126).

[24] Face imagery runs through the sermon, e.g., SC 31.5, 8.

he is" (*videre sicuti est, quam esse sicuti est*).²⁵ Seeing, one becomes like; becoming like, one sees more clearly. Ultimately the two are one.

For Bernard, then, seeing is a metaphor for a kind of knowing with the whole of one's being, through the lens of one's likeness to God. In a later expression, also explicating 1 John 3:2, he writes of "that likeness that accompanies the vision of God and *is itself* the vision." He explains, "This vision is charity, and the likeness is charity." In heaven "there will be a oneness of spirit, a reciprocal vision, and reciprocal love. . . . Then the soul will know as it is known and love as it is loved."²⁶ There is simultaneous unity and reciprocity. Ultimately the *ad imaginem* is so conformed to *imago* that God loves through it, as when Bernard writes of his deceased brother Gerard, "his whole being somehow changed into a movement of divine love."²⁷

## Three Visions

In Sermon 31, Bernard describes three "visions" through which God reveals himself: through creation to the philosopher, through dreams to the prophet, and through mystical visitation to the bride. Though Bernard presents them comparatively, stressing the superiority of the last to the two former types of contact, the earlier, less intimate visions nonetheless convey something of God's reality. Reasoning from creation, he tells his reader, "you are made aware beyond all doubt that he exists, and that you must seek him."²⁸ That is, creation not only makes one aware of God "beyond all doubt" but provokes

---

²⁵ Bernard, SC 31.3 (SBOp 1:221; CF 7:126).
²⁶ Bernard, SC 82.8 (SBOp 2:298; Bernard of Clairvaux, *On the Song of Songs IV*, trans. Irene M. Edmonds, CF 40 [Kalamazoo, MI: Cistercian Publications, 1980], 178–79).
²⁷ Bernard, SC 26.5 (SBOp 1:173; CF 7:63).
²⁸ Bernard, SC 31.3 (SBOp 1:221; CF 7:126).

the quest for him. By means of "images or the spoken word" (*imagines exstrinsecus apparentes seu voces sonantes*), he says, the Patriarchs "were graciously admitted to sweet communion with God, who became present to them,"[29] an expression suggesting a greater degree of personal intimacy and presence for Hebrew believers than medieval Christian authors generally allow. Bernard presents the three visions as increasingly privileged and personal. Unlike the vision of creation available to all (*videndi communi*), the dreams and locutions received by the patriarchs were "not apparent to everybody [*non . . . communis*]," and the mystical visitation enjoyed by the bride is rarer and more intimate still.

As Bernard explains, the third form of *divina inspectio*[30] is "very different" from the first two as it takes place "in the interior."[31] Interestingly, it is characterized by the silence of the Word, "who penetrates without sound, who is effective though not pronounced, who wins the affections without striking on the ears."[32] In this case "God himself" (*seipsum*) comes to the soul "that seeks him." There is a two-way movement: the soul seeking and God visiting. The sign of God's impending visit, he writes, is the "fire of holy desire" (*sancti desiderii ardor*). Here, as in the fuller account of mystical visitation in SC 74, God is known through the medium of the soul's inner movements: "It was not by any movement of his that I recognized his coming; it was not by any of my senses that I perceived that he had penetrated to the depths of my being. Only by the movement of my heart . . . did I perceive his presence."[33] God is not seen directly, but he moves the soul, and by the way the soul is moved one can discern something of God.

---

[29] Bernard, SC 31.4 (SBOp 1:221; CF 7:127).

[30] An interesting shift in vocabulary, contrasting with God's outward *demonstratio* to the patriarchs; *inspectio* keeps the sense of vision but one directed inward.

[31] Bernard, SC 31.4 (SBOp 1:221; CF 7:127).

[32] Bernard, SC 31.6 (SBOp 1:223; CF 7:129).

[33] Bernard, SC 74.6 (SBOp 2:243; CF 40:91).

Bernard compares the departure of the Word, and the corresponding waning of desire, to the removal of fire from under a boiling pot.[34] In Sermon 31 the fire of desire burns away "the rust of bad habits" to prepare the soul for the visitation, an encounter only possible for souls suitably disposed.[35] Bernard pictures an angelic go-between mediating the exchange between bride and bridegroom, "making known the desire of one, bearing the gifts of the other."[36] He presents visions of God, then, that are increasingly interior, silent, intimate, and mutual.

The three "visions" Bernard describes—through creation, in dreams and voices, and in mystical visitation—bear a resemblance to the three types of encounter with God he presents in SC 23.[37] There God appears as a teacher, judge, and bridegroom. Each image of the Word corresponds to a different state of soul.[38] Both schemes begin with reason seeking God through creation, move to fear encountering God through visions,[39] and advance to the intimate encounter of bride and bridegroom. In SC 23 the bridegroom appears under the aspect of Wisdom arranging all things sweetly in "weight, measure, and number," and stirs the bride to a kind of mixed contemplation such that "she experiences a repose full of sweetest surprise and wondrous peace, but her wakeful heart endures the lassitude of avid desire and laborious effort."[40] Surprise, wonder, and intellectual effort to grasp the created world then charac-

---

[34] Bernard, SC 74.7 (SBOp 2:243; CF 40:92).

[35] Bernard, SC 31.4 (SBOp 1:221; CF 7:127).

[36] Bernard, SC 31.5 (SBOp 1:222; CF 7:128).

[37] The three visions also correspond to pagan, Jewish, and Christian understandings.

[38] On this sermon, see M. B. Pranger, *Bernard of Clairvaux and the Shape of Monastic Thought: Broken Dreams* (Leiden: Brill, 1994), 51–84; and Mette B. Bruun, *Parables: Bernard of Clairvaux's Mapping of Spiritual Topography* (Leiden: Brill, 2007), 39–44.

[39] Bernard connects the time of the Old Testament with fear and the New Testament with grace (e.g., SC 45.6).

[40] Bernard, SC 23.11 (SBOp 1:146; CF 7:35).

terize this first level of encounter with God. While the lowest tier on Bernard's mystical ascent, it is nonetheless a more positive appraisal of the role of the intellect than one tends to associate with Bernard.

Bernard considers the dread-inspiring Judge and the fear he evokes to be an advance on this sort of contemplation, however: "For there we listen to Wisdom as a teacher in a lecture-hall, delivering an all-embracing discourse, here we receive it within us; there our minds are enlightened, here our wills are moved to decision. Instruction makes us learned, experience makes us wise [*Instructio doctos reddit, affectio sapientes*]." This second stage is more interior, less busy and laborious, more voluntary, and less speculative. The attraction of "avid desire" now propels reason's pursuit of Wisdom, the Word as Creator apprehended through the order of the universe. The soul still knows by affinity—the restless student sees a "busied" (*sollicitus*) God—but only the existential dread inspired by the real prospect of one's own Judgment makes one conscious of the reciprocal relationship between God and the soul. Self-knowledge is demanded in the second vision, whereas in the first the seeker could continue in an abstract fascination with the Logos and its workings.

As with the three visions in Sermon 31, the ascent culminates in the intimacy enjoyed by the bride: "But there is a place where God is seen in tranquil rest, where he is neither Judge nor Teacher but Bridegroom."[41] Here Bernard presents unchanging Wisdom as the power that turns all things to good in time: "God's purpose stands fast; the peace he has planned for those who fear him is without recall. Overlooking their faults and rewarding their good deeds, with a divine deftness he turns to their benefit not only the good they do but even the evil."[42]

---

[41] Bernard, SC 23.15 (SBOp 1:148; CF 7:38).
[42] Bernard, SC 23.15 (SBOp 1:148; CF 7:38–39).

### In Umbra

Bernard links the appearance of the Word in images, *similitudinibus adumbrari*, to a favorite verse from Lamentations (4:20), "Christ the Lord is a spirit before our face; under his shadow [*in umbra*] we shall live among the nations," which he connects in turn to 1 Corinthians 13:12: "Now we see in a mirror dimly and not yet face to face." In heaven, Bernard writes, taking up the refrain of 1 John 3:2, "we shall see him as he is [*sicuti est*], in the form of God, no longer in shadow."[43] "Just as we say that our ancestors possessed only shadows and images [*umbram figuramque*], whereas the truth itself shines on us by the grace of Christ present in the flesh, so also no one will deny that in relation to the world to come, we still live in the shadow of the truth [*veritatis umbra*]."[44] Bernard does not aim to diminish the reality or value of Jesus' humanity, or his presence in the Eucharist; in the context of the sermon, he considers these under the aspect of representation, modes of communication with a God who transcends corporeality and every human conception. What is striking is that because of the incarnation, because of the Eucharist, appearances interpreted by faith can genuinely communicate something of the unseen God. For both Jesus' mortal body and his sacramental presence are shadows that require the shadow of faith to be understood. Both are modes of communication that will no longer be necessary in heaven, when God will be seen as he is.

Indeed, in the Christian view, Christ is already risen in glory: his mortal humanity, the mysteries of his life on earth, are to be recalled with love and devotion, but Bernard steers mature worship toward the reality of Christ living now in risen glory. Indeed, in the ardor and eloquence of his devotion to Jesus' mortal humanity there are few to equal Bernard. It may even be precisely because he senses the horizon of glory so keenly

---

[43] Bernard, SC 31.8 (SBOp 1:225; CF 7:131).
[44] Bernard, SC 31.8 (SBOp 1:225; CF 7:131).

that he can best appreciate the gift of Christ's appearance to us in shadow. Not only the corporeal mediation of God but also the highest form of mystical contact remain a vision "in a mirror and a riddle."[45] This is the case, it seems, because experience still passes through the medium of a self imperfectly like God. Once again he declares, "That the faith is shadowy is a blessing, it tempers the light to the eye's weakness and prepares the eye for the light; for it is written: 'He cleansed their hearts by faith.' Faith therefore does not quench the light but protects it. . . . If you cannot yet grasp the naked truth is it not worthwhile to possess it wrapped in a veil?"[46] Faith through its work of interpreting the figures of Scripture stores up glory and accustoms the eye to its light. As desire burns away the rust of vice, faith similarly cleanses the heart.

This passage recalls the metaphor of the sun and corporeal vision earlier in the sermon.[47] Faith tempers the light, allowing the eye slowly to grow in likeness, to acclimate to the sun's brilliance. Faith's movement is reciprocal, twofold, recalling that of the angel who serves as go-between for lover and beloved. It adapts the light to the eye's weakness by taking shape in figures, and it "prepares the eye for the light" by its work of interpretation, in which the soul is "likened" to the bride, "imagining" itself toward fulfillment.

## SC 48

Bernard's Origen-inspired reading of Lamentations 4:20 also features powerfully in Sermon 48. It begins by commenting on Song 2:2: "As a lily among thorns, so is my love among maidens," as spoken by the bridegroom. It then progresses to 2:3, in the first part of which, in Bernard's interpretation, the bride replies in kind: "As an apple tree among the trees of the

---

[45] Bernard, SC 48.8 (SBOp 2:72; CF 31:20).
[46] Bernard, SC 31.9 (SBOp 1:225; CF 7:132).
[47] Bernard, SC 31.2 (SBOp 1:220; CF 7:126).

wood, so is my beloved among the sons." The first image suggests the fragility of virtue in a fallen world, and of nonviolence amid violence: "It is no small proof of virtue to live a good life among the wicked, to retain the glow of innocence and gentleness of manners among the malicious, above all to show that you are peaceful with those who hate peace and a friend to your very enemies."[48] The second prompts Bernard to ask why Christ is likened to a mere apple tree and compared, although beyond comparison, to wild trees: "Should he thus receive praise by measure who has not received the Spirit with measure?"[49] Other trees cast shade, but, Bernard writes, "Alone among the trees of the wood the Lord Jesus is the tree that bears fruit."[50] Texts like those in SC 48 where the bride regards Christ as in no way diminished when "his loving goodness is lauded in terms of his frailty"[51] balance Bernard's preference for the spiritual Christ.

Bernard's artful use of shadow language for the humanity of Jesus also clarifies the manner in which the incarnation simultaneously provides relief and darkens the brilliance of the divine. Continuing with Song 2:3, "In his shadow, for which I longed, I am seated, and his fruit is sweet to my taste," he hears in "shadow" the series of texts joined by Origen (Luke 1:35, the overshadowing of Mary; Lam 4:20; Isa 9:2). In the course of his own explication of this miniature catena Bernard writes of Christ, "His shadow is his flesh; his shadow is faith." He then explains that as Mary was overshadowed by the flesh of Christ and dwelt in the shadow of faith, believers now "walk by faith and not sight" and are overshadowed by the flesh of Christ in the Eucharist.[52] The shadow is not a stopping point but a path, a *ductus*: "The first thing is to come to the shadow,

---

[48] Bernard, SC 48.2 (SBOp 2:68; CF 31:13).
[49] Bernard, SC 48.3 (SBOp 2:69; CF 31:14).
[50] Bernard, SC 48.4 (SBOp 2:69; CF 31:15).
[51] Bernard, SC 48.4 (SBOp 2:69; CF 31:15).
[52] Bernard, SC 48.6 (SBOp 2:71; CF 35.17).

and then to pass on to that of which it is the shadow, because he says, 'Unless you believe you will not understand.'" Faith, he writes, is the shadow cast by knowledge, knowledge in the sense of more immediate experience of divine majesty. It is as if the blinding light of glory is broken by the obstruction of "measure," embodiment, to cast the shadow of Christ's flesh. Faith is to vision as shadow to light.

For Bernard, faith is stretched by the work of interpretation that the shadow demands, developing the capacity for knowledge: "The eye that would see God must be cleansed by faith." That is, he understands that hearing (the channel of faith) makes the heart pure so that it can see (knowledge/experience).[53] In turn, the occasional experience of ecstasy, the leap beyond the frame, recapitulates and makes transparent the realm of shadows, leading to a profusion of images resonant with the world of glory.[54] The more believers experience that reality, the stronger their faith becomes to further trust what cannot yet be seen, and the greater their faith, the more disposed they become to the self-forgetfulness experienced in contemplation, martyrdom, or loving service, in each of which one seems to pass beyond measure.[55] So it becomes easier to see the divinity within the humanity of Jesus the more one has passed beyond it in contemplation, so that one no longer reflects on a mental image of Jesus but has become one spirit with him.

---

[53] Bernard, SC 28.5 (SBOp 1:195; CF 7:91); see also SC 45.5.

[54] Bernard, SC 41.3 (SBOp 2:30; CF 7:207): "But when the spirit is ravished out of itself and granted a vision of God that suddenly shines into the mind with the swiftness of a lightning flash, immediately, but whence I know not, images of earthly things fill the imagination, either as an aid to understanding or to temper the intensity of the divine light. So well adapted are they to the divinely illuminated senses, that in their shadow the utterly pure and brilliant radiance of the truth is rendered more bearable to the mind and more capable of being communicated to others."

[55] "Seems" at the level of experience where in reality the soul remains distinct.

For Bernard, following Paul, flesh and spirit correspond to ways of knowing rather than ontological states. Thus he declares that faith already attests the life of Christ in the soul, but in a veiled fashion: "Faith is both life and the shadow of life."[56] More fully, he explains, "Through his flesh he is the shadow of faith; through his spirit he is the light of the mind. He is flesh and he is spirit. He is flesh to those who remain in the flesh, but 'a spirit before our face,' that is, in the future, provided we forget what lies behind and strain forward to what lies ahead, where on arriving we may experience exactly what he said, 'The flesh is of no avail; it is the spirit that gives life.' "[57] For Bernard, the incarnation corresponds to and educates the believer's faith, where the spirituality of the risen Lord accords with the knowledge that comes through experience. So Bernard interprets the words of Paul, who after being rapt out of himself could say, "Even if we did know Christ in the flesh, that is not how we know him now."[58] That Paul never knew Jesus in his earthly ministry suggests that for him "in the flesh" refers to a fleshly way of knowing rather than to the state of the one known.

Just as throughout the commentary Bernard poses a creative tension between the audacity and the temerity of the bride, he also creates a parallel tension between those texts inciting his audience to aim for the heights of spiritual experience of Christ and others, like this one in Sermon 48, that counsel remaining humbly in his shadow: "We, however, who have not yet merited to be rapt into Paradise, into the third heaven, let us meanwhile be fed with the flesh of Christ, let us honor his mysteries, follow his footsteps, and preserve the faith, and we will cer-

---

[56] Bernard, SC 48.7 (SBOp 2:71; CF 31:18); the New Testament realities are shadows, but shadows containing life.

[57] Bernard, SC 48.7 (SBOp 2:72; CF 31:19).

[58] 2 Cor 5:16, a verse that recurs when Bernard or Origen discusses the humanity of Jesus.

tainly be living in his shadow."[59] The bride's audacity, he implies, is the right form of what in worldly philosophers is a vain seeking after majesty. They, by contrast, in their pride, are unable to recognize the Lord who comes in humility, as a child, and so are overwhelmed by the unfiltered light of glory.

Bernard distinguishes those who simply are in the shadow, those who live there, by virtue, and the bride, who rests and is seated there. Even the bride's contemplation remains "in a mirror and in a riddle." The shadow is intrinsically provisional and temporary, made to give way to the light of glory: "A time will come however when the shadows will wane and even entirely fade away with the advance of dawn, and a vision as clear as it is everlasting will steal upon her, bringing not only sweetness to her taste but fulfillment to her heart, yet without surfeit: 'In his longed-for shadow I am seated, and his fruit is sweet to my taste.' "[60]

---

[59] Bernard, SC 48.7 (SBOp 1:72; CF 31:19).
[60] Bernard, SC 48.8 (SBOp 1:72–73; CF 31:20).

# 3. Beyond Measure: The Human Imagination of God

Bernard is customarily noted for his affective devotion to the humanity of Jesus manifest in his early ministry, a devotion that strongly influenced later developments in the history of spirituality. His focus on the risen and ascended Christ, however, complements and balances this devotion.[1] Just as the first disciples had to surrender the immediate presence of Jesus' humanity when he ascended in order to receive the outpouring of his Spirit, so believers, he argues, may grow from a carnal attachment to the memory of Jesus' earthly humanity to a spiritual communion with the risen Lord. The incarnation is the means by which God can lure the affections of carnally minded human beings away from perverse attachment to material realities and toward the divine. Such carnal love for Jesus pushes out other carnal loves, Bernard says, "as one nail drives out another,"[2] as though Jesus' unique human nature were the one sensible reality that could not become (or at least remain) an idol. Like the bronze serpent in the desert, because Christ is both God and man, even when idolatrous desire locks onto him it cannot ultimately reduce Jesus to itself but is instead transformed into him. The transformation of Jesus' humanity (an event that renews the cosmos) effects a corresponding transformation in the awareness of believers. Bernard's escha-

---

[1] See Bernard McGinn, "The Mystery of the Ascension in the Sermons of Saint Bernard," CSQ 25, no. 1 (1990): 9–16.
[2] Bernard, SC 20.4 (SBOp 1:117; CF 4:150).

tological vision of the glorious mysteries holds riches worth recovering for contemporary theology.

Just as one may hold either a carnal or a spiritual attitude toward the mortal humanity of Jesus, so too with regard to all sensible realities. Because of Christ's ascension, the created world has been recapitulated, made transparent by his light. For those whose love is carnal, sensible realities (including the types and figures of Scripture) remain opaque. For those with a more spiritual love of Christ, not only Jesus' humanity but, through it, all created things become transparent. This fact helps to explain the seeming contradiction in Bernard's use of image-packed rhetoric to recall and kindle desire for an experience of ecstatic prayer that lies beyond images.

Some readers are nervous about what they perceive as a move beyond the material, seeing that step as perhaps the vestige of a spiritualizing tendency in patristic literature to be discarded in favor of a more purportedly incarnational approach. In fact, however, the Jesus of the New Testament is always and intrinsically pointing beyond himself. The mortal humanity of Jesus is the expression of his divine nature as the Second Person of the Trinity; as Son he points to the Father: he is the image of another. The state of Jesus in his earthly ministry is entirely provisional and leads, through the cross, to Easter and the ascension. In the same way, for believers the current experience of embodiment is incomplete and deficient, a shadow of the real and lasting embodiment to be gained at resurrection. Further, the New Testament itself presents the earthly Jesus through the lens of the church's living experience of the risen Christ. Bernard's writing is true to this perspective.

Bernard often returns to the verse, "A spirit before our face is Christ the Lord; in his shadow we live among the pagans."[3] As the figures of the Old Testament are shadows and types of

---

[3] See chapter 2 on SC 31.

realities revealed in the New, so New Testament realities such as the humanity of Jesus and the Eucharist are shadows of what can only reach full realization in the age to come. Far from degrading the human, Bernard esteems it so highly that he keenly feels the degree to which its present condition falls short. The post-Enlightenment commonplace that desire for heaven erodes the value attached to life in time has seeped into western Christian culture. Only such desire, however, can "set love in order." Bernard's highly spiritual slant retains a powerful idea of the created order, principally the humanity of Christ, as "overflowing measure," transparent form.

## Mediation

In his study on the place of Jesus' humanity and the mediation of images in Christian mystical experience, Paul Mommaers articulates several pertinent questions: "Is it the case that full-fledged contemplatives are gifted with imageless experience that does away once and for all with all images or necessarily reduces them to inane substitutes? And if, on the contrary, the images do not need to disappear from the full-grown experience, then how can the imageless go together with the imaged? To put this in a more general way, how does immediacy relate to mediation?" He continues, noting the particular importance of these questions in a Christian context in which Jesus is "the image of the invisible God" (Col 2:9): "Is Jesus himself only a 'temple image' or even an 'encumbrance'? Does the most conducive of images turn in the contemplative's experience into the most subtle of idols? And anyway, even if Jesus appears to be the right 'Door,' what happens to him in the experience of those who have passed through it?"[4]

Mommaers provides a helpful discussion of different aspects of image in Christian tradition. In his view, the idea that

---

[4] Paul Mommaers, *The Riddle of Christian Mystical Experience: The Role of the Humanity of Jesus* (Louvain: Peeters Press, 2003), 7–8.

human beings are made "in the image" of God refers not to a visible similarity but to the fact that they can act like God. No inert idol but only the free, active, living human being can represent the living God.[5] This way of situating the likeness is significant for Bernard, for whom the *imago dei* is connected to free choice, and union with God is principally a union of wills.

Mommaers distinguishes the ontological (a son is an image of his father) and the psychological (a photograph of the father) understandings of image and points out that both aspects are present in mystical writing. He gives the example of a person passing from meditation on an image of Jesus to an awareness of Christ's life within.[6] The interaction of these two aspects of image appears in an interesting way in Bernard. Different metaphors (what Mommaers calls psychological images) for God (teacher, bridegroom, judge) correspond to different levels of spiritual awareness, the degree to which people have realized their likeness to God (the ontological image).[7]

Mommaers champions Jan Ruusbroec as the writer who best blended the mediate and the immediate and who integrated the humanity of Jesus into his account of the mystical heights. In Mommaers' view, Bernard fails in this regard and on a number of counts. Mommaers acknowledges the pivotal role played by Bernard in the advent of twelfth-century humanism and notes that themes like self-knowledge, friendship, human dignity, and the experience of God, "the humanity of God," are prevalent in Bernard's writings. Yet ultimately he finds that Bernard's perspective leaves too extreme a disjunction between the fleeting "rest" of mystical contact and the restlessness of active love. Bernard's "ecstasy," he says, cannot be reconciled with life in the world.

---

[5] Mommaers, *The Riddle*, 11, 13.
[6] Mommaers, *The Riddle*, 18.
[7] Mommaers derives from Jean-Paul Sartre the conclusion that "imagining is, in the very first place, an act, the act of *intending*" (*The Riddle*, 25).

Mommaers arrives at this perspective through a series of steps. He begins by observing Bernard's great devotion to the humanity of Jesus and the value Bernard gave to the affective element in this devotion. After citing SC 74.6, in which Bernard extols meditation on the human life of Jesus, Mommaers notes and comments on the centrality of the words *experientia* and *affici* in Bernard's mystical vocabulary: "The 'experience' he has in mind consists in the kind of knowledge a person can be favoured with only in loving, and this love-experience is in the first instance a matter of feeling."[8] The first statement is clearly true, and "love itself is knowledge" is a theme running throughout Bernard's works. But to say that mystical experience is for Bernard "in the first instance" a matter of "feeling" is at best misleading, especially as Mommaers uses the word here in relation to the kind of feeling associated with imaginative reflection on the human life of Christ.

For Bernard, the love that gives knowledge is in the first instance a matter of *will*, and the carnal love born of imagining Jesus' human life is only the springboard for deeper experience. Mommaers himself describes the manner in which for Bernard carnal love for Jesus' humanity cedes to love at the level of the "soul," then to love characterized by "strength."[9] These later modes of love, he says, "relativize" the value of the more immediately affective kind of prayer, but essentially leave it intact. For Bernard, however, carnal love is not (only) relativized by soul and strength love, but is taken up into and transformed by them. The ecstatic leap beyond the frame recapitulates what came before it. One may then have at least two attitudes toward the humanity of Jesus: the affective experience of the beginner, in which the emotional attachment to Jesus remains enmeshed in the lover's own projections, and

---

[8] Mommaers, *The Riddle*, 119.
[9] Mommaers, *The Riddle*, 121, following Bernard's scheme explained in SC 20.

the *affectus* of one whose desire has matured.[10] Both perspectives are open to readers of Bernard's writings on Jesus, one in which the humanity of Christ is practically opaque, the other in which it is transparent to the light of glory.

In his reading of Bernard, Mommaers worries that the movement "beyond the material images" (*phantasmata corporearum similitudinem*) leaves no way back to them: "Apparently, ecstatic contemplation, 'alone or principally called contemplation,' does not fully integrate the non-ecstatic aspects of the contemplative's existence. There seems to be no organic unity between the lofty quiet of this angelic state and the lowly restlessness of the human condition. Mystical 'death' does not tolerate day-to-day life, and far from enhancing activity the 'rest' has rather to be protected from it." The ex-cellence of the *ex-cessus* involves a loss in value of the human and thus of the Humanity."[11] The mystic, he goes on, is left at the whim of irreconcilable forces: "Ascent into heavenly rest is bound to alternate in arbitrary fashion with descent into earthly restlessness."[12]

Why "arbitrary"? Bernard repeatedly ties the ups and downs of the spiritual life to the activity of a divine providence that through the very alternation of longing and contact hones the desire of the person seeking God. Similarly, the material demands of life challenge one to grow in the same charity that is built up in another way by experience in prayer. The *rara hora et parva mora* of mystical experience is never the chief or final goal for Bernard, but rather growth in love.

In fact, ecstasy in Bernard does not involve the devaluation of the human but its exaltation, as the prominence of the ascension in his theology, for instance, attests. While the self-forgetfulness of intense spiritual experience may seem to eclipse human awareness (and awareness of the human) in the mystic's perception, Bernard never confuses the natures of

---

[10] See the discussion of SC 20 and 50 below.
[11] Mommaers, *The Riddle*, 127–28.
[12] Mommaers, *The Riddle*, 128.

God and the human pray-er.[13] He plays, rather, on the tension between the experiential and the ontological registers, and failure to discern his treatment of the two can easily mislead. For Bernard, because experience of God is mediated by human being in the image, a more or less realized likeness, it will always pass through the measure of the human. But Mommaers fails to recognize this fact, concluding his treatment of Bernard by stating, "The father of medieval monasticism, who was also the one who put the Godman at the heart of the contemplative's endeavour, does not explain how the Humanity and the human can be part and parcel of contemplation in the strict sense."[14] But in fact, Bernard demonstrates precisely the mediating role of the Humanity and the human in his conception of "overflowing measure," as is best seen in his portrayal of the ascension, which he shows as not eliding but rather fulfilling and recapitulating all creation.

## Ascension

Jean Leclercq has pointed out the prevalence of sermons by Bernard on the ascension.[15] While he describes their Christology as basically centrist and traditional vis-à-vis the disputes of his time, they also provide a striking literary-theological vision that lights up Bernard's other writings and has practical value for believers today. For Bernard, the feast of the Ascension is the "consummation and fulfillment" (*consummatio enim et adimpletio*) of every other feast.[16] He insists that Christ's ascension does not leave creation behind but rather brings all

---

[13] See the discussion in Étienne Gilson, *The Mystical Theology of St. Bernard*, trans. A. H. C. Downes (London: Sheed and Ward, 1940), 119–52.

[14] Mommaers, *The Riddle*, 129.

[15] Jean Leclercq, "The Mystery of the Ascension in the Sermons of Saint Bernard," CSQ 25, no. 1 (1990): 9–16, here 11.

[16] Bernard, Asc 2.1 (SBOp 5:127; Bernard of Clairvaux, *Sermons for the Summer Season*, trans. Beverly Kienzle, CF 53 [Kalamazoo, MI: Cistercian Publications, 1991], 32]; see also Asc 4.1 for "goal and fulfillment" (*finis et adimpletio*).

things, that is, the cosmos, to fullness: " 'The one who descended is the very one who ascended' today 'above all the heavens to bring all things to fulfillment'" (*ut ad impleret omnia*).[17] The ascension, he says, makes it possible for the measure of the cosmos to be filled and even to overflow. Just as the meaning of Jesus' earthly ministry is recast in light of Easter, so too in his ascension the entire created order becomes transparent to the light of glory.

Throughout these sermons on the ascension Bernard draws a parallel between the mysteries of Jesus' life and the life of the church. The "seamless garment" of Christ's trajectory through the universe, from the authority over the elements he exercised on earth through the descent into hell, is completed by his ascension to heaven, he writes, which in turn brings "the integrity of our faith to wholeness."[18] This connection between events in Jesus' life and the lives of believers is more than a superficial comparison. The Christian stands in the place once occupied by the pre-ascension Christ. Jesus thus becomes less an external object of meditation and more one whose life is nearer to believers than they themselves are.[19]

Spiritual transformation involves the whole human being. In sermons 3 and 6 on the Song of Songs Bernard treats *de intellectu et affectu*: "There are two parts of ourselves then, understanding and inclination, that must be purified: the understanding, that it may know; and the inclination, that it may will." He explains that Christ enlightens the minds of his disciples by his earthly ministry, but only with the gift of the Spirit can their inclination be healed and their zeal for virtue

---

[17] Bernard, Asc 2.1 (SBOp 5:127; CF 53:32), citing Eph 4:10.

[18] The "seamless garment" (John 19:23) is itself an image of the church for Bernard: see, e.g., Apol 6; see also Asc 2:3 and, especially, Asc 3:1, where the sun in a robe is the image of the risen Christ, as in Apol 6–7.

[19] Conversely, participation in the life of Christ makes imitation possible. On this point, see Roch Kereszty, "Relationship between Anthropology and Christology: St. Bernard, A Teacher for our Age," *Analecta Cisterciensia* 46 (1990): 271–99, here 286, 287.

kindled: "Still, having grown accustomed to that most holy flesh of his, they could not listen to a word about his departure: that the one for whom they had left everything would leave them. What is the reason for this? [Their] understanding was enlightened, but [their] inclination was not yet purified [*Quia intellectus illuminatus erat, sed nondum purgatus affectus*]."[20]

This passage could seem to contradict the idea so frequently attested in Bernard's work, that knowledge cannot be reached without virtue. However, in the present case it is not knowledge of God that is in question but knowledge of what is to be done. Christ has shown the disciples how to live, but their power to effect this new way of life depends on his departure and the gift of the Spirit. Bernard's reference to the Spirit "who leads us into all the truth" (John 16:13) suggests that new awareness will accompany the new virtue that Christ will make possible.[21] Otherwise, understanding and inclination splinter the self, so that one is drawn upward by knowledge of what ought to be and downward by lack of zeal.[22] It is exactly this inner division that is healed not only by intellectual seeking but also by affectively savoring what is above.[23]

Thus Bernard describes a condition of "exceedingly bitter conflict," a "divided state so difficult to endure" (*intus amarissima contradictio et divisio molestissima*), "when from the one side [understanding] we are drawn upward, and from the other [inclination] we are dragged back down again." Returning to the notion that while all monks know the course they should take, not all are equally zealous to travel it, Bernard finds the difference in the perspective of hope opened to those who are "repeatedly looking up to heaven."[24] He compares the ascension of Jesus to that of Elijah in Kings, with the two-

---

[20] Bernard, Asc 3.4 (SBOp 5:133; CF 53:39).
[21] Bernard, Asc 3.9 (SBOp 5:137; CF 53:43).
[22] See also Bernard, Asc 6.7.
[23] Bernard, Asc 6.7–8 (SBOp 5:153–54; CF 53:60–61).
[24] Bernard, Asc 6.6 (SBOp 5:153; CF 53:60).

fold spirit poured out on Elisha being the Holy Spirit, who after Jesus had enlightened the minds of his disciples would heal and encourage their wounded inclination: "The sight of him leaving made twofold his spirit, when, visibly caught up to heaven, he bore with him every desire of Elisha, so that he too would then begin to savor the things that are above, not those on the earth. The sight of [Elijah] leaving made twofold his spirit, so that to spiritual understanding was joined spiritual inclination, which was caught up to heaven with the very flesh to which it was so strongly clinging."[25] So one spirit guides both understanding and inclination, and inner division is healed by casting one's longing gaze beyond the measured frame of the familiar.

But the perfection of this unity must of course await the next life. With endearing realism, Bernard observes that the best one can do on earth is to steer one's thoughts and inclinations as they arise, in a "piecemeal" fashion: "Assuredly, as long as our hearts are divided and found to have many recesses, and do not appear at all consistent with themselves, we must lift them up piecemeal and somehow part by part. The purpose is that they may be brought together in that celestial Jerusalem 'which is banded together in unity,' where not only individuals but all alike begin to dwell together as one, undivided not only within themselves, but undivided also among themselves."[26] The humanity of Christ educates affection so that minds can understand. Without understanding, the mind remains locked in carnal attachment. Bernard compares carnal affection's rising beyond itself to understanding with the serpent Moses lifted up in the desert, where the creature that wounds becomes an agent of healing:

> [Christ] aroused the disciples' inclination toward his own flesh because, without some modification of will, their

---

[25] Bernard, Asc 6.14 (SBOp 5:158–59; CF 53:66–67).
[26] Bernard, Asc 6.5 (SBOp 5:152–53; CF 53:59).

minds could not be directed toward understanding of faith, and [they] did not yet have the strength to rise up toward what is spiritual. Thus they would cling to [this] man [who was] performing wondrous deeds and uttering wondrous words with a human sort of love [*amore quodam humano*]. Assuredly [their] love was still carnal, but so strong as to prevail over all other loves. This was surely the serpent of Moses that devoured all the serpents of the Egyptian magicians. Moreover, "Behold," they say, "we have left everything and followed you."[27]

Here Bernard presents the more familiar notion of the will's needing to be healed for understanding to arise. Jesus is so attractive on a strictly human level, he says, that the affections of the disciples are pried away from every other emotional attachment: they have left everything to follow Christ. The ascension then leaves the disciples in an affective void.

Such interior emptiness and affective hollowing is a precondition for the growth of love into a more spiritual phase. Bernard explains that the soul filled up with material distractions is hereby closed to spiritual awareness: "Now a soul subject to these distractions cannot be satisfied by the Lord's visitations. The more it is emptied of the [distractions], the more fully will it be satisfied by the [visitations]. If [it is] greatly [emptied], [it will be] greatly [satisfied]; if it is barely [emptied], [it will be] barely [satisfied]. . . . *When the oil did not meet with an empty vessel, it had to stop flowing*."[28] As Bernard memorably puts it in another place, "If you do not give up what you love, you will not have what you desire" (*Si non dederitis quod amatis, non habebitis quod desideratis*).[29] Christ has ascended *ut ad impleret omnia*. Further stressing the value of emptiness, Bernard

---

[27] Asc 6.11 (SBOp 5:156; CF 53:63–64).
[28] Bernard, Asc 3.7 (SBOp 5:135; CF 53:41), citing 2 Kgs 4:3, 6, my emphasis; see Asc 3.9, which also mentions the serpents being swallowed and suggests that the oil refers to the anointing of the Spirit.
[29] Bernard, Pent 3.2 (SBOp 5:172; CF 53:82).

writes, "In preparation for that grace, let us strive, dearly beloved, in the measure our littleness allows, *to empty ourselves of all things* [Phil 2:7] and to rid our hearts of wretched pleasures and transitory consolations."[30] This focus corresponds to what may be called a whole poetics in Bernard, a theological imagination attuned more to the void of desire than saturation with sensory overload.

## Distance

Jean-Luc Marion touches on a number of the key themes that have emerged in this discussion. In his early work *The Idol and Distance* he describes Bernard's portrayal of the disciples at Jesus' ascension, underlining the way carnal attachment precludes spiritual understanding:

> The attachment of the disciples to the immediately corporal presence of the Christ remains a "carnal love" that attempts to take possession of it, with the infantile frenzy of a strained, distracted, impotent desire. In approaching the Christ thus, "carnal love" effaces the withdrawal and misses the testimony of the filial withdrawal . . . the attachment to the body of Christ is "carnal" here not because a mark of infamy would taint corporeal reality—Christ sanctified it in assuming it—but because, in the familiarity of a close proximity, the body is banalized, with the result that one misses the divinity that delivers itself therein.[31]

For Marion, in losing the distinction between the two natures of Christ and the corresponding modes of knowing, the disciples also collapse the Son's distinction from the Father:

---

[30] Bernard, Asc 6.15 (SBOp 5:159; CF 53:67), my emphasis.
[31] Jean-Luc Marion, *The Idol and Distance: Five Studies*, trans. Thomas A. Carlson, Perspectives in Continental Philosophy No. 17 (New York: Fordham University Press, 2001), 116–17.

> The corporeal face of Christ here, when men venerate it with a puerile covetousness, masks, in the Christ himself, the revealed face of the divine—the icon, under a solar gaze, again becomes an idol. In the end, the face of Christ, for "carnal" love, is identified with our habitual habitat, and there makes us assume or keep our usual habits. Thus ignoring the mediate approach to the Christ ("spiritual" and filial love), the disciples miss the mediate relation of the Christ to the Father.[32]

The loss of distinction Marion describes includes a loss of the distance that is the condition of right desire, distance built into the paschal event: "The cross manifests the withdrawal as distinction, and the Resurrection, the same withdrawal as union." Indeed, he suggests, the incarnation itself embodies this distance: "The Christ incarnates distance, not only for us, to whom he presents himself 'mediately in the Holy Scriptures' . . . but already with his Palestinian incursion into the history of men."[33] Marion importantly identifies the spiritual as a "mediate" form of love and speaks of "the mediating measure of our relation to the divine."[34] Conversely, for Bernard carnal love for Jesus' humanity has a unique power to "draw all things to itself" and cast out lesser loves as the serpent made from Moses' staff devours the serpents of Pharoah's magicians. In place of a grasping carnal affection, the ascension works a pedagogy of desire, carving out a space of waiting in which a free, strong, and chaste love can blossom. Through waiting, the disciples find themselves and one another as "sons in the Son." As Marion writes, "Affiliation joins them together in the trial; in the waiting prepared by the Son—the withdrawal of the Father, they discover themselves as Sons."[35]

---

[32] Marion, *The Idol*, 117.

[33] Marion, *The Idol*, 115, citing Friedrich Hölderlin, his main subject in these pages.

[34] Marion, *The Idol*, 118.

[35] Marion, *The Idol*, 129.

## Measure Beyond Measure

In the sermons on the ascension, when Bernard speaks of the way Jesus' earthly ministry enlightened the minds of his disciples, he shows that illumination to be the fruit of reflection on the apparent incongruity of Jesus' divine and human nature. He is in fact fond of rhetorically accentuating this point: "Who can sufficiently ponder how the Lord has come before us, come to us, come to our assistance, and how his unparalleled Majesty willed to die that we may live, to serve that we may reign, to live in exile that we may be brought home again, and even to stoop to the most menial actions so as to set us over all his works."[36] Bernard here also accents the high vision of human possibility, the noble status to which human beings are called. The scandal of the cross, that God in human form underwent humiliation, is the key that opens the Scriptures: "Does it not seem to you that he enlightened their understanding when he opened their mind[s] to understanding of the Scriptures, making known that the Christ had to suffer these things and rise from the dead, and so enter into his glory?"[37]

Bernard underlines the tension between the two natures not from a low estimation of the human but to accent the ironic dimension of faith. Just as spectators at a play are aware of elements in the narrative that the figures onstage cannot perceive, the faith-filled reader of Scripture perceives the reality of Jesus' full divinity as it acts through his human deeds and inflects them with another dimension of meaning. Bernard associates the carnal, only-human knowledge the disciples initially had of Jesus with a stage in the spiritual life where beginners are attracted to the human Jesus but effectively fail to perceive him in a way that is spiritual, that is, with living

---

[36] Bernard, Asc 3.2 (SBOp 5:132; CF 53:38).
[37] Bernard, Asc 3.3 (SBOp 5:133; CF 53:39).

faith. Faith transforms the quality of one's affection and changes the manner of one's relation to visible realities.

Bernard's disparaging remarks about the body and human realities pertain to the body in its fallen state and are not comments on the intrinsic nature of embodiment.[38] When he speaks of "the frightful prison of the filthy body," he has in view the postlapsarian body insofar as it is dominated by disordered passion. In one passage, after a string of invectives against "the enticements of the flesh," he argues that the disciples could not receive the Spirit "while [they were] with the flesh of the Word." The obstacle is not the flesh of Jesus, which of course is free of sin, but the fleshly orientation of the disciples, as he clarifies in the sentence that follows: "Anyone is completely mistaken to think that heavenly sweetness could be mixed with these ashes, divine balm with this poison, or the gifts of the Spirit with enticements of this type."[39] *Ashes* and *poison* do not refer to the body in itself, for in Jesus it is joined to the Spirit. So when Jesus ascends, "He did not indeed put aside the substance of his sackcloth, but its decrepitude, its decay, its misery and its worthlessness, [when] he consecrated the first-fruits of our resurrection."[40] In another place: "Was [the Spirit] shrinking from any involvement with [Christ's] flesh? From the Spirit and by the Spirit was [Christ] conceived in the Virgin, and born from a virgin mother. It was nothing of the sort! [Christ] was showing us the path along which we were to walk, and putting before us the form by which we were to be impressed."[41] In a similar vein, he writes: "Did the Holy

---

[38] Emero Stiegman argues that in Bernard's vocabulary the binary of body versus soul is used in the Pauline sense of flesh versus spirit: "*Corpus* represents the fragility of man as *caro; anima*, though it too is a mere creature and therefore *caro*, represents man's capacity for union with the divine *Spiritus* and, as such, is associated dynamically with the *spiritus* of the Scriptural dichotomy" (Emero Stiegman, "The Language of Asceticism in Bernard of Clairvaux's Sermones Super Cantica Canticorum," PhD dissertation, Fordham University, 1973 [Ann Arbor: University Microfilms], 151–52).

[39] Bernard, Asc 6.13 (SBOp 5:158; CF 53:65).
[40] Bernard, Asc 4.1 (SBOp 5:138; CF 53:44).
[41] Bernard, Asc 3.4 (SBOp 5:133; CF 53:39).

Spirit shudder at cohabiting with the Lord's flesh, which, as we know from the Angel's message, could not have been conceived without the Spirit's coming upon Mary?"[42]

All of Bernard's monks know via Jesus' earthly ministry how they are to act, the observances they are to follow, and so on, but each follows this course with more or less zeal. For the diligent, the yoke seems light, to the sluggish, heavy:

> Some not only walk but also run, or rather fly; so that to them their vigils seem brief, their foods sweet, their clothing soft, and their labors not only bearable but even appealing. Others are not like this. Instead, with withered hearts and rebellious dispositions, scarcely are they dragged to these [exercises]; scarcely are they compelled by fear of hell. . . . What then is the reason? Clearly it is this, that they do not see Christ when he is taken up from them; in other words, they do not ponder how he left them orphans, that they are pilgrims and strangers on earth, that as long as they are still held in the frightful prison of this filthy body, they cannot be with Christ. . . . They never breathe fully in the light of the Lord's mercies and in the Spirit's freedom, which alone makes [our] yoke easy and our burden light.[43]

So he implies that they lack the experience of absence, the experience of distance that would relativize their human schemes and open a space for authentic desire. This experience of radical poverty and dejection (a dimension of yearning) colors the entire poetics of Bernard's mysticism and characterizes the Cistercian style in everything from observance to architecture. Spiritual emptiness serves as a precondition to fruitfulness.

---

[42] Bernard, Asc 6.12 (SBOp 5:157; CF 53:65).
[43] Bernard, Asc 3.6 (SBOp 5:135; CF 53:41). This reading of the yoke of monastic observance made light by willingness echoes Cassian's Conf 24 and is another instance of moral quality's shaping perception in Bernard. See also SC 43.1 and Asc 3.9, where the Spirit "makes light and broad whatever seems difficult and confining in this wicked world."

The humanity of Jesus and all of his actions indicate meaning in a new and singular way. His actions are not haphazard but deliberate, and they express a hidden sense and purpose, as Bernard explains: "For just as a writer arranges everything for specific reasons, so the things that are from God are appointed; and especially those performed by Majesty present in the flesh."[44] Bernard's comparison here of God's work to that of a writer suggests that the life of Jesus is dramatic, rhetorical, and expressive in a way that an ordinary human life, which is more of an improvisation, cannot be. Jesus communicated through parables and prophetic deeds. Because he was the Word of God, whatever he said or did carried multiple levels of meaning. His human nature was a means of communication in the way that the figure or image employed by a writer is; indeed Jesus' human nature had a figural meaning: it pointed beyond itself to the invisible God. It held this dimension precisely as human, since human beings are "in the image of God," but it was clearest in him as he was perfectly human. It is the very meaning of the human person to point beyond itself to another, so it is no betrayal to move beyond the human when human nature is iconic and intended to point beyond itself. Even in his divine nature, Jesus the Son points beyond himself to the Father.

The iconicity of human nature and especially the humanity of Jesus has a literary parallel in Bernard's work. Natalie B. Van Kirk identifies a congruence of rhetorical and christological aims in Bernard, using sermons on the ascension for examples. She writes of the importance of rhetorical *ductus* for Bernard, the movement and directional flow of a text:[45] "As Saint Bernard recounts the events of the Incarnation he is

---

[44] Bernard, Asc 4.2 (SBOp 5:139; CF 53:45).

[45] Natalie B. Van Kirk, "Finding One's Way Through the Maze of Language: Rhetorical Usages that Add Meaning in Saint Bernard's Style(s)," CSQ 42, no. 1 (2007): 11–35. Regarding *ductus*, she draws on Mary Carruthers, *The Craft of Thought: Meditation, Rhetoric and the Making of Images, 400–1200* (New York: Cambridge University Press, 1998), 77–81.

showing his hearers the meditative path along which they ought to proceed. The peril of the impure will is that it seeks its own path. Bernard is showing his hearers/readers the steps to follow as they create or follow the *ductus* of the Incarnation and illuminating the perils of failure to follow the proper way."[46] She goes on to discuss the orthopraxy of monastic life as a journey along which monks travel, associating the flesh with fantasies and mental associations that pull the mind away from the path of meditation.[47] Her phrase "the *ductus* of the Incarnation" is striking vis-à-vis Bernard's own comparison of the writer's artistry with the works of God, especially those "performed by Majesty present in the flesh."

Following Origen, Bernard distinguishes Christ as the Image from human beings "in the Image."[48] Christ alone, he says, receives the Spirit "without reserve": "The Spirit is given with reserve to everyone except Christ, yet the abundance of the measure that runs over seems somehow to exceed measure."[49] This seeming to pass beyond measure is akin to the experience of ecstasy, in which one experiences absorption in God while remaining ontologically distinct and entirely human. Bernard associates the ascension of Jesus with the contemplative's arrival at a vision of peace: "Let us follow him even as he ascends, which means to seek and savor the things that are above. . . . Do you want to know what things are there? It is a vision of peace: 'Praise the Lord, Jerusalem, Zion, praise your God'; 'he has established peace in your borders,' O peace that surpasses all understanding! O peace even beyond peace! O measure beyond measure, pressed down and shaken together, and running over!"[50] This peace surpasses human understanding yet dwells within the limits of the human measure. On the cosmic

---

[46] Van Kirk, "Finding," 25.
[47] Van Kirk, "Finding," 20.
[48] Henri Crouzel, *Origen: The Life and Thought of the First Great Theologian*, trans. A. S. Worrall (San Francisco: Harper and Row, 1989), 93.
[49] Bernard, Asc 5.2 (SBOp 5:150; CF 53:55–56).
[50] Bernard, Asc 6.4 (SBOp 5:152; CF 53:58–59).

level, the seamless garment of Christ's mysteries comes to fulfillment in the ascension, which recapitulates all that led up to it.

## Origen

Origen's influence on Bernard has been studied in some detail.[51] Jean Leclercq wrote of Bernard's use of Origen, "He not only preaches on him but like him: the same themes borrowed from holy scripture and particularly the Old Testament, the same understanding of the rapport between the Old and the New Testaments, the same allegorical exegesis; above all, the same imagination."[52] This last remark, that Bernard shared above all Origen's imagination, is especially apt. Bernard was particularly fond of Origen's exegesis of Lamentations 4:20, "A spirit before our face is Christ the Lord; in his shadow we live among the pagans."[53] This verse and its Origenist interpretation shape Bernard's view of Jesus' humanity. He takes up the notion that as the images of the Jewish Scriptures were realized in the incarnate Word, so too the human life of Jesus and its extension through the ages in the Eucharist are shadows of the glorious reality to come. The human Jesus is not a stop-

---

[51] E.g., Luc Bresard, "Bernard et Origène commentent le Cantique," *Collactanea Cisterciensia* 44 (1982): 111–30, 182–209, 293–308; James W. Zona, "'Set Love in Order in Me': *Eros*-Knowing in Origen and *Desiderium*-Knowing in Saint Bernard," CSQ 34, no. 2 (1999): 157–82; Jean Danielou, "Saint Bernard et les Peres Grecs," in *Saint Bernard Théologien: Actes du Congrès de Dijon 15–19 Septembre, Analecta SOC* 9 (1953): 46–55.

[52] "Il prêche non seulement *sur* lui, mais *comme* lui: mêmes thèmes empruntés à l'Écriture Sainte et particulièrement à l'Ancien Testament, même conception des rapports entre l'Ancien et le Nouveau Testament, même exégèse allegorique; surtout, même imagination" (Jean Leclercq, "Saint Bernard et Origène d'après un manuscrit de Madrid," *Révue Bénédictine* 59 [1949]: 183–95, here 195).

[53] See Jean-Marie Déchanet, "La Christologie de S. Bernard," in *Saint Bernard Théologien*, 78–91, here 87, n. 1.

ping point but always contains this movement forward, as, correspondingly, the believer's spiritual goal is not life in a mortal body but the risen glory promised by Easter and shared now, but "in a mirror, dimly."

Henri Crouzel, writing of Origen but in words that are equally true of Bernard's work, underlines the centrality of the *imago dei*: "The theology of the image of God, at the root of the possibility of knowing God, is the foundation of the whole of Origen's mysticism."[54] Therefore, he says, humanity (preeminently the human nature of Jesus) is "in" the Image, as the divine nature of the Word being the Image of the invisible God.[55] The humanity of Christ is the "image of the image."[56]

Crouzel stresses that for Origen, the fact that humans are "in the image" is central. Relationship with God and the movement to become like him form the heart of being human. This energetic, relational quality is also prominent in Bernard's conception and is inseparable from the role both authors give to freedom.[57] For both Origen and Bernard, it is through imagehood, the degree of likeness, that one knows God. Sinful humanity forgetful of its divine likeness likens itself to beasts,[58] but the image remains ineradicable and cannot be lost, however disfigured.[59] That one knows in and through the image and the degree of likeness, says Crouzel, makes knowledge a matter of union and participation.[60] In another place, he

---

[54] Crouzel, *Origen*, 98.

[55] See chapter 1 above on SC 8.81; and Crouzel, *Origen*, 93.

[56] Crouzel, *Origen*, 93.

[57] Crouzel, *Origen*, 95.

[58] Crouzel, *Origen*, 96; Bernard, Dil 15 (SBOp 3:131–32; Bernard of Clairvaux, *On Loving God with an Anaytical Commentary by Emero Stiegman*, CF 13B [Kalamazoo, MI: Cistercian Publications, 1995], 18).

[59] Crouzel, *Origen*, 96–97, and Bernard, SC 83.1 (SBOp 2:298–99; CF 40:180–81).

[60] Crouzel, *Origen*, 99, my emphasis, the last phrase recalling Gregory's *amor ipse notitia est* (Gregory the Great, *Forty Gospel Homilies*, trans. David Hurst, CS 123 [Kalamazoo, MI: Cistercian Publications, 1990], 215).

explains, "knowledge is a vision or a direct contact, it is participation in its object, better still, it is union, 'mingling' with its object, and love . . . dispensing with the mediation of the sign, the image, the word, which are rendered necessary here below by our corporeal condition."[61]

Crouzel goes on to explore "the close connection between literality and corporeality" and the place of symbolism in the divine pedagogy.[62] Sin, he says, is essentially a failure to follow the inherent direction, the *ductus* of scriptural images.[63] Not only the spiritual or carnal quality of intention, but also the quality of affection colors the reader's reception of the word. He describes Origen's "strongly emotional devotion" to the Word made flesh.[64] The coincidence of such devotion with a highly spiritual outlook is characteristic of Bernard as well. Far from dampening the ability to feel, the distance afforded by the spirit frees the vigor and health of *affectus*.

Perhaps most important, Bernard derives from Origen his sense of Jesus' humanity as both ineradicable and iconic. Crouzel claims that for Origen, the humanity of Jesus is moved through but never left behind: "One must start from the incarnate Logos to reach the Logos-God and there is no stage, even in the final state of blessedness, when the humanity of Christ can be lost from sight; even if the attention is directed more and more to his divinity the latter is still contemplated through his transfigured humanity." Bernard uses the image of the humanity of Christ in heaven as a kind of altar, the place of exchange and mediation par excellence, supporting the soul's eternal contemplation of God.[65] Crouzel notes the possibility

---

[61] Crouzel, *Origen*, 116; Crouzel (118) notes that the Hebrew sense of the verb *to know* is very much in Origen's mind when he speaks of love as knowledge.

[62] Crouzel, *Origen*, 106.

[63] Crouzel, *Origen*, 107.

[64] Crouzel, *Origen*, 118.

[65] *St. Bernard's Sermons for the Seasons and Principal Feasts of the Year*, trans. Ailbe J. Luddy (Westminster, MD: The Carroll Press, 1950), 2:345 (SBOp 5:305).

of unending advance in such contemplation, with Origen anticipating the *epektasis* of Gregory of Nyssa as yet another idea taken up by Bernard.

For both Bernard and Origen, God's self-revelation in the incarnate Word coincides with the nature of the biblical text and its figural interpretation. Each requires a hermeneutic of faith that powers an "iconic" reading of the symbol, which appears ambiguous insofar as it depends on the quality of the interpreter's desire. The divine pedagogy of the incarnation demands that knowers' state conditions their knowledge. Bernard's distinction between carnal and spiritual love is thus akin to Origen's idea of both a temporal and an eternal gospel. Crouzel finds in this surprising notion of the two gospels traditional "Christian sacramentalism," the distinction between sign and reality: "It must be repeated that, according to the measure of spiritual progress made, the veil of 'image' which still covers the mystery in the temporal Gospel becomes more and more transparent, revealing the truth that it holds. When one turns to the Lord, the veil is taken away, gradually no doubt, and the divinity of Christ shows more and more through his humanity, the flesh no longer forming a screen for those who have 'spiritual eyes' capable of perceiving the divinity."[66]

## The Center

Bernard's fascination with the way the quality of people's desire shapes their perception of God leads to the christological heart of his monastic-theological poetics. He creatively adapts and appropriates Origen and shares basic features of his biblical imagination. Bernard's view and presentation of the spiritual are highly charged and dynamic: the seeker is always falling back or straining forward to the goal, moving through conformity with Jesus crucified to transformation from glory

[66] Crouzel, *Origen*, 112.

to glory. The degree of the seeker's conformity determines the accuracy of his or her perspective on images and the sensible world. The education of desire towards the eternal sets love in order and heals inner division. Bernard teaches that in his ascension Christ elevates and transforms the love of those who look longingly after him as he carries their desire with him into heaven. This notion of an evolving capacity for God flows naturally into a vision of heaven characterized not by static rest but by the expansion and energy of *epektasis*, another dimension of Bernard's Origenist imagination.

Bernard's view, also drawn from Origen, that even the highest realities in this life, such as the humanity of Jesus and the Eucharist, are only shadows of the glory to be revealed, does not denigrate life in time but recalls the high destiny to which human beings have been called in Christ. Everything on this side of the veil is transitional: Jesus' mortal humanity and our own. Yet the goods of this world are not left behind, but taken up into a higher fulfillment both begun and prefigured by the ascension. Bernard's highly spiritual focus is not elitist but realistic. Jesus crucified becomes in effect the one idol, the worship of whom, because he is also the Word, draws idolaters toward the living God, cleansing their desire and revealing the icon within the idol. The incarnate Word thus becomes, says Marion, "the unsurpassable measure of what man can know of God. His body . . . became the actuality of measure, and hence the poetic center of the world."[67]

---

[67] Marion, *The Idol*, 108.

# 4. Amor Carnalis

Bernard presents the movement from carnal to spiritual love for the humanity of Jesus in a variety of schemes. In general they portray emotional attachment growing into a zeal for virtue that in turn grows into a mature spiritual affectivity that culminates in martyrdom, where ecstatic mystical love and zeal for virtue merge.

In a series of articles, Marsha Dutton argues that Bernard's impulse to move beyond the earthly visage of Jesus is motivated by "anxiety" over the dangers of remaining stuck at this phase of encounter. Bernard's protégé Aelred of Rievaulx, she claims, offers a more developed approach, one more at home with the humanity of Jesus, readier to find God in, rather than through, it. Far from being merely a matter of sensibility, however, Bernard's manner of presenting the humanity of Christ goes straight to the heart of his entire outlook and attests his creative appropriation of texts from Origen.

After acknowledging the extent of Bernard's influence on Aelred and listing elements on which they agree, Dutton claims they differ on "the effect of the Incarnation for humankind in this world," and on how it is that Jesus' love leads to God. For Aelred, Dutton claims, love for Jesus is not a first step to love for God, but an expression of it: "As Bernard's love for Jesus in his humanity results from and is evidence of human frailty, itself a result of the Fall, he reaches ever beyond it, longing to transcend love of God in flesh so as to arrive finally at the love of God in spirit."[1] In fact, however, Bernard is concerned to transcend a fleshly love of Jesus considered as man, one that lacks a living sense of what it means for him to also be Son of God, a love that is preoccupied with its own gratification and projections through which it is unable to accurately perceive Jesus. He aims for a spiritual love of God "for his own sake" and *sicuti est*.

As the previous chapter's discussion of the ascension sermons has shown, Bernard links parts of the seamless garment of Jesus' mysteries with corresponding states of soul in the believer. When he speaks of carnal love for the pre-Easter Jesus he faults the quality of human affection rather than some deficiency in Jesus' human nature. Of course, as the mystery of the ascension demonstrates, Jesus' mortal humanity was not a stopping place but was destined for glory. Like attracts like, and those whose faith is weak are inclined to remain within the safety of a familiar way of being. They are drawn to Jesus the man insofar as he is "just like them," and so they resist the dizzying prospect of his glory. This resistance corresponds to a fearful self-limitation of the believers' own human possibility, to their own destiny as foreshadowed in Jesus' ascension, and constitutes a rejection of the real otherness and transcendence of God. Consistent with his broader poetics, Bernard underlines the artifice of the incarnation, the step taken by ironic imagination in the movement of faith, so accenting the disparity between appearance and being. That he so places the accent is not the result of disdain for the flesh; the distance between appearance and being is required to secure the integrity of each. The emptiness of distance creates the space for longing, steered by the hope of glory revealed in the ascension.

---

[1] Marsha L. Dutton, "The Face and Feet of God: The Humanity of Christ in Bernard of Clairvaux and Aelred of Rievaulx," in *Bernardus Magister*, ed. John R. Sommerfeldt, CS 135 (Kalamazoo, MI: Cistercian Publications, 1992), 205.

There is both a spiritual and a carnal love of humanity for Bernard. Mystical experience "beyond images," he says, occurs rarely and for a brief moment (*rara hora, parva mora*), an ecstasy that is the gift of God and beyond human power to produce. Just as Jesus' ascension reinterprets and recapitulates the events of his ministry, ecstasy transfigures the visible for the mystic, including the memory and imagination of Jesus' earthly life. If the humanity of Jesus no longer had any value for Bernard after his taste of the God beyond images, Bernard would no longer continue to write about Jesus as he did. That human contact with the divine remains mediated for Bernard is supported by his frequent refrain that in this life we see "in a mirror." Jean-Marie Déchanet emphasizes this point: "It is clear that the highest revelations, the most sublime ecstasies, the most exalted mystical graces, will never exempt the Christian soul from returning to the flesh of Christ, to Christ by way of the flesh, the only way to the Father, the one bridge from earth to heaven, from the 'land of unlikeness' to 'the fatherland'; between a human being tied by sin to a body of flesh and the God who is Spirit and the father of spirits."[2] Further, a believer's shifting focus away from the humanity of Jesus can mean not a lessening of closeness to him but an increase. Christ becomes no longer an object of meditation, something external, but rather one lives with the very life of Christ and is animated by the Spirit with Jesus' own zeal for virtue and yearning for the Father.

---

[2] "C'est dire clairement que les révélations les plus hautes, les extases les plus sublimes, les graces mystiques les plus relevées, ne dispenseront jamais l'âme chrétienne de revenir à la chair du Christ, au Christ selon la chair, unique voie pour aller au Père, unique pont de la terre au ciel, de la 'region de la dissemblance' à la 'patrie'; entre l'homme lié par le péché à un corps de chair, et Dieu, Esprit et père des esprits" (Jean-Marie Déchanet, "La Christologie de S. Bernard," in *Saint Bernard Théologien: Actes du Congrès de Dijon 15–19 Septembre, Analecta SOC 9* [Rome: Curia Generalis S.O.C., 1953], 78–91, here 91).

Prayerful Christian reflection on memories and images of Jesus' mortal human nature is always with a view to communion with the living, risen Christ in glory. Consideration of Jesus' life on earth is inseparable for the Christian from encounter with his risen presence here and now. The New Testament presents no direct access to Jesus' human nature as it existed before Easter. Memory of that nature is always, including and especially in the gospels, in and through the light of glory. Bernard presents Jesus to an audience that includes monks more and less advanced on the way of love, for whom Jesus' humanity is more or less opaque. Accordingly, his rhetoric oscillates between pedagogical styles, using an array of methods, always with the end goal of stirring desire for the presence of the risen Christ.

This manner of proceeding, however, can give the impression of a Christ compartmentalized into flesh and spirit, concrete and abstract. Dutton, for instance, writes, "So Bernard, often credited with originating twelfth-century devotion to the humanity of Christ, reveals himself as augustinian in his efforts to maintain a clear hierarchical distinction between God known in the flesh, available to because necessary to spiritual beginners, and God known in spirit. He is always less drawn finally to the man Jesus, infant, boy, or crucified lord, than to the fruits of his flesh, faith and salvation."[3] This passage however, again collapses the object and the quality of love. The Christ with whom the believer is now in communion, through or without the mediation of images of Jesus' life on earth, is the risen Christ, whose body is spiritual. If the manifestation of God in mortal flesh had been a stopping point, God would have stopped there, but he did not! The suggestion here is that Bernard bypasses the concrete (infant, boy, lord) for an abstraction (faith, salvation); however, it is only through faith that one begins to come into contact with the living God, to gain a sense

---

[3] Dutton, "The Face," 212.

of what it means that Christ is Lord. Bernard's concern is not with an abstraction but with what is most immediate to the believer: his own experience of salvation, through participation in the life of Christ.

Further, Dutton contrasts a disposition of tenderness with moral force in a way that is alien to Bernard's (and Aelred's) mentality. After citing a passage in which Bernard speaks of the great value meditation on Jesus' suffering has held for him, she complains that he advocates reflection on these sufferings "for their moral benefit rather than for increased love or knowledge of God."[4] Yet for Bernard these two are inseparable: growth in the moral life, the education of desire, is the way to greater love and knowledge. There is a modern tendency to equate the moral with moralizing; however, in Bernard's world, the ethical and the aesthetic are fused. He and his readers took delight in the art of living and its creative refinement, and this delight comes through in the texts, for the sympathetic reader.[5]

If there is a false distinction drawn between love and virtue, there is also a tendency to collapse distinctions in Dutton's language. She cites a passage in Aelred in which he states that "the Son of God entered into our mortality, bringing about so great a unity between himself and our human nature that, according to our catholic faith, he did not clothe himself with man but became man." He speaks of how "between the garment and the wearer there should be no difference." She praises the fact that Aelred "accents the indistinguishability between God as the garment—Christ's humanity—and its wearer—Christ's divinity—by moving briefly from the metaphor of the tunic and its wearer to simple propositional insistence that all that Christ in his humanity does, Christ in his

---

[4] Dutton, "The Face," 211.
[5] See Emero Stiegman, "A Tradition of Aesthetics in Bernard of Clairvaux," in *Bernardus Magister*, ed. John Sommerfeldt, CS 135 (Kalamazoo, MI: Cistercian Publications, 1992), 134.

divinity does as well: 'God sleeps, God thirsts.'"[6] A garment and its wearer may seem indistinguishable, and yet they are distinguished. The reason sleep and thirst can be attributed to God is of course that the personhood of Christ is divine, with the garment of a human nature joined to it.

Bernard is not worried about loving "God in the flesh." By "carnal" love he means an immature attachment to what is safe and familiar in the human Jesus in a way that precludes, or drastically reduces the scope of, faith. To recognize that Jesus is God is ultimately to recognize that he is Spirit (and that his risen body is spiritual).[7] Dutton, however, ties carnal love to the object of love (Jesus' humanity) rather than seeing it as a way of loving: "It is not then necessary for Aelred to leave behind God known and loved in flesh, to put off the carnal love for Jesus in order to love God in spirit. It is only necessary to recognize that Jesus is in fact God and so to love him as God. The tunic, the veil of flesh assumed by God, only works to hide God, perhaps, from those who are not truly looking."[8] Similarly: "For Aelred the contemplative's vision of Jesus the man is a vision of Jesus who is God, and as he is known now in meditation and in occasional contemplative vision he will be known in eternity."[9] In this last passage "vision" is unclear. If it means a sensible memory or imagining, or even a mystical vision, will the quality of the encounter with Christ in heaven not be more direct—face to face rather than through an image?

Aelred shares Bernard's "anxiety" about carnal love. In a passage cited by Dutton he writes: "The love that comes about through feeling is pleasant but dangerous. . . . Love induced

---

[6] Dutton, "The Face," 215–16; on the iconic nature of Jesus' humanity, Jean-Luc Marion writes, "The reference of human nature to the divine nature expresses, in the very person of Christ, the reference of the Son to the Father. Without this reference, the Son, denying himself as Son, masks the Father, and collapses as God" (*The Idol and Distance: Five Studies*, trans. Thomas A. Carlson [New York: Fordham University Press, 2001], 117, n. 45).

[7] Dutton, "The Face," 222.

[8] Dutton, "The Face," 221.

[9] Dutton, "The Face," 220.

by mere feeling may well be good, but what we love in this way we love because it is pleasant and nothing more. But in the full and perfect love [that comes from the collaboration of reason, feeling, and will] we love not because it is pleasant to do so, but because it is the love of something worthy."[10]

While Aelred may indeed stress the "visible and palpable physicality" of the incarnation in a distinctive way, he yet imagines a movement through and beyond the physical to the spiritual. As Elias Dietz observes, "it is worth noting that Aelred does not allow this emphasis to become an imbalance. Along with Bernard—for whom the theme was important—Aelred reaffirms Saint Paul's teaching about the need to progress from *amor carnalis* to *amor spiritalis*. Aelred mentions this need less frequently than Bernard and is perhaps gentler in his approach, but he was equally convinced about the importance of this progression."[11] He proceeds to give a passage from Aelred that celebrates the "greater joy" of those who can say,

---

[10] Marsha L. Dutton, "Intimacy and Imitation: The Humanity of Christ in Cistercian Spirituality," in *Erudition at God's Service: Studies in Medieval Cistercian History, XI*, CS 98 (Kalamazoo, MI: Cistercian Publications, 1987), 56, citing Aelred, Spec car 3:20.

[11] Elias Dietz, "Aelred on the Humanity of Christ: A Theology in Images," CSQ 45, no. 3 (2010): 277. The article begins by mentioning the three essays by Dutton. It also refers (277, n. 15) to Bernard McGinn's evaluation of Aelred's view on the subject, which reads in part, "Aelred's sustained attempts to rouse his readers to an affective but still spiritual devotion to the beauty and love of Jesus gives his mode of expressing the *amor carnalis Christi* a different flavor from what we have seen in Bernard and the other Cistercians. It has also been claimed that he differed from Bernard in rejecting any real distinction between love in the flesh and love in the spirit, that is, that he was not interested in encouraging the kind of transition from *amor carnalis* Christi to the *amor spiritalis* that Bernard felt was the true goal of the contemplative. To be sure, the Englishman seems to have a stronger sense of the fact that in loving Christ's flesh we are already loving God and that this form of love is one that will always be needed in this life, but the presence of texts in which Aelred, like Bernard, speaks of spiritual love as a higher form indicates that one should beware of making any sharp distinction between the abbot of Rievaulx and the abbot of Clairvaux on this point" (Bernard McGinn, "The Growth of Mysticism," *The Presence of God: A History of Western Christian Mysticism*, vol. 2 [New York: Crossroad, 1994], 315–16).

"'Even if we know Christ in the flesh, now we no longer know him in this way.' A great joy it is to see how our Lord lay in the manger, but a much greater joy it is to see how the Lord reigns in heaven."[12]

### De quattuor modis dilectionis

A careful reading of key texts in which Bernard describes the movement from carnal to spiritual love supports this view. In the short sermon *De quattuor modis dilectionis* he elucidates his understanding of carnal and spiritual love.[13] He states that there are two kinds of love, spiritual and carnal, and that these include four modes, in ascending order: (1) a carnal love of the carnal, (2) a carnal love of the spiritual, (3) a spiritual love of the carnal, and (4) a spiritual love of the spiritual. After giving examples of each from the gospels, where the disciples show love for Jesus in each of these four ways, he provides four corresponding ways in which his readers can love—not Jesus, interestingly, but themselves—in each of the different modes. He illustrates the first mode by the fact that when God was made flesh and lived among and spoke with the disciples they first loved him as a man among men.

In the second mode, Bernard explains that when the disciples realized that Jesus was willing to lay his life down for them, they loved his spirit but in a "carnal" way. The illustration Bernard selects for this example is instructive: "Moreover, when he was willing to lay down his life for his friends, they

---

[12] Dietz, "Aelred," 277, citing Aelred's S 20.4 (CF 58:276).

[13] Bernard, Div 101 (SBOp 6/1:368; Bernard of Clairvaux, *Monastic Sermons*, trans. Daniel Griggs, CF 68 [Collegeville, MN: Cistercian Publications, 2016], 376–77). Helpful context is supplied by Damien Boquet, *L'ordre de l'affect au Moyen Âge: autour de l'anthropologie affective d'Aelred de Rievaulx* (Caen, France: Crahm, 2005), 119–49, "À la jonction de l'âme et la corps." Boquet distinguishes a spiritual/ascetical dualism (as in Bernard) from a metaphysical one.

were already loving the spirit, but still in a carnal way. So even Peter responded thus to Christ when he spoke about his passion: 'Far be it from you! Look out for yourself!'"[14] Peter has just confessed that Jesus is the messiah and Son of the living God (Matt 16:16); his understanding is shown to be carnal in that he advises Jesus to look out for himself, that is, to love in the way he, Peter, loves. He thus demonstrates faith of a sort, but reduced to a human level. Peter's own self-concern prevents him from imagining anything different for (or from) Jesus. He has a carnal love for the spiritual. In other words, faith allows him to see that Jesus is more than a man among men, but it is a weak faith, so limited by carnal affection that Peter does not really grasp the spirit that leads Jesus to lay down his life. Like seeks like, and love's knowledge is by affinity. Carnal (self-seeking, narcissistic, centripetal) love draws the beloved to be like itself, but spiritual love is transformed according to the image of Christ (2 Cor 3:18).

In the third mode, Bernard explains that spiritual love of the carnal characterizes the disciples' love for Jesus crucified once they recognize that his death is for their redemption. That Bernard considers this to be a higher love than the previous one makes it clear that it is the mode of love rather than the nature of what it is directed toward—flesh or spirit—that determines its value. The disciples see Jesus crucified not as a man among men, but as the manifestation of divine love and the means of their redemption; they see a physical reality with the eyes of faith, in a spiritual way—a spiritual reality in a carnal fact. Finally, for the fourth mode, the resurrection and ascension make possible spiritual love of the spiritual Christ: "When, however, he rises again and ascends, they love the spirit spiritually, and joyfully they sing, 'And if we have

---

[14] Bernard, Div 101 (SBOp 6/1:368; CF 68:376): *Cum autem pro amicis suis animam ponere vellet, iam spiritum diligebant, sed adhuc carnaliter. Unde et Petrus loquenti de passione sua respondit: "Absit a te! Propitius esto tibi."*

known Christ according to the flesh, now we know him so no longer.'"[15]

Bernard then applies the same modes of love to modes of self-love. For the first mode, that one loves oneself carnally is clear in that one "gratifies his desires." This expression, significantly, alludes to Galatians 5:16 and implies its context: Christ has set Christians free, and if they live by the Spirit they will not gratify the flesh; the two are opposed. This clarification shows that Bernard is mapping out "carnal" and "spiritual" love in a Pauline context. But whereas gratifying one's own desires comprises carnal love for the self, one loves one's spirit in a carnal way by compunction, in which physical/emotional outpourings express and further the life of the spirit.

Moving on to the two forms of spiritual self-love, Bernard argues that a spiritual relationship to the carnal appears in one who performs good works, in the material sphere, with spiritual discernment. Intriguingly, one reaches the fourth and highest love, spiritual love of the spiritual, when one places the needs of one's brothers before one's own spiritual exercises: "[We love] the spirit spiritually when out of charity we postpone even our spiritual pursuits for fraternal benefit."[16] In a way this example is surprising, as the love described seems to place material needs, that is, carnal, ahead of a spiritual goal. However the *utilitati* Bernard indicates could be what is spiritually needful for the community, as when Bernard puts aside his own restful contemplation for the business of preaching. It is not God who takes second place to human needs, but one's own spiritual exercises (*spiritualia studia*), such as meditating on the passion. In this fourth stage, however, one's own spiritual realization coincides with loving others, *eros* with *agape*,

---

[15] Bernard, Div 101 (SBOp 6/1:368; CF 68:376), citing 2 Cor 5:16: *Resurgente autem eo et ascendente, spiritum spiritualiter amant laetique decantant: Et si cognovimus Christum secundum carnem, sed nunc iam non novimus.*

[16] Bernard, Div 101 (SBOp 6/1:368; CF 68:376–77): *Spiritum spiritualiter, cum ipsa etiam spiritualia studia nostra fraternae utilitati ex caritate postponimus.*

and one has begun to love not only as God loves, but with God's own love: "For him, to be nourished is to nourish," Bernard says, and "to nourish is to be nourished."[17]

This fourfold scheme is similar to the four stages of love in Bernard's treatise *On Loving God*. Carnal love of the carnal corresponds with love of oneself for one's own sake, carnal love for the spiritual with love of God for one's own sake, spiritual love of the carnal with the love of God for his own sake, and spiritual love of the spiritual with love of oneself only insofar as one is loving and loved by God. Setting these two schemes side by side strengthens the identification Bernard makes in the first step of *De diversis* Sermon 101 of *carnal* with selfish. In the second stage one loves God "for one's own sake" to some extent when craving the emotional release of consolation in prayer. The third degree of love in *On Loving God* describes a transition in which delight in the goodness of God, manifest in the gifts by which he meets humans' material needs, begins to outweigh the urgency of those needs themselves.[18] So Bernard writes, "The needs of the flesh are a kind of speech, proclaiming in transports of joy the good things experienced," a language that becomes meaningful only when the center of gravity has shifted from oneself to God. Such a shift changes the appearance of sensible realities for the lover, transforming them from idols on which he models himself into a sacred, iconic language praising God. "This love is pleasing because it is free," Bernard writes, rather than driven by self-concern and the urgency of material want.[19] The last stage, loving oneself only in relation to God, is akin to the spiritual love of the spiritual expressed in putting what is useful to others ahead of even one's spiritual *studia*.

---

[17] Bernard, SC 71.4 (SBOp 2:216–17; CF 40:51).
[18] For the believer Jesus crucified attests divine love with singular power; see Bernard of Clairvaux, Dil 7.
[19] Bernard, Dil 26 (SBOp 3:141; CF 13B:28).

The degree of one's freedom then transforms one's relationship to material realities. Bernard connects likeness with God to a stability whereby one learns to cooperate with him in turning all things to good (Rom 8:28).[20] God *sicuti est* is unchanging, and the soul that is like God develops a stable disposition whereby that soul turns whatever occurs, trials or consolations, to good. Creation cooperates with the person who cooperates with God. Such a one, "made in the image and likeness of his Creator," Bernard writes,

> deems it unworthy to be conformed to a world that is waning. Instead, following Paul's teaching, he strives to be reformed by the renewal of his mind, aiming to achieve that likeness in which he knows he was created. And as is proper, this purpose of his compels the world itself, which was made for him, to become conformed to him by an admirable change of relationship, according as all things in their true and natural form begin to cooperate for his good. They become aware of the Lord for whose service they were created, and shed every trace of degeneracy.[21]

By conforming oneself to Christ one finds that all things begin to conform to oneself, so that the words of Jesus apply to believers as well, "And when I am lifted up from the earth I shall draw all things to myself." Bernard underlines the fact that everything belongs to those who are truly poor: "These possess earthly things but with the spirit of men who possess nothing; in reality they possess all things, not like unhappy beggars who get what they beg for, but as masters, masters in the best sense because devoid of avarice. *To the man of faith the whole world is a treasure-house of riches: the whole world, because all things, whether adverse or favorable, are of service to him; they*

---

[20] At SC 43.2, meditation on the humanity of Jesus anchors one between prosperity and sorrow.

[21] Bernard, SC 21.6 (SBOp 1:125–26; CF 7:8).

*all contribute to his good.*"[22] What is said here of material riches applies to all images and created realities: when one has been lifted up in conformity to the Image, all images become transparent and serve to help one on one's way. Bernard shows the literal lifting up of martyrdom to be the highest expression of love and the place where active and ecstatic love combine.

## Martyrdom

Bernard's sermon on the four modes of love (Div 101) continues material from an earlier sermon (Div 29) that begins by assuring the audience that the Father will provide a threefold love to exclude and replace the lust of the flesh, eyes, and world spoken of by John (1 John 2:15-16). It is threefold on the pattern of the command to love the Lord with all one's heart, soul, and strength, a love at the level of carnal affection, a discerning soul, and then a free and strong spirit. Affection for the humanity of Jesus excludes lesser carnal attachments, discernment (which creates distance from the passions) excludes the lust of the eyes, and the martyr's strength, embracing humiliation, replaces worldly ambition.

According to Bernard, the incarnation hides the wisdom and strength of God while at the same time revealing his goodness in a way that attracts the heart.[23] He does not hold affection to be intrinsically corrupt, though it can lead one astray if it lacks discernment (*si desit prudentia*).[24] Rather, this wisdom is hidden in the incarnation by the folly (*stultitiam*) of the Word, who goes to his death forgetful of himself and drunk on the wine of love: "Was he not drunk with the wine of charity and

---

[22] Bernard, SC 21.7 (SBOp 1:126; CF 7:9); my emphasis; see also SC 22.8, where the verse is interpreted to mean the humanly attractive power of the love revealed in Jesus' passion, and SC 76.1, where after the lifting up of the passion the ascension will draw all things up with divine power.

[23] Bernard, Div 29.3 (SBOp 6/1:212; CF 68:168).

[24] Bernard, Div 29.4 (SBOp 6/1:213; CF 68:169).

unmindful of himself, against the advice of Peter, who said, 'Take care for yourself' "?[25]

Bernard returns to this moment between Jesus and Peter later in the sermon. Peter's attempt to dissuade Jesus from going to the cross when he first announces his impending passion shows that Peter loves with affection but without wisdom. Similarly the disciples, Bernard writes, are sorrowful at the prospect of Jesus' ascension: "They both love and do not love; they love sweetly, but they do not love wisely."[26] Additionally, he says, Peter loved wisely but without force when he promised he would die with Jesus but in the event deserted him.[27]

For, Bernard continues, the strong do not seek worldly honor but instead suffer for justice. Only those are fit to lead others who, drunk on the wine of love, forget themselves and burn not for what is their own but for the things of Christ: "For one who is intoxicated and burning with the wine of charity should lead others, unmindful of himself, so that he 'seeks not things that are his own but rather things that are Jesus Christ's.' "[28] In that way Christ becomes less an external object for meditation and more another life within one's own; the things that concerned him—the care of the flock, even to laying down one's life—are now one's own: "It is no longer I who live but Christ lives in me."[29] This is the *unity of spirit*, a voluntary union or conformity that for Bernard is always the goal.

Thus natural affection has passed through the crucible of freedom, the work and wisdom of virtue, to become spiritual

---

[25] Bernard, Div 29.3 (SBOp 6/1:212; CF 68:168): *Nonne ebrius erat vino caritatis, et immemor sui, contra Petri consilium dicentis: "Propitius esto tibi"?*

[26] Bernard, Div 29.5 (SBOp 6/1:213; CF 68:169): *Et diligunt, et non diligunt: diligunt dulciter, sed non sapienter.*

[27] Bernard, Div 29.5 (SBOp 6/1:213; CF 68:169–70).

[28] Bernard, Div 29.5 (SBOp 6/1:213; CF 68:170): *Ille enim praesse debet aliis, qui vino caritatis debriatus aestuat, immemor sui, ut non quaerat quae sua sunt, sed magis quae Iesu Christi.*

[29] Gal 2:20.

*affectus*, a new delight that flows from and includes union of purpose with the risen Christ. Significantly, Bernard fuses the ecstatic and contemplative associations of wine with active martyrdom. It is not contemplation alone, but the experience of the martyr, a blend of active and ecstatic love, that represents the summit for him. His example of spiritual love for the spiritual is illustrative: the brothers' concerns trump one's own. The essential thing is that love has become centrifugal. Whether one is drawn out of oneself in the ecstasy of contemplation or by the needs of others, one's center of gravity is outside. One grows in love and the freedom that constitutes being in the image of God by being drawn out of oneself in this way, living with the life of the Word who leapt out of himself and entered time in an ecstasy of love, and who reached the summit of love not in contemplation but on the cross. For Bernard too, the Christian experience of martyrdom is the height of love, a fusion of the mystical and active, where the ecstasy of service and the ecstasy of erotic contact are one.

## Love's Order: SC 20

In sermons 20 and 50 on the Song of Songs Bernard presents other patterns describing the development of love. These patterns are never rigid for him, however. A person could be said to be characteristically in one phase more than another, but to some extent each phase remains present at all stages and can even be integrated into and elevated by later development.[30] As there is pliability within a given ordering, so too in the comparison of one arrangement with another. There need not be one-to-one harmonization. Indeed, Bernard allows the different schemes to almost, but not quite, line up in suggestive ways.

---

[30] Bernard makes this point clear in Dil 38 by the way he shows fear and self-interest as taken up into and refined by love.

Sermon 20 includes key ideas and allusions from Div 29 in a more polished format and provides a natural starting point for discussions of Bernard's view of Jesus' humanity and the transition from carnal to spiritual love. If there were any doubt that Jesus is God (and vice versa) for Bernard, the first few sections of this sermon ought to allay them as he compares the works of redemption and creation, claiming that the labor of Jesus on the cross was greater than that of the Creator at the beginning of time. The realization that Jesus is God makes him so attractive: "How sweet it is to see as man the Creator of humanity."[31] Bernard continues, "His love was sweet, and wise, and strong. I call it sweet because he took on a human body, wise because he avoided sin, strong because he endured death. Even though he took a body, his love was never sensual, but always in the wisdom of the Spirit. 'A Spirit before our face is Christ the Lord,' jealous of us but with the jealousy of God, not man, and certainly not like that of the first man, Adam, for Eve."[32] In this passage the love of the incarnate Word follows the pattern Bernard develops in Div 29, moving from carnal love to wise to strong. Again he links strength to martyrdom and describes the incarnation as "sweet," a gracious expression of divine humility.

As in Div 29, in this passage too Bernard offers as examples of carnal affection both Peter's attempt to hold Jesus back from the cross (Mark 8:31-32) and the sadness of the disciples on Jesus' ascension.[33] Similarly, the gap between Peter's promise to die with Jesus and the strength to carry this out recurs here.[34] So Bernard emphasizes that Christians are to learn from Christ how to love Christ.[35] He goes on to compare this threefold love to the love of heart, soul, and strength (Deut 6:5):

---

[31] Bernard, SC 20.2, 3 (SBOp 1:115; CF 4:148).
[32] Bernard, SC 20.3 (SBOp 1:115; CF 4:148).
[33] Bernard, SC 20.5 (SBOp 1:117–18; CF 4:150–51).
[34] Bernard, SC 20.5 (SBOp 1:117; CF 4:151).
[35] Bernard, SC 20.4 (SBOp 1:116; CF 4:149).

The love of the heart relates to a certain warmth of affection, the love of the soul to energy or judgment of reason, and the love of strength can refer to constancy and vigor of spirit. So love the Lord your God with the full and deep affection of your heart, love him with your mind wholly awake and discreet, love him with all your strength, so much so that you would not even fear to die for him. . . . Your affection for your Lord Jesus should be both tender and intimate, to oppose the sweet enticements of sensual life. Sweetness conquers sweetness as one nail drives out another.[36]

The simultaneity of the three modes of love in this account suggests that advance in love in a given phase involves the experience of love predominantly rather than exclusively. Bernard describes one love in a multifaceted process of transformation, as for instance when he speaks of carnal love's "becoming" rational and spiritual: "But that carnal love is worthwhile since through it sensual love is excluded, and the world is condemned and conquered. It becomes better when it is rational, and becomes perfect when it is spiritual."[37] Yet one love remains higher than another: "We know that the love of the heart, which we have said is affectionate, is sweet indeed, but liable to be led astray if it lacks the love of the soul. And the love of the soul is wise indeed, but fragile without that love which is called the love of strength." While it is love for Jesus in view here, the process described remains an interiorization of Jesus' love. As Bernard writes towards the close of this sermon, "Of course love for Christ is a gift, a great gift of the Spirit. I have called it carnal with comparison to that other love which does not know the Word as flesh so much as the Word as wisdom, as justice, truth, holiness, loyalty, strength, and whatever else could be said in this manner."[38] The

---

[36] Bernard, SC 20.4 (SBOp 1:116; CF 4:150).
[37] Bernard, SC 20.9 (SBOp 1:120; CF 4:154).
[38] Bernard, SC 20.8 (SBOp 1:120; CF 4:154).

examples he gives suggest that far from referring to justice, truth, and so on in the abstract, Bernard has in mind Christ as a force living these qualities in and through the believer: "In giving me himself, he gave me myself."[39]

Indeed the cultivation of right desire, a pedagogy of the heart, is the motive for the incarnation in Bernard's view: "I think this is the principal reason why the invisible God willed to be seen in the flesh and to converse with men as a man. He wanted to recapture the affections of carnal men who were unable to love in any other way, by first drawing them to the salutary love of his own humanity, and then gradually to raise them to a spiritual love." He then returns to his examples of the disciples' resistance to the passion, then the ascension: "So it was only by his physical presence that their hearts were detached from carnal loves."[40]

### Love's Order: SC 50

Commenting on the verse, "He set love in order in me" (Song 2:4), in SC 50 Bernard presents another threefold order of love, still basically related to love of "heart, mind, and strength."[41] In this presentation, however, he gives the first sort of love as a kind of concupiscence so intractably turned in on itself that it is incapable of transformation. Next he describes a dutiful but "emotionless" love that shows concern for those most in need.[42] But the highest love, imperfectly realized on earth, matches feeling to virtue. What one performs dutifully in the active mode is done with delight at the level of spiritual *affectus*.

For Bernard, someone in the second, active mode places the practical necessities of life in the distorted order of a fallen

---

[39] Bernard, Dil 15 (SBOp 3:132; CF 13B:18).
[40] Bernard, SC 20.6 (SBOp 1:118; CF 4:152).
[41] Bernard, SC 50.6 (SBOp 2:87; CF 31:35).
[42] "Emotionless," but zealous and "still vehemently aflame with the love of love itself" (Bernard, SC 50.4 [SBOp 2:86; CF 31:33]).

world ahead of what the spirit most enjoys and what is of itself a higher goal, desire for God. It follows the truth of love, where the higher order operates by love of truth. The active level seems to involve adhering to and performing the truth of what charity indicates ought to be done, from a zeal for virtue, a "love of love," where the third delights, without resistance, in showing love for others. Here *eros* and *agape* are one. This alternative scheme complicates things considerably, and it is easy to see how it could lead to confusion. A key to its interpretation lies in Bernard's statement that the higher, affective love "always leads the ordering from the first."[43] This love, he goes on, "is the wisdom by which all things are experienced as they are; as, for example, the higher the nature the more perfect the love it evokes; the lower evokes less, the lowest nothing."[44]

Active love, then, is for Bernard a transposition of spiritual *affectus* into another mode, one required by postlapsarian life. It is love "as a confused reflection in a mirror":

> Now the active prefers what is lowly, the affective what is lofty. For example, there is no doubt that in a mind that loves rightly, the love of God is valued more than the love of men, and among men themselves the more perfect more than the weak, heaven more than earth, eternity more than the flesh. In well-regulated action, on the other hand, the opposite order frequently or even always prevails. For we are more strongly impelled toward and more often occupied with the welfare of our neighbor; we attend our weaker brothers with more exacting care.[45]

Thus *eros*—spiritual affect—leads from the first and motivates the zeal, the love of love that characterizes the active mode. Martyrdom, the expression of "strong" love in Div 29 and SC

---

[43] Bernard, SC 50.6 (SBOp 2:87; CF 31:35).
[44] Bernard, SC 50.6 (SBOp 2:87; CF 31:35).
[45] Bernard, SC 50.5 (SBOp 2:87; CF 31:34).

20, is the height of the erotic love that values God over every lesser good, even one's own life. The martyr, like God himself in his incarnation, is drunk on the wine of love and completely self-forgetful. So the martyr scorns what is allegedly higher—e.g., worldly honors—and embraces humiliation, glad to suffer for the kingdom.

In *On Loving God* Bernard describes the fourth and highest degree of love in terms of transcending material necessities. As in Div 101 he expresses this idea in the language of inebriation and self-forgetfulness, as a fragile state soon interrupted by the weaknesses of the flesh, "and sometimes with greater violence than these, brotherly love." He goes on to state that love with all one's heart, soul, and strength cannot be attained beneath the press of material needs, but concludes, "All the same, do we not think the holy martyrs received this grace, at least partially, while they were still in their victorious bodies? The strength of this love seized their souls so entirely that, despising the pain, they were able to expose their bodies to exterior torments. No doubt the feeling of intense pain could only upset their calm; it could not overcome them."[46] The summit of spiritual love is found then not in leaving behind the humanity of Jesus but in becoming it, in being so united with his Spirit that one loves and dies as he did. Martyrdom blends the two modes of love (*actus* and *affectus*).

Bernard holds that meditation on the passion of Jesus leads to strength for martyrdom, a belief he illustrates by his portrayal of the Bride's manner of meditation: "All her affections are preoccupied with the wounds of Christ; she abides in them by constant meditation. From this comes endurance for martyrdom, for this her immense trust in the Most High. The martyr need not be afraid of raising his bloodless and bruised face to him by whose wounds he is healed, to present to him a glorious likeness of his death."[47] In the ecstasy of love, then,

---

[46] Bernard, Dil 29 (SBOp 3:144; CF 13B:31).
[47] Bernard, SC 61.7 (SBOp 2:152; CF 31:146–47).

martyrs love themselves only in relation to God to such a degree that they are willing to undergo torments in their mortal bodies:

> While gazing on the Lord's wounds he will indeed not feel his own. The martyr remains jubilant and triumphant though his whole body is mangled; even while the steel is gashing his sides he looks around with courage and elation at the holy blood pouring from his flesh. Where then is the soul of the martyr? In a safe place, of course; in the rock, of course; in the heart of Jesus, of course, in wounds open for it to enter. . . . Nor should we wonder if, exiled from the body, it does not feel bodily pains. Insensibility does not bring this about, love does. For the feelings are not lost, they are leashed. And pain is not absent, it is scorned. From the rock therefore comes the courage of the martyr, from it obviously his power to drink the Lord's cup. And this intoxicating cup—how wonderful it is! Wonderful, I say, and sweet, no less to the commander looking on than to the conquering soldier. "For the joy of the Lord is our strength."[48]

The martyr has thus become identified more with the risen life of Christ within him than with his own mortal body. Through the memory of the material wounds of Jesus each martyr becomes one spirit with Christ, receiving in himself courage and power. Bernard's "intoxicating cup" recalls the wine of love (Div 29 and 101) that propelled the Word to leap out of himself and enter time in a radical embrace of measure at its most impoverished: the height and depth, length and breadth of the cross.

Bernard's account of martyrdom makes clear that the active and the spiritually affective dimensions in the life of the monk are united by love and freedom, one love and freedom, one likeness with God that grows by being stretched by both

---

[48] Bernard, SC 61.8 (SBOp 2:153; CF 31:147).

contemplative prayer and the demands of service. The goal is to love with God's own love. In the divine love that became flesh and went to the cross, "drunk on the wine of charity," delight is found precisely in giving oneself away. The descent of the Word in becoming man coincides with the ascent of the man Christ Jesus, whose longing for union with the Father culminates in his gift on the cross. So Bernard can write of the incarnation of the Word, "he ascended in this very act of descending."[49]

---

[49] Bernard, Asc 4.3 (SBOp 5:139; CF 53:46).

## 5. "Black but Beautiful": Bernard's Incarnational Poetics

In one of his best known works, Sermon 26 *On the Song of Songs*, Bernard appears to violently break off his commentary on the text (Song 1:4, "I am black but beautiful, daughters of Jerusalem, as the tents of Kedar, as the curtains of Solomon") to lament the recent death of his brother Gerard. But far from being a total disjunction, Bernard's lament continues his commentary on the Song by means of his personal meditation on the experience of grief.[1] The apparent contradiction of a suffering (black) but grace-filled (beautiful) bride reverberates through a series of contraries—carnal and spiritual for instance, or affection and faith—that structure his lament. His method throughout is to intensify the opposition between these contraries before revealing them as fused in the tangle of mortal human life. He is better able to express such complexity in the form of lyrical reflection on experience than in more conventional or scholastic methods. As he shifts into the lament he asks, "I, whose life is bitterness, what have I to do with this canticle?" He then answers his question in a way that shows the Song to be the very best remedy for his sorrow, and he then demonstrates its deep relevance to the human condition.

---

[1] Wim Verbaal also sees the sermon as a commentary but focuses on the reader's experience of the text. See Verbaal, "Preaching the Dead from Their Graves: Bernard of Clairvaux's Lament on His Brother Gerard," in *Speculum Sermonis: Interdisciplinary Reflections on the Medieval Sermon* (Turnhout: Brepols, 2004), 113–39.

Bernard portrays the movement from a carnal to a spiritual perspective in both his struggle with his own grief and the divinization of Gerard's love for his bereft brother. In the first case he dramatizes his effort to stoically restrain carnal grief but arrives at a poignant vindication of an affectivity not opposed to faith but acting as its existential anchor. In the second while it appears to him at first that Gerard must have moved beyond concern for those he loved on earth, ultimately the spiritualization of his love makes it infinitely more powerful and personal. Similarly, Bernard sharply contrasts material and moral beauty, the visible and the invisible, only to celebrate their fusion in the bride. He opposes his personal, existential manner of lyrical exegesis to the approach of those whom he calls philosophers and whom he accuses of being motivated by curiosity and a lust for glory to probe into mysteries beyond rational understanding.

### From Carnal to Spiritual—and Back: Compassion and Grief

Appearance and reality, visible and invisible, practical and contemplative, ugly and virtuous, Bernard and Gerard: these apparent contraries are among the versions of "black but beautiful" that Bernard presents in these sermons, in each case moving from their strict opposition to their entanglement in mortal life. Bernard at first portrays Gerard as having moved beyond the measure of human concern: "You feel our absence as no loss. You have no cause to complain that we have been cut off from you, favored as you are by the constant presence of the Lord of Majesty and of his heavenly friends." But by the end of the paragraph he is convinced that "since love never ends, you will not forget me forever."[2] What transpires in the short space between is a particularly compressed instance of

---

[2] Bernard, SC 26.5 (SBOp 1:173; CF 7:63).

the way Bernard often pushes contraries to extreme opposition before showing how they merge in a higher resolution.

Bernard sets the immediacy of his sense of loss against his presentation of Gerard become wholly spiritual—raised above concern for those still in exile. From the snapshot of Gerard impervious in glory Bernard wrenches the frame to his own bitter suffering and, undermining the initial presentation, begins to wonder aloud, "Perhaps you still give thought to our miseries, now that you have plunged into the abyss of light, become engulfed in that sea of endless happiness." At this point he holds in tension the hope of connection and the radical contrast between Gerard's happiness and Bernard's misery. Here Bernard injects what is perhaps his favorite text for depicting the move from carnal to spiritual: "It is possible that though you once knew us according to the flesh, you now no longer know us" (1 Cor 5:16). Gerard, he says, has found "his whole being somehow changed into a movement of divine love," and so "your love has not been diminished but only changed." Bernard thus formulates a compact, culminating argument as he reflects on Gerard's fully "spiritual" love vis-à-vis his own:

> He no longer has the power to experience or relish anything but God, and what God himself experiences and relishes, because he is filled with God. But God is love, and the deeper one's union with God, the more full one is of love. And though God cannot endure pain, he is not without compassion for those who do [*porro impassibilis est Deus, sed non incompassibilis*]; it is his nature to show mercy and pardon. Therefore you too must of necessity be merciful, clasped as you are to him who is mercy, and though you no longer feel the need of mercy, though you no longer suffer, you can still be compassionate. Your love has not been diminished but only changed; when you were clothed with God you did not divest yourself of concern for us, for God is certainly concerned about us. All that smacks of weakness you have cast away, but not

what pertains of love. And since love never comes to an end, you will not forget me forever.³

The spiritual of which Bernard writes here is divine love expressed by incarnation. If the eternal life of the Trinity, complete and unhindered in itself, is in some way intrinsically higher and freer than its revelation in time, there is yet a singular beauty and goodness proper to the Incarnate Word. Similarly, in SC 50, Bernard describes erotic love for God alone as intrinsically higher than love for others while recognizing that in time the demands of charity often trump the desire for contemplation. Such practical love has its own proper integrity, and even beauty. Indeed, Bernard portrays Gerard as the practical one, who made possible the abbot's own forays into contemplation. Gerard's industrious zeal was the "curtain of Solomon" that allowed Bernard the privacy to enter the Holy of Holies.⁴ The curtain was "black," weathered by its exposure to material cares, and in its blackness, as the grief-stricken Bernard now perceives so keenly, "beautiful."

Reflection in faith has allowed Bernard to reach this consoling vision of Gerard, who now takes on a maternal aspect: "It seems to me that I can almost hear my brother saying: Can a woman forget the son of her womb? And if she should forget, yet I will not forget you" (Isa 49:15). But immediately he is yanked back from the perspective of faith to the urgency of the moment, "In every emergency I look to Gerard for help, as I always did, *and he is not there.*" In this way he dramatizes the tension between genuine faith and the pressure of experience. The process recalls the basic pattern seen for instance in

---

³ Bernard, SC 26.5 (SBOp 1:163; CF 7:63).
⁴ Bernard, SC 26.6 (SBOp 1:174; CF 7:65): "Your involvement in the business of the house gave me the leisure and privacy for more prayerful absorption in divine contemplation, for more thorough preparation of doctrine for my sons. Why should I not rest secure in my cell when I knew that you were my spokesman with the people, my right-hand man, the light of my eyes, my heart and my tongue?"

SC 50: from a threatened explosion of carnal grief, through its stoic suppression, to an affection elevated and purified by faith, a faith that has owned and integrated the power of affection and the fuller truth of concrete experience.

In his lament for Gerard Bernard solicits from his readers "not mere conventional respect but . . . human affection." He distinguishes his own grief, sifted by reflection in faith, from those who weep "solely for the loss of earthly glory." He continues: "Can it be possible I am one of them? My emotional outburst is certainly like theirs, but the cause, the intention differs."[5] Bernard claims that the spiritual bond between him and Gerard ran deeper than their physical kinship: "We were of one mind, and it was this, not blood relationship, that joined us as one. That he was my blood-brother certainly mattered; but our spiritual affinity, our similar outlooks and harmony of temperaments, drew us more close still."

Death separates; love reunites. Bernard enacts these movements in his language in a way that continues and extends the both/and logic of the black-but-beautiful theme. No sooner has he neatly divided the carnal from the spiritual than he complicates and retracts this separation in a rhetorically loaded vindication of the human measure found in grief, affection, friendship:

> My very heart is torn from me, and shall it be said to me: "Try not to feel it?" But I do feel it intensely in spite of myself, because my strength is not the strength of stones nor is my flesh of bronze. I feel it and go on grieving; my pain is ever with me. He who chastises me will never be able to accuse me of hardness and insensibility. . . . I have made public the depth of my affliction, I make no attempt to deny it. Will you say then that this is carnal? That it is human, yes, since I am a man [*Ego humanum non nego, sicut nec me hominem*]. . . . If this does not satisfy

---

[5] Bernard, SC 26.8 (SBOp 1:176; CF 7:68).

> you, then I am carnal, sold under sin, destined to die, subject to penalties and sufferings. I am certainly not insensible to pain; to think that I shall die, that those who are mine shall die, fills me with dread. And Gerard was mine, so utterly mine. . . . I feel it, the wound is deep.[6]

Bernard would concede that he is carnal rather than relinquish the truth in his experience of grief. The alternative he prefers is that such grief, informed by faith, is not only to be tolerated but is the proper human response to loss. This vindication of spiritual *affectus* is followed a moment later by a similar defense of friendship, also in terms of the human: "It is but human and necessary that we respond to our friends with feeling [*Humanum, inquam, et necesse affici erga caros*]: that we be happy in their company, disappointed in their absence. Social intercourse, especially between friends, cannot be purposeless; the reluctance to part and the yearning for each other when separated indicate how meaningful their mutual love must be when they are together."[7] The rhetorically clinching argument for Bernard and the theological ground is incarnational: Jesus himself wept.[8]

Bernard describes Gerard's singing for joy on his deathbed, his future, heavenly exultation in the heavenly choir spilling over into the world of time, and this deathbed song becomes an image for Bernard's own rhetorical lament. Amazed to find someone so close to death singing, Bernard reflects that such singing turns dying into song: "A man dies as he sings, he sings by dying." Death separates body from soul, lover from beloved. So Bernard's sermon depicts the violent separation of flesh and spirit. But death becomes the gate of heaven (Song 26.11) and the song of Bernard's commentary a way for eternal

---

[6] Bernard, SC 26.9 (SBOp 1:177; CF 7:68–69).
[7] Bernard, SC 26.10 (SBOp 1:178; CF 7:69).
[8] Bernard, SC 26.12 (SBOp 1:180; CF 7:72); the blackness but beauty of the Crucified is the model for that of the bride: see Bernard, SC 25.8 (SBOp 1:168; CF 7:56).

life to infuse and raise up the carnal, here and now. Death itself is a black reality made beautiful by the Paschal mystery of the Word incarnate. The poignancy of Gerard's deathbed song derives from its context—this liminal moment where the frailty and need of carnal humanity at its most vulnerable is lit from within by the radiance of eternal life spilling over from beyond the frame.

## The Curtains of Solomon

Just as grief and the other affections can be primarily carnal or spiritual, so too with the manner of portraying and reflecting on experience. Bernard sets up his ostensibly spontaneous irruption of grief and distinguishes his indirect, literary, personal manner of reflecting on it from what he calls "rash curiosity" of philosophers seeking glory. He begins by underlining the ambiguity of the verse: "I am black but beautiful, as the tents of Kedar, as the curtains of Solomon." It can be read either with *black* corresponding to tents and *beautiful* to the curtains or with both adjectives applying to both objects. He opts to pursue both interpretive lines, hinting in these first sentences at the way he will fuse apparent opposites (appearance and reality, carnal and spiritual) throughout the sermon.

To frame the lament for Gerard, Bernard first associates *tents* with *our bodies*. At once, however, he digresses to stress the impermanence of human life on earth: "Our bodily dwelling-place therefore, is neither a citizen's residence nor one's native home, but rather a soldier's tent or traveler's hut. This body, I repeat, is a tent, a tent of Kedar, that now intervenes to deprive the soul for awhile of the vision of the infinite light, permitting that it be seen 'in a mirror dimly, but not face to face.'" The tent of the body both obscures and allows a glimpse of direct reality, he says,[9] noting that the press of necessity so burdens

---

[9] Bernard, SC 26.1 (SBOp 1:169–70; CF 7:59).

the virtuous that one might even long for death.[10] He depicts the sacred as enclosed by the curtains of the tabernacle just as the "concealed fire" of glory lies within the folds of his own grief. Just so, a spiritual seed, he says, lies buried in carnal affection: "This is why the bride said she is black like the tents of Kedar. But how can she be beautiful like the curtains of Solomon? I feel that something beyond imagining, something sublime and sacred is so caught up in these curtains of Solomon that I dare not approach them at all, except at the bidding of him who hid it there and sealed it. For I have read 'he that is a searcher of majesty shall be overwhelmed by glory.'"

Bernard hints at his intention to continue commenting on his text from the Song while lamenting the death of Gerard when he asks, "I, whose life is bitterness, what have I to do with this canticle?"[11] In the very gesture by which he appears to break off from the Song he embeds his lament within its horizon. He depicts Gerard, the ever-practical cellarer, as a curtain drawn away from Bernard the contemplative abbot poring over the Scriptures in contemplative calm.[12] At first, "clothed in priestly vestments," he draws the curtain of ritual over his grief. But while ritual (and art) provide a certain distance from the passions, Bernard is reduced to a state in which reality and appearance, grief and its expression are placed in

---

[10] This statement could function as a way to excuse Gerard's faults discreetly, to hint that Gerard himself longed to depart, pure as he was and sensitive to his own faults (Bernard SC 26.2 [SBOp 1:170; CF 7:59]).

[11] In SC 26.7 Bernard provides a similar example of a rhetorical question calling attention to his purpose by asking, "But why have I described Gerard as a mere extern worker, as if he were ignorant of the interior life and devoid of gifts?" Why indeed! Precisely because Bernard is starkly contrasting Gerard as effective and himself as affective (as in SC 50), dramatizing their separation to set the stage for reunion.

[12] In his discussion of this sermon, M. B. Pranger perceptively observes the way the suspension of contemplative desire by the demands of the active life can serve, by deferral, to strengthen that very desire (Pranger, *Broken Dreams*, 190–206).

unbearable tension: "I could control my tears but could not control my sadness." Of course, Bernard the rhetorician is in fact effectively gaining distance from his grief through the rhetorical, ritualizing power of his art. He gives an artful performance of being out of control.

In this passage, then, Gerard is the black but beautiful curtain, worn and darkened by exposure to worldly affairs and shielding Bernard in his shadow. He is also "the spokesman" of the abbot, mediating his contact with others: "a wise heart, a judicious tongue. . . . 'The mouth of the righteous utters wisdom and his tongue speaks what is right.'" Gerard is thus at once a shield and mouthpiece of his brother.[13] He is blackened perhaps from his exposure to constant business, but in that very blackness he is beautiful in his heroic willingness to forgo his own longing for deeper prayer in order to protect the special gifts of Bernard.

At the start of his sermon and just before breaking into the lament for Gerard, Bernard abstains from peeking behind the "curtains of Solomon" lest, he says, like a "searcher after majesty," he be "overwhelmed with glory." These expressions recall the other places where he speaks of those philosophers whose rationalism conceals a lust for glory and blinds them to the God who comes in humility as a human child. He instead proposes a discourse powered by what he calls the "respectful knock" of prayer rather than by the "rash curiosity" of logicians. Bernard feigns concluding his exegesis—"Besides all that, the sorrow that oppresses me since my bereavement compels me to come to an end"[14]—but precisely at that moment launches into a demonstration of his alternative to the crass probing of the conventional philosopher. His own charged, personal but artful reflection on his brother's death is a mode of real inquiry into human grief and loss through the lens of

---

[13] See Pranger, *Broken Dreams*, 202–3, on the way Bernard describes the brothers' switching places in this sermon.

[14] Bernard, SC 26.2 (SBOp 1:171; CF 7:60).

his own experience, one that is held accountable to its truth. Marshaling all his resources, Bernard dramatizes grief from within the enigma of mortal life and arrives at a vindication of the human measure, its affectivity and incompletion. The art Bernard proposes and demonstrates is supremely pliable and responsive to life, open to both invasion by grief and saturation by the "infinite light," unable to exhaust either pole of experience but able to advance on the path and to steer others along it by means of his work. His art is open to its own abbreviation and silencing by grief, and to the healing of sorrow by the light of glory.

## The Immediate Context: SC 25, 27, 28

Just as in SC 26 Bernard affirms the rightness of human affectivity in the midst of confusion, loss, and incompletion, so in the surrounding sermons he makes the case for a kind of beauty ("black but beautiful"), an aesthetic proper to life "in-between." The free human being emerges from these as the measure of all created beauty, while the Crucified Jesus is the measure of free human being. Bernard folds this distinctive chiaroscuro loveliness into an ethical expression:

> How lowly! Yet how sublime! At the same time tent of Kedar and sanctuary of God; an earthly tent and a heavenly palace; a mud hut and a royal apartment; a body doomed to death and a temple bright with light; an object of contempt to the proud, yet the bride of Christ. She is black but beautiful, daughters of Jerusalem; for though the hardship and sorrow of prolonged exile darkens her complexion, a heavenly loveliness shines through it, the curtains of Solomon enhance it. If the swarthy skin repels you, you must still admire the beauty; if you scorn what seems lowly, you must look up with esteem to what is sublime. Indeed you must note the prudence, the great wisdom, the amount of discretion and sense of fittingness generated in the bride by that controlled interplay of low-

liness and exaltation according as occasion demands, so that amid the ups and downs of this world her sublime gifts sustain her lowliness lest she succumb to adversity, while her lowliness curbs her exaltation, or good fortune will bring it toppling down. These poles of her life act so harmoniously. Though of their nature opposites, they will work with equal effectiveness for the good of the bride. They subserve her spiritual welfare.[15]

In the same vein, in SC 25 Bernard writes, "And the saints glory not only in their inward light, but even in the unsightliness of their outward appearance; nothing in them is without its use, 'everything works for good.'"[16]

Just as Bernard vindicates grief by an appeal to the example of Jesus, so he conceives an order of beauty, an "aesthetics of ambiguity," based on the Crucified. In SC 28 he envisions a soteriological scheme in terms of beauty: "The blackening of one makes many bright. . . . It is better . . . that he himself should suffer the ignominy of the cross, grow pale in death, be totally deprived of beauty and comeliness, that he might gain the Church as a beautiful and comely bride, without stain." So he argues that the ugliness taken on by Christ is not proper to him but is the image of human sin. Similarly he likens Jesus to an attractive Jacob clothed in the hairiness of Esau: "These hairy hands are the sign of my likeness to sinful men. These hairs are my very own: and in my hairy skin I shall see God my Savior."[17] Implicit here is the fact that Jesus assumes not only sin in the abstract but also the ugliness of limits and distortions foisted upon his countenance by human projection. He willingly undergoes subjection to the ambiguity of appearances to light them up from within by the purification of human desire. Made beautiful in heaven, he draws human perception beyond its earthly frame:

---

[15] Bernard, SC 27.14 (SBOp 1:191; CF 7:86).
[16] Bernard, SC 25.7 (SBOp 1:167; CF 7:55).
[17] Bernard, SC 28.2 (SBOp 1:194; CF 7:90).

> She therefore will touch me worthily who will accept me as seated with the Father, no longer in lowly guise, but in my own flesh transformed with heaven's beauty. Why wish to touch what is ugly? Have patience that you may touch the beautiful. Things will be beautiful then that are now ugly: ugly to the touch, ugly to the eye, ugly even to you in your ugliness, you who are so bound to the senses, so indifferent to faith. Become beautiful and then touch me; live by faith and you are beautiful [*Esto formosa, et tange me; esto fidelis, et formosa es*]. In your beauty you will touch my beauty all the more worthily, with greater felicity. You will touch me with the hand of faith, the finger of desire, the embrace of love; you will touch me with the mind's eye. But shall I still be black? God forbid! Your beloved will be fair and ruddy, strikingly beautiful.[18]

In such passages Bernard, addressing one still locked in the senses, opposes spiritual and material beauty to stress the radically distinct quality of the former, which the novice has barely begun to imagine. Even for the more advanced, he suggests, it is only in longing for the absolute that the full value of the relative, made transparent by right desire in the gaze of faith, can emerge.

While in these passages Bernard's emphasis on the spiritual can seem extreme, without some intuition of the other as an ethical agent with an inner life of his or her own, there remains only the crude reduction to the opacity of an idol. "How did the centurion [at the foot of the cross] *see* the beauty of the crucified?" Bernard will ask. The centurion sees, so to speak, by the hearing that comes with faith. Because he can imagine beyond the sensory frame, he can fittingly esteem what seems ugly: "He did not despise what he saw because he believed in what he did not see."[19] He saw meaning and value in the body of the Crucified that were inaccessible without faith and the

---

[18] Bernard, SC 28.10 (SBOp 1:198–99; CF 7:96–97).
[19] Bernard SC 28.5 (SBOp 1:195; CF 7:92).

loving reverence it prompted. Jean-Luc Marion has aptly captured the manner in which "love makes visible":

> The lover alone sees something else, a thing that no one other than he sees—that is, what is precisely no longer a thing, but, for the first time, just such an other, unique, individualized, henceforth torn from economy, detached from objectness, unveiled by the initiative of loving, arisen like a phenomenon to that point unseen. The lover, who sees insofar as he loves, discovers a phenomenon that is seen insofar as it is loved (and as much as it is loved).[20]

"The eye that would see God must be cleansed by faith," he goes on, faith that comes through hearing and demands practice as obedience. Interior attitude opens the scope of what can be seen. Conformity to the Crucified leads to transformation, obedience to vision: ultimately the vision of heaven, but here and now, too, one can see the things of this world with increasing accuracy.

Bernard is a literary rather than a visual artist, who gives priority to the meaning and context of a work of art rather than considering its materiality in itself. He understands that the fittingness of a given work as an expression of the community from which it emerges is integral to its value and part of what makes it in a broad sense beautiful. That the quality of viewers' desire is so involved in what they see undergirds this prioritization of meaning and destabilizes an artwork's claim to a completely intrinsic value, a worth independent of the human context that engendered it. In the perspective of Bernard's twelfth-century-Renaissance humanism, the raw material beauty of a ruby-studded chalice, considered in itself, cannot compete in beauty with an action in which the freedom of the

---

[20] Jean-Luc Marion, *The Erotic Phenomenon*, trans. Stephen Lewis (Chicago: The University of Chicago Press, 2007), 80–81.

virtuous human being made in the *imago dei* shines forth.²¹ The reality of human freedom (the *imago dei*) is the most beautiful element in creation, the measure of created realities and the lens through which their beauty is perceived. Beautiful actions and works of art are those that best express and reflect human freedom, which is in turn dynamically iconic, an image of divine creativity. Love is the supreme expression of freedom qua freedom.

As there is a carnal and spiritual affection, so there is a carnal and spiritual measure.²² While there are material limitations on what the physical senses can experience, human freedom (*imago dei*) admits of infinite development. Reflecting on Mary Magdalene's encounter with the risen Christ—a favorite image in distinguishing carnal from spiritual affection—Bernard has Christ ask, "Why do you want to touch me now? Would you measure the glory of the resurrection by a physical touch?" He sets up this exchange with the statement just before it: "[Sensory] experience is deceptive." Faith by contrast grasps a spiritual measure: "With its fuller comprehension, faith will define it more worthily and more surely. In its deep and mystical breast it can grasp what is the length and breadth and height and depth: 'What eye has not seen, nor ear heard, nor the heart of man conceived, is borne within itself by faith, as if wrapped in a covering and kept under seal.'"²³ That human beings, in the degree of their likeness to God, are the carnal or spiritual measure becomes clear at SC 27.10:

> The soul must grow and expand that it may be roomy enough for God [*Deinde necesse est eam cresceri et dilatari, ut sit capax Deo*]. Its width is its love, if we accept what the

---

²¹ "For must not outward radiance, no matter how radiant, seem to an enlightened mind to be cheap and ugly when compared with the inward beauty of a holy soul?" (Bernard, SC 27.1 [SBOp 1:182; CF 7:75]).

²² So too Bernard contrasts the material and spiritual "curtains" in SC 27.1–5.

²³ Bernard, SC 28.8, 9 (SBOp 1:197–98; CF 7:95, 96).

Apostle says: "Widen your hearts in love." The soul, being a spirit, does not admit of material expansion, but grace confers gifts on it that nature is not equipped to bestow. Its growth and expansion must be understood in a spiritual sense; it is its virtue that increases, not its substance. Even its glory is increased. And finally it grows and advances toward "mature manhood, to the measure of the stature of the fullness of Christ." The capacity of any man's soul is judged by the amount of love he possesses.[24]

So the movement is not from carnal measure to formless void but to a spiritual measure, and this series of sermons culminates not in a final polarization of carnal and spiritual but in their fusion. Bernard indeed praises the bride for seeking beauty in blackness:

> Here, then, we must pay tribute to the prudence of the bride, and the profound wisdom of her words. She sought her God under the image of the curtains of Solomon, that is, in the flesh. She sought life in death, the summit of glory and honor in the midst of shame, the whiteness of innocence and the splendor of the virtues under the dark vesture of the Crucified. Those curtains, black and despicable as they were, contained beneath them jewels more precious and more brilliant than a king's riches. How right not to have been put off by the blackness in the curtains, when she glimpsed the beauty beneath them.[25]

The proud "seekers of majesty" who out of "rash curiosity" disdain the human condition in their quest for the absolute are overwhelmed by glory, lacking the education of desire that Bernard advances through his more personal, existential, and literary reflection on experience.

---

[24] Bernard, SC 27.10 (SBOp 1:189; CF 7:83).
[25] Bernard, SC 28.11 (SBOp 1:199–200; CF 7:97–98).

# 6. The Poetics of *Apology*

We answer no meaningful question by asking how many times the word *pulchrum* occurs in Bernard's text. If we ask, instead, whether Bernard has an aesthetic approach to reality—if we ask for his evaluation of that which affords delight in its contemplation—then we must answer that, for this author, everything in existence was seen in an *analogia pulchri, sub specie gloriae*, in the light of beauty.[1]

In Bernard's view, just as one's inner state makes the experience of grief and the other affections carnal or spiritual, so too one's relation to art varies with the quality of one's desire. Bernard's epistolary treatise *Apology to Abbot William* (ca. 1125) was written in response to conflict between the monastic reform movement of which he was a leading light and the monastic establishment. Bernard criticizes the self-righteousness of some in his own camp before launching a scathing satire of the excesses to which certain traditional Benedictine monks were allegedly prone. The extravagant art and architecture of some Benedictine abbeys was a particular target of Bernard's attacks and has led to the mistaken impression that Bernard was hostile to art altogether. In fact Bernard's own style and

---

[1] Emero Stiegman, "A Tradition of Aesthetics in Saint Bernard," in *Bernardus Magister*, ed. John R. Sommerfeldt, CS 135 (Spencer, MA: Cistercian Publications, 1992), 139–40 (also published as *Cîteaux: Commentarii Cistercienses* 42 [1991]). Stiegman here cites Nat 2.1 (SBOp 4:251).

sensibility is highly artistic. As Étienne Gilson remarked, "One has to have a manuscript for a heart not to sense that he was an artist."[2]

Commentators attempting to present a Bernard more favorable to art steer readers away from the *Apology*: "It is not in the satiric lines of the *Apologia* that one must look for Bernard's aesthetics."[3] But it is in the *Apology* that Bernard reveals his distinctive contemplative aesthetic of monastic reform. Far from being indifferent to questions of art and the beautiful, he uses essentially aesthetic categories in his critique of artistic excess. In effect, he opposes one aesthetic vision to another and does so within a particular integration of monastic and artistic sensibility. Indeed his entire treatise operates within the field of such themes as proportion, variety in unity, necessity, purpose, and the correspondence of inner and outer. He articulates his discussion of monastic lifestyle and values in terms of a poetics of monastic life, one that reveals the close connection between ethos, art, and the beautiful for him.[4] The

---

[2] Cited by Stiegman, "A Tradition," 131.

[3] Elisabeth Melczer and Eileen Soldwedel, "Monastic Goals in the Aesthetics of Saint Bernard," in *Studies in Cistercian Art and Architecture*, vol. 1, ed. Meredith P. Lillich, CS 66 (Kalamazoo, MI: Cistercian Publications, 1982), 31–44, here 40.

[4] Stiegman, "A Tradition," 134–35, writes of the link between ethos and aesthetic, "What is properly proportioned, whether ontologically or morally, is one beauty." See also 135–36. M. B. Pranger speaks of Bernard's "monastic poetics," by which he understands a certain "convergence of image and structure," a correspondence between the images Bernard employs and the "image" of the monastic setting. See M. B. Pranger, *Bernard of Clairvaux and the Shape of Monastic Thought: Broken Dreams* (Leiden: Brill, 1994), 13. Pranger also speaks of the "artificiality" of monastic life (11, n. 13). He cites Robert of Basevorn's description of Bernard's work as *semper devote, semper artificialiter*. While *artful* is part of what is meant by the word, and *artificial* today carries a connotation of *inauthentic*, there is value in retaining the surprise that the word holds. The monastic life, highly structured and formal in its skeleton, can be thought of as an artificial way to be genuine. Pranger's use of the term springs in part from a concern to resist an easy identification of author and the sentiments expressed rhetorically in his text (*Bernard of Clairvaux*, 170).

early sections of the treatise frame this discussion within an ecclesial/eschatological vision mapped out in aesthetic terms.[5] The fusion of horizons in the work—ethical/monastic, artistic, literary, and theological—is part of the reason his use of art in his critique of art has been overlooked. In addition, much can be learned of his own literary art, not only in his discussion of visual art but through the treatise as a whole. The use he makes of satire and the related play in the space between appearance and reality gains a particular shading, situated as it is within the theological horizon Bernard establishes in the opening part of the work.[6]

## Art and Life

Faith and artistic sensibility are inseparable for Bernard. Writing of the *Apology*, however, Jean Leclercq states that Bernard's criticisms of Black Monks in this work are inaccurate and unfair. He qualifies that criticism by stating that while they are inaccurate on a literary level they are true on the spiritual: "If the *Apologia* wishes to paint a picture of monastic behavior, it is false and inaccurate. But on the plane of the spiritual,

---

The present chapter adopts and adapts both expressions. By "monastic poetics" I have in view the literary aesthetic that accords with Bernard's sense of what reformed monasticism ought to be; in regard to the "artificiality" of monastic life I consider the way the made quality of things is accented both in the life itself and in the way Bernard writes about it.

[5] In his art-historical study of the *Apology*, Conrad Rudolph helpfully maps the basic structure of the treatise as follows: chapters 1–3, preface; 4–9, the apologia proper; 10–15, criticism of detractors; 16–27, the "small things" (i.e., material excesses); 28–29, the "things of greater importance" (e.g., art); 30–31, conclusion (Conrad Rudolph, *The "Things of Greater Importance": Bernard of Clairvaux's* Apologia *and the Medieval Attitude Toward Art* [Philadelphia: University of Pennsylvania Press, 1990]).

[6] For historical background, see Rudolph, *"Things"*; and Dianne J. Reilly, "Bernard of Clairvaux and Christian Art," in *A Companion to Bernard of Clairvaux*, ed. Brian Patrick McGuire, Brill's Companions to the Christian Tradition, vol. 25 (Leiden: Brill, 2011), 279–304.

which was Bernard's natural habitat, the *Apologia* rings true."[7] Leclercq's manner of distinguishing the spiritual from the literary is problematic. Far from being a naïve and otherworldly dreamer unaware of the effect of his words, Bernard was a literary artist keenly alert to the artificiality of his *Apologia*. The work was meant as caricature and has the corresponding sort of accuracy and distortion.[8] Leclercq states, "The literary skill which Bernard lavished on the tract is *only* a means of expressing an ideal, for which monks of all ages should be grateful."[9] He goes on, further separating Bernard's faith and imagination: "It is necessary to appreciate the double aspect of Bernard's greatness; on the one hand, his literary genius which enabled him to handle satire, humor and sarcasm with much mastery, on the other the purity of his experience of the mystery of Christ which gave him a basis for distinguishing the essential from what was peripheral."[10] In fact, these two elements are much more closely identified than Leclercq allows. Bernard's "experience of the mystery of Christ"—revelation itself—includes an understanding of the relationship between inner and outer, of irony, and of other aesthetic features. In other words, the way Bernard handles satire is shaped by his specifically Christian experience. Conversely, the way in which he distinguishes the essential from the peripheral is an element of his artistry.

Kilian Hufgard supports the position that Bernard's aesthetic view of reality demands harmony between art and life: "To Bernard the purpose of a work of art ought to be related essentially to a particular pattern of life, endorsing the implied principle of an integration between a way of life and a mode of art. The forms of art which serve and surround the daily life

---

[7] Jean Leclercq, Introduction, in *Bernard of Clairvaux: Treatises I*, CF 1 (Kalamazoo, MI: Cistercian Publications, 1970), 20–21.

[8] A good political cartoon, for example, can be at once exaggerated and remarkably accurate.

[9] Leclercq, Introduction, 21.

[10] Leclercq, Introduction, 29.

of monks ought to harmonize with that life . . . monastic art emerges from, serves, and conforms to monastic life."[11] This integration of art and life coupled with the already highly artificial nature of monastic life—characterized as it is by ritual, liturgy, and horarium—allows us to speak of a "monastic poetics." Pranger has identified a crucial point of intersection between life and art in Bernard in the concept of "measure":

> If we look for measure in Bernard it has to be found in the form and nature of his monastic existence . . . it is in the shape of that existence that "measure," both in its literary and existential sense, has to be found. Bernard's asceticism was materially rooted in the scenery in which he founded his monasteries; monasteries that, in their turn, are known for the austerity of their architecture. The fact that exuberance and the threat of a life without measure are to be seen as constitutive elements of Bernard's mindset becomes evident if one takes into account not only the "exuberance" of his style and the exuberance of his behaviour but also the spatial setting of his asceticism.[12]

Life and art are "measured" in the *Apology* in a variety of ways, principally by necessity (the human needs of the community generating the work) and purpose.

What is unmeasured, in a negative sense, is superfluous. Hufgard observes that the attack on "superfluities" in the second part of the *Apology* is grounded in Bernard's anthropology:

---

[11] Kilian Hufgard, *Saint Bernard of Clairvaux: A Theory of Art Formulated from His Writings and Illustrated in Twelfth-Century Works of Art* (Lewiston, NY: Edwin Mellen, 1989), 20–21.

[12] M. B. Pranger, "Bernard the Writer," in *A Companion to Bernard of Clairvaux*, ed. Brian Patrick McGuire, Brill's Companions to the Christian Tradition, vol. 25 (Leiden: Brill, 2011), 243–44. Moving beyond or outside of measure can suggest a life unregulated by monastic observance, which threatens Bernard because of his many travels. His rhetoric was described by a near contemporary as *modus sine modis*, and similarly, his treatise *On Loving God* begins by stating that God is to be loved "without measure."

Even before the transgression Adam lived by a preventive law of simplicity: "the first man was forbidden to admit anything superfluous." After the transgression, a remedial law of simplicity was given man; "it commanded him to cut off and remove from him the superfluities already admitted." Superfluities (objects of an inordinate and insatiable passion for pleasure), according to Saint Bernard, are unnatural to man because they never have been a true part of his nature. Man has lost his native simplicity. Through Adam's fall, love, man's "innate natural affection," "has missed the way and is unable to find it again unless it be retaught."

Later she cites Bernard further: "Remove what is superfluous and thou shalt see an increase in what is good and necessary. What thou subtractest from superfluity is added to utility." It is not only life context but the subjective state of the viewer that determines the value of a given work of art. As Hufgard writes, "[Bernard] remarks that beauty itself, rooted in being, is objective; but the experience of beauty, which is dependent on the state of the observer's intuition is subjective."[13] Conceding the ambiguous (not exclusively negative) character of visual art works in church decoration, Bernard allows in the *Apology* that "even if they are harmful to the shallow and avaricious, they are not to the simple and devout."[14] Thus in the field of visual art as in the exegesis of Scripture the quality of one's desire shapes one's imagination.

## Aesthetic Elements in the *Apology*

Bernard's text is at once a treatise, a satire, and, as the dedication indicates, an epistle addressed to William of Saint-Thierry. Conrad Rudolph suggests that the initial impetus

---

[13] Kilian Hufgard, *Bernard of Clairvaux's Broad Impact on Medieval Culture* (Lewiston, NY: Edwin Mellen, 2001), 14.

[14] Bernard, Apol 28 (SBOp 3:106). Throughout this chapter I use the translation by Rudolph in *"Things,"* 283.

originated with Oger, a canon of Mont Saint-Eloi, but it was only with the additional pressure of William's entreaty that Bernard was finally prompted to write. It was politic of Bernard to address a satire against the Benedictines to a Benedictine. At the same time, as Rudolph brings out, the controversy was not so much between Benedictines and Cistercians as it was between a monastic reform movement and the status quo.[15]

Necessity is one of the key ordering principles of both art and life for Bernard. He claims at the outset of the *Apology* that "necessity itself" has given him confidence to write, despite his lack of expertise (*fiduciam dante ipsa necessitate*). The idea of necessity recurs throughout the work as a guiderail on which one can reliably lean, in the moral sphere as in the aesthetic. It provides a norm that shows up the superfluous. Hufgard articulates the way the limitations of everyday life ground and foster creativity for Bernard:

> The very constraint of necessity, in man's case, becomes a virtue that guides him to ordered production—for in man's necessities the arts are seen to have their final cause, their origin. Order in a work of art is the result of the coordination of the knowledge of craftsmanship and the knowledge of purpose. When the second cause of art, the knowledge of craftsmanship, is respectful, so to speak, of the necessities of man and recognizes them as a primary source, the first cause of art, then the work of art will be truly ordered.[16]

Because necessity compels him, Bernard claims, whether he writes "skillfully or clumsily" (*vel perite, vel imperite*) is immaterial. This opening passage, in which Bernard artfully calls attention to literary art while at the same time dismissing it, recurs later in the treatise.[17]

---

[15] Rudolph, "*Things*," 161–93.

[16] Hufgard, "Saint Bernard," 52.

[17] See Appendix 3 for the way this strategy appears in two letters of Bernard to Oger that form part of *Apology*'s genesis.

Just as in Sermon 26 on the Song Bernard pushes contraries into extreme opposition before resolving them in a surprising synthesis, so in the opening lines of *Apology* he begins a process of polarization, caricaturing both sides in the dispute, by means of an allusion to Jerome: "from [our] holes, as he says, [we] are alleged to pass judgment on the world, and what is, among other things, more intolerable even to disparage your most glorious Order, to detract impudently from the holy men who live commendably in it, and to insult the luminaries of the world from the shelter of our low position."[18] If a hint of sarcasm inflects the characterization in the too-exuberant praise for the Black Monks ("luminaries") and belittling of the White (in their "holes"), it does not detract from the force of the coming blast against (White) detractors.

Right from the outset, the *Apology* plays on the relation between appearance and reality. Natural, visible beauty in itself remains ambiguous for Bernard. Moral beauty can appear in the worn and weathered features of an apostle tried by struggle, and the beauty of God's self-revelation occurs through the ugliness of the cross. At the same time the measure and right order, the proportion and harmony of natural creation, reveal the Creator's wisdom. The beauty that appears in the cross requires a particular quality of faith-inspired irony for appreciation.[19] The coarse food and poor clothing of Cistercian monks can be considered beautiful in the light of the ironic reversal made possible by faith. Yet the reversal is reversed when such monks pass judgment on others. If the stricter monks seek to appear strict only to win praise, then like the Pharisees "they have had their reward." Quoting 1 Corinthians 15:19, Bernard asks, "Do we not in fact hope in Christ for this

---

[18] Bernard, Apol 1 (SBOp 3:81; Rudolph, "*Things*," 233): *de cavernis, ut ille ait, dicimur iudicare mundum, quodque inter cetera intolerabilius est, etiam gloriosissimo Ordini vestro derogare, sanctis, qui in eo laudabiliter vivunt, impudenter detrahere, et de umbra nostrae ignobilitatis mundi luminaribus insultare?*

[19] See William Lynch, *Images of Faith: An Exploration of the Ironic Imagination* (South Bend, IN: University of Notre Dame Press, 1973).

life only, if from the service of Christ we seek temporal glory only?"[20] At one level his *Apology* is a work on the meaning of monastic life; here he introduces the point that this life can only be rightly interpreted, its beauty or ugliness judged, in the light of heaven, its measured way of life in view of the unmeasured and eternal.

At the beginning of *Apology* 2, the tension Bernard has been establishing between appearance and reality continues to grow. He shifts grammatically from the first person plural to the first person singular as he steps into, dramatizes, and exaggerates the role of the self-righteous monk who works so hard "to be—or rather not to seem to be—like other men." He adopts and subverts the position his accusers have assigned him by making it ridiculous. Those who choose the way of temporal pleasure, he argues, at least have some delight, however fleeting. The austere but hypocritical monk, however, lacks even this consolation. Bernard characterizes the disparity between appearance and reality in such monks and suggests the association with art by means of the image of a harp: "How unfortunate it is for those who do not carry their own cross like the Savior, but carry another's like the Cyrenian! How unfortunate it is for those who do not play their own harps like the men of the Apocalypse, but play another's like hypocrites! . . . they share in his [Christ's] Passion but neglect to follow his humility!"[21] The cross of a stricter way of life, then, is not proper to them, does not express their interior state. Their hypocrisy reverses the ironic reversal whereby spiritual beauty shines through poverty. The image of the harpists from the Apocalypse invokes the otherworldly reward for virtuous suffering.

---

[20] Bernard, Apol 1 (SBOp 3:82; Rudolph, "Things," 235).

[21] Bernard, Apol 2 (SBOp 3:82; Rudolph, "Things," 235). *Vae portantibus crucem, non sicut Salvator suam, sed sicut ille Cyrenaeus alienam! Vae citharoedis citharizantibus, non ut illi Apocalypsi, in citharis suis, sed vere, ut hypocritae, in alienis! Vae semel, et vae iterum pauperibus superbis! Vae, inquam, semel, et vae iterum, portantibus crucem Christi et non sequenti Christum: qui nimirum cuius passionibus participantur, humilitatem sectari negligunt.*

Hypocrites enjoy their reward now and so play a harp, enjoying an esteem that does not belong to them, a reward for this life only.

The harp in this passage, however, also suggests the world of art and beauty. Implicitly, the hypocrite presents an image—an aesthetic, a monastic way of life, akin to a musical performance—that does not genuinely express and support his inner being. The beauty of a work of art for Bernard takes account of its total meaning in context, in harmony with the life it manifests. Proportion or concord between being and appearance is an element of what makes something beautiful, and yet Bernard is keenly aware of the way outward ugliness can reveal moral beauty. Hypocrisy is ugly because of the discrepancy between appearance and reality, but the visible in itself is ambiguous, so the range of factors that contribute to its meaning must be held in view. These include not only personal but social justice, as appears in Bernard's outrage that gaudy churches "feast the eyes of the rich while the poor go hungry."[22] The treatise, and indeed Bernard's whole theological aesthetic, play in this space between appearance, reality, and the different kinds of congruence and incongruence between them. Arguably, by using satire Bernard intentionally distorts and exaggerates the disparity between reality—whether the self-righteousness of the White monks or the excesses of the Black—and the cartoon appearances he parades. Rather than poor taste or an "unfair" presentation (*pace* Leclerq), this approach can be read as ridiculing both parties and the futile polemicizing between them. Bernard himself, who in his caricatures presents appearances out of tune with fact, here assumes the role of the rhetorical arch-hypocrite.

Compression and expansion form another set of aesthetic categories Bernard exploits. He compares the stricter observance of the White monks to the constriction of the swaddling

---

[22] Bernard, Apol 28 (SBOp 3:106).

clothes of the child Christ: "What is Pride doing in the swaddling clothes of Christ's humility? Does not human malice have anything with which to cover itself except that with which the infant Savior was wrapped? How does the impostor, Arrogance, squeeze herself into the manger of the Lord, and utter malicious detractions there in the place of the cries of Innocence?"[23] Elsewhere Bernard writes of the incarnation in terms of the *verbum abbreviatum*, the eternal Word compressed to the dimensions of humanity.[24] His entire poetics is grounded in the incarnation: *"The Word was made flesh and even now dwells among us.* It is by faith that he dwells in our hearts, in our memory, our intellect, and penetrates even into our imagination. What concept could man have of God if he did not first fashion an image of him in his heart? By nature incomprehensible and inaccessible, he was invisible and unthinkable, but now he wished to be understood, to be seen and thought of."[25]

In this view the immensity of the Word is contained in the measure of the flesh so that humanity can move through the flesh to the boundless Word. Bernard's own incarnational rhetoric embodies this blend of compression and ecstatic expansion. He moves between densely packed figural miniatures and long, rambling digressions. Like the cross, the incarnation involves an ironic reversal in which the beautiful finds expres-

---

[23] Images of food and clothing in the first part of the treatise foreshadow the more concrete discussion of monastic diet and dress in the second. Apol 3 (SBOp 3:83): *quid enim facit superbia sub pannis humilitatis Iesu? Numquid non habet quo se palliet humana malitia, nisi unde involuta est infantia Salvatoris? Et quomodo intra praesepium Domini simulatrix arrogantia se coarctat, ac pro vagitabus innocentiae malum inibi detractionis immurmurat?*

[24] See Pranger, *Broken Dreams*, 247–57.

[25] Bernard of Clairvaux, *In Nativitate B. Mariae* (SBOp 5:282): *Verbum caro factum est, et habitat iam in nobis. Habitat plane per fidem in cordibus nostris, habitat in memoria nostra, habitat in cogitatione, et usque ad ipsam descendit imaginationem. Quid enim prius cogitaret homo de Deo, nisi forsitan idolum corde fabricaretur? Incomprehensibilis erat et inaccessibilis, invisibilis et excogitabilis omnino. Nunc vero comprehendi voluit, videri voluit, voluit cogitari.*

sion in the worn contours of human weakness. So the false immensity of swollen Arrogance's wrapping itself in "the swaddling bands of Christ's humility" is a richly suggestive image on several levels; it develops the portrait of pride by inverting the reversal of the divine pedagogy that reveals beauty in poverty. Hypocrisy thwarts the imagination's progress from the visible to the invisible, and asceticism is likewise undermined: for Bernard the whole pattern of spiritual life moves from conformation to the poor Christ to transformation to the risen Christ's glory. The hypocrite possesses outward conformation without interior transformation.

Bernard then shifts from the allegorical personification of Arrogance to a direct address of William while continuing to play on the tension between appearance and reality. Having just in effect shown the ambiguity of all utterance, including his own, he worries that he may be held in suspicion as one of the detractors (see *Apology* 15), and he appeals to William to guarantee his sincerity. As an intimate friend and a Benedictine, William can attest that what Bernard has declared in public corresponds with his private views. Bernard says that he writes since he cannot address each of his accusers individually, and yet the work, like all art, all visible phenomena, remains fundamentally ambiguous. It requires (or so Bernard says) William's witness to Bernard's character to prove that Bernard genuinely disavows the hypocrisy he has just so expertly caricatured. The letter is addressed through William, in effect, to those critical of Bernard. William is invoked as guarantor of the likeness between private speech—in which true intention can be more directly expressed—and public writing, which is necessarily rhetorical.[26]

---

[26] This theme also appears in Bernard's Ep 93.1 to Oger (Appendix 3). There is some irony in Bernard's claiming to tell it as it is while indulging in wild caricatures, even if they were intended as such and would so have been recognized.

## The Beauty of the Church

The rich ecclesiological aesthetic that Bernard weaves in the first part of *Apology* forms the interpretive horizon in which he frames the details of controversial monastic practices concerning diet, clothing, and art. Unity in diversity, for instance, the holding together of apparent contraries, can be one dimension of beauty: the two natures of Christ in the incarnation, matter and spirit in the human being, and, as now appears, unity and diversity in the church. Emero Stiegman speaks of this theme in Bernard:

> "What an artist!" he exclaims. *Qualis artifex, qualis unitor rerum, ad cuius nutum sic conglutinantur sibi limus terrae et spiritus vitae!* Bernard is in awe of what he sees as the highest possible achievement of creativity, bringing unity to the most varied of elements, matter and spirit. Unity in variety as the essence of beauty defines that aesthetics of proportion which reigned in the ancient world and in the Middle Ages until the beginning of the thirteenth century. . . . a classic statement of it is found in Galen: "Beauty does not consist in the elements, but in the harmonious proportion of the parts . . . of all parts to all others." Beauty was transcendent, in the sense that every visible beauty was a proportionate participation in the good.[27]

Bernard declares the absurdity of people in different states of ecclesial life disparaging one another simply because of their difference, likening the church to the spiritual Joseph's coat of many colors: *Notissima quippe est, quia polymita, id est pulcherrima varietate distincta.*[28] The beautiful coat has been dipped in the blood of an innocent lamb, a comparison that picks up the

---

[27] Stiegman, "A Tradition," 133, citing Nat 2.1 (SBOp 4:251).
[28] Bernard, Apol 5 (SBOp 3:85; Rudolph, *"Things,"* 241). In the same passage Bernard underlines that this "Joseph" (that is, Christ) saves not only the body but the soul and, by extension, both appearance and reality.

earlier sheep/lamb imagery, suggesting the quality of a Christian beauty that has passed through the irony of the cross.[29] So Bernard contrasts a body torn by rivalry with the diversity in unity of the church as it is meant to be. Christians in time conform with either the church in glory or its caricature. The beauty of the church is not an end in itself but looks toward "the consummation of the saints and the attainment of the perfection of man, in the measure of the fullness of Christ" (*in mensuram aetatis plenitudinis Christi*).[30] So Bernard more broadly situates his discussion of visual art and monastic poetics in an ecclesial and eschatological understanding of beauty. He himself comically dramatizes the ugliness of rivalry (the caricature of this ecclesial vision) by the rhetorical hypocrisy of satire.

Rather than competing factions, each clutching for itself an identity against all others, the robe that adorns Christ, that is, the church, is itself Christ's gift and the fruit of his paschal mystery. Bernard describes a church that combines the diversity of Joseph's coat of many colors and the unity of Christ's seamless garment: it is "a many-colored robe, both seamless and woven from top to bottom, many-colored because of the distinct ways of life of her many Orders, seamless because of the indivisible unity of her indestructible love."[31] He continues, developing his scriptural portrait of the church as a diverse unity: "For although from many and different parts, my dove, my beauty [*formosa mea*], my perfect one is still one." White and Black monks belong together, "unless perhaps—may it never happen—mutually envious and provoking we gnaw at each other in turn and in turn we are devoured."[32] That Bernard intends this vision of the church as the horizon within which

---

[29] Luigi Giussani: "Beauty without the cross is a mask of violence." The passage in *Apology* picks up the earlier imagery of harps and martyrdom from the book of Revelation (Apol 2).

[30] Bernard, Apol 5 (SBOp 3:85; Rudolph, "*Things*," 241).

[31] Bernard, Apol 6 (SBOp 3:86; Rudolph, "*Things*," 243).

[32] Bernard, Apol 7 (SBOp 3:87; Rudolph, "*Things*," 245).

his audience is to read the more concrete critique of monastic practices to follow is underscored by his use of clothing and eating imagery: gnawing fleas, mutual devouring in envy, and the gourmandizing of the Black Monks, the swaddling clothes of the infant Christ, the robe of Joseph, and the delicate silk robes of decadent monks.

Ultimately for Bernard it is love that makes possible the fruitful tension of unity and diversity in the church. He invokes a favorite verse from the Song of Songs: *Ordinate in me caritatem* (Song 2:4), here with a more social meaning than his usual application, the setting now in order of ecclesial, communal love. The church, he writes, is "one in love yet divisible in arrangement" (*una in caritate, divisa tamen sit in ordinatione*). In his breadth of spirit, Bernard, who just before personified the hypocrite, now aims to model the ordered charity that allows one to see and share in the many-colored robe of the church. He demonstrates that such participation in love allows an appreciation of the diversity that to the envious may become the cause of contention.

So the coat of many colors is at once an adornment and reward of the Son, and the fruit of his gift. The church, insofar as it truly is the church, is a tapestry of divine gifts, diverse expressions of one love, expertly interwoven. Bernard powerfully energizes the extended metaphor of the coat by fusing it with the image of the sun—"Nothing is concealed from its warmth"—and the image of Wisdom, who "Reaches mightily from one end to the other, and orders all things well." The very being of the church is gratuitous reward and adornment celebrating the triumph of the Son; the coat wraps the extent of the body and holds in warmth; the Sun extends across the heavens, setting love in order. The comparison recalls that of the boundless Word that submits to abbreviation within the swaddling clothes of the infant Jesus. There is the simultaneous sense of terrific light and energy bursting from within the embrace of the coat, and of the sun clothing the heavens in warmth. The risen Christ is the Wisdom of the Father, who "sets love in order," the supreme artist harmonizing the diverse colors of the robe as well as the bridegroom who receives it as a wedding-gift.[33]

Continuing to develop the notion of the church's diversity in unity, Bernard distinguishes the diversity found while one is a "pilgrim" and "in exile," moving through the different states of life, from the *discordem concordiam* found in heaven, where the order is based on merit as opposed to social status. The apparent superiority of any one state in life over another, indeed the whole sense of ecclesiastical hierarchy, is dramatically relativized by the horizon of eschatological Judgment. It is this horizon alone that gives the monastic life its meaning and purpose. The entire poetics of the life opens onto and steers toward heaven, where appearances will at last yield to reality. Both the moral and the aesthetic dimensions of monastic life are ordered by this orientation to heaven; that is what the "ordination of love" is about. The poetics of monastic life, ordered to heaven—and the hierarchy of merit vs. appearance—intrinsically subverts every trace of hypocrisy. That is, to boast that one's way of life is superior when the entire impetus of that life points toward Judgment and the order of merit in heaven is self-defeating.

The treatise naturally moves at this point (§§10–14) against detractors, those in Bernard's own order accused of attacking the laxity of the Black Monks. He criticizes them first for judging "before the time," for failing to suspend Judgment, to defer to the light of that Sun of Righteousness who alone can reveal the reality beneath appearance.[34] This ethical stance has a contemplative and aesthetic parallel, as Stiegman explains: "When, ascetically, Bernard turns away from some beautiful things, it is only that, contemplatively, he may leave open his inner space. Experience has taught him that this inner space is coveted and reserved by Beauty Himself."[35]

---

[33] Bernard, Apol 6–7 (SBOp 3:86–88; Rudolph, *"Things,"* 243–47).

[34] Bernard, Apol 10, citing 1 Cor 4:5.

[35] Emero Stiegman, "The Aesthetics of Authenticity," in *Studies in Cistercian Art and Architecture II*, ed. Meredith Parsons Lillich, CS 69 (Kalamazoo, MI:

Perhaps anticipating the objections of the Black Monks, Bernard highlights the importance of the inner meaning of the Rule over mere observance. However, even while detailing examples of monastic laxity he states their relative unimportance alongside the inner attitude of pride: "By detracting from your brothers, you lose humility in that you exalt yourself; in that you deprecate others, you lose love."[36] The spiritual cannot, however, he says, be reached without external observance; he continues, citing a favorite verse, *Non prius quod spirituale, sed quod animale, deinde quod spirituale* (1 Cor 15:46): "And as is said in the psalm, 'Begin the song and play the drum,' which is to say, begin spiritual things, but first give attention to physical things. Indeed, the best man [*optimus*] is he who performs discreetly and harmoniously [*discrete et congrue*] both the one and the other."[37] He introduces music again as an image of the spiritual life, as with the harps in *Apology* 2, with physical observances as the percussion undergirding the melody. This connection to the earlier image links the world of art

---

Cistercian Publications, 1984), 3. Both the self-righteous detractors and the self-indulgent concentrate on externals to the detriment of interior realities; the former fail to suspend judgment, while the latter clog their bellies with food and the stomach of their memories with lavish images. Bernard invokes a series of gospel images (the publican and the Pharisee; the splinter and the beam in the eye) to challenge the detractors to "know themselves" (see the end of Apol 11). Stiegman comments on the centrality of this Christian Socratism for Bernard: "Self-knowledge *is* the Cistercian quest for the beautiful" (Stiegman, "Aesthetics," 8). In *Apology* Bernard frames the discussion in terms of "order": the disparity between the outward order of the stricter Order with the inner dis-order of its pride. The plank of self-righteousness obscures the detractor's vision of those whom he accuses. The familiar idea that the state of one's soul colors what one sees is here placed center stage, being part of the ambiguity of all appearances.

[36] Bernard, Apol 13 (SBOp 3:93; Rudolph, "Things," 257).

[37] Bernard, Apol 14 (SBOp 3:94; Rudolph, "Things," 259): *Unde rursus in Psalmo: Sumite psalmum, et date tympanum, quod est dicere: Sumite spiritualia, sed prius date corporalia. Optimus autem ille, qui discrete et congrue et haec operatur, et illa.*

with the ecclesial/eschatological horizons of the first section, the martyrs rejoicing in heaven.

## *Apology* and Monastic Practice

In the part of *Apology* (§§16–29) directed *contra superfluitates*, Bernard describes how what is "necessary," proportionate to the "measure" of healthy monastic life, becomes covered over by "excess" in externals (food and drink, bedding, and so on). Bernard's sense of monastic poetics sees the articulated measure and definition of the structured life as opening onto and making way for encounter with the "immeasurable" goodness of God and even the "wilderness" of unconscious desire, a kind of thickly articulated speech that opens onto silence. "Excess" instead of measure in externals, he says, clogs the pores of memory and obscures the monastic ethos/aesthetic. Instead of ordered love, indulgence is a "love that destroys love" (*caritas destruit caritatem*).[38] Over-concern for the body "is to feed the maid [concupiscence] and kill the mistress [virtue]," and one who does so "feeds the barren childless woman and does no good to the widow."[39] Like the detractors, he argues, the self-indulgent stop at externals; both are hypocrites, as appears in the way the latter rename their laxity as virtue.

Bernard continues to use the language of feeding and overloading in the section *De commessatione* (Apol 20). He says that while in the early days of desert monasticism monks "took the bread of the soul from each other with such avidity that on many occasions they passed the entire day with empty stomachs, but not spirits [*ventribus, sed non mentibus*], having completely forgotten the food of the body," now they are glutted with both food and talk: "During meals, just as gullets are feasted with food, so ears are feasted with gossip so engrossing

---

[38] Bernard, Apol 16 (SBOp 3:95; Rudolph, "*Things*," 261).
[39] Bernard, Apol 16 (SBOp 3:95; Rudolph, "*Things*," 261), citing Job 24:21.

that you know no moderation in eating."[40] Gossip covers over the natural appetite, the level of necessity, just as "novel seasonings" cultivate an overlay of superfluous desires that obscure normal appetite. Noting the *accuratione et arte* with which meals are prepared and that "the palate, as long as it is enticed by novel seasonings, gradually loses its attraction to the familiar and is hungrily restored in its desire by foreign spices as if it had fasted until now," Bernard continues:

> The stomach, as long as it is unfamiliar with these [new seasonings and spices], is overloaded, but variety removes any weariness. This is because as long as one thing and another are blended together in many different ways, we treat unadulterated food—as nature has made it—with disdain and, having scorned the natural qualities which God has bestowed on these things, the appetite is roused by certain adulterated flavors: the limit of necessity is of course passed by, but the capacity for pleasure is not yet exhausted.[41]

Here Bernard links the attractive power of "variety" both backward to the description of the coat of many colors and ahead to the "variety of contradictory forms" (*diversarum formarum . . . varietas*), the monstrous figures populating the cloisters of Cluny, the latter representing a distortion of the aesthetic principle of diversity in unity exemplified in the structure of the church, God's work of art. In the case of the "excessive" visual arts, it is as though the stomach of memory were crammed and the native desire of the soul stifled.

---

[40] Bernard, Apol 19 (SBOp 3:97; Rudolph, "Things," 265).

[41] Bernard, Apol 20 (SBOp 3:97; Rudolph, "Things," 265): *Venter, quidem, dum nescit, oneratur; sed varietas tollit fastidium. Quia enim puras, ut eas natura creavit epulas fastidimus, dum alia aliis multifarie permiscentur, et spretis naturalibus, quos Deus indidit rebus, quibusdam adulterinis gula provocatur saporibus, transitur nimirum meta necessitatis, sed necdum delectatio superatur*; and see Apol 21 on similarly adulterated wine "steeped with honey and sprinkled with ground spices."

In architecture the Cistercians generally emphasize the native grain of building materials rather than painting over or encrusting them with ornament, incorporating their natural qualities into the design. Similarly, as mentioned, the structural elements supporting the buildings are accented rather than covered: what is useful and necessary, showing its purpose, becomes an element of beauty. Implicit in this "aesthetics of authenticity," to borrow Stiegman's phrase, is an understanding of the interior life in which holiness coincides with "simplicity," the integrity of ordered love. The natural desire of the soul is for God; cupidity complicates the simplicity of this one desire that is meant to order the others with an overlay of spurious, superfluous longings.

An apparent contradiction arises between Bernard's stated ideal and his literary practice. In terms of the current discussion, Bernard can appear like a rhetorical chef whose food is seasoned so thickly that the simplicity of native appetite is lost. The limit of necessity and measure does not play out, however, in the same way with spiritual desire as with the needs of the body. God, he says, is to be loved "without measure." Bernard's alternation between compressed lexical units and rambling ecstatic digressions dramatizes and arouses the spiritual desire of the soul, transcending and expanding the measure of its capacity. His rhetoric aims at cultivating the heart's palate, developing the spiritual sense of taste; if the means, the "spices," are various, the hunger they feed is single. While material food is meant simply to nourish and satisfy the body, spiritual food of the sort Bernard seeks to provide in his writings is meant both to satisfy and to stir hunger, to stretch both the capacity and the sensitivity of desire. As is suggested by his comparison of the desert fathers eating the bread of the soul with the lavish banquets of contemporary monks, sensuality displaces the care for spiritual discourse and the cultivation of the heart's native desire to which it (and all monastic culture) is ordered. Of course, material food can never satisfy immaterial desire, or vice versa: "What do material things mean to the mind? The body cannot live on ideas or the mind subsist on meat."[42] Bernard suggests the encroachment of one field of desire on the other when he complains,

> The properties of these foods are prepared to show their appearance in such a way that their sight is no less pleasing than their taste [*non minus aspectus quam gustus delectetur*]. Although the stomach proclaims itself filled by repeated belching, curiosity is not yet satisfied. But while the eyes are enticed by the colors and the palate by the taste, the unfortunate stomach—which neither sees the colors nor is allured by the tastes—is forced to receive it all and, having been smothered, is more overwhelmed than refreshed [*magis obruitur quam reficitur*].[43]

Again, Bernard underscores the similarity between such a description of cuisine and the language he uses to critique the visual arts because the stomach is a favorite image of memory, the spiritual sense the monk ought to be engaging while reading in the cloister instead of gawking at monstrous sculptures. Mary Carruthers suggests that for Bernard, monks trained in the art of memory are not iconoclastic but privilege interior images over exterior ones: "Decoration is vital to moral life, but it is interior. It is created lavishly in the mind, out of all that is precious and rich in the images invoked through recollective technique alone." In her view, by eliminating distraction/superfluity, the absence of exterior decoration supports

---

[42] Bernard of Clairvaux, *On Loving God* (with an Analytical Commentary by Emero Stiegman), CF 13B (Kalamazoo, MI: Cistercian Publications, 1995), 24.

[43] Bernard, Apol 20 (SBOp 3:98; Rudolph, "*Things*," 267): *Ipsa deinde qualitas rerum talis deforis apparere curatur, ut non minus aspectus quam gustus delectetur, et cum iam stomachus crebris ructibus repletum se indicet, necdum tamen curiositas satiatur. Sed dum oculi coloribus, palatum saporibus illiciuntur, infelix stomachus, cui nec colores lucent, nec sapores demulcent, dum omnia suscipere cogitur, oppressus magis obruitur quam reficitur*. Later he depicts monks examining fine silk for robes "with both fingers and eyes" (Apol 26).

the work of developing an interior temple, decorated by elaborate figural images according to the genius of the individual monk, and the apparent contradiction between stark cloister walls and ornate rhetoric dissolves.[44]

When Bernard next attacks those who loll about in the infirmary pretending to be sick in order to be dispensed from a vegetarian diet, his words ironically recall his earlier remark that he chose the more austere order of the Cistercians over the Benedictines not from disdain for the latter but rather from his need for a stronger remedy (Apol 7). While not himself a knight, he was from a military family, and his scorn for the self-indulgent is clear: "What faintheartedness is this, good soldiers? While your comrades are whirling about in the blood and gore, you are enjoying a delicate meal or taking your early morning sleep."[45]

## Clothing

Bernard sets up his more concrete discussion *De vestitu superfluo vel superbo* in the last pages of *Apology* by a series of images around clothing, including Pride wrapped in the swaddling clothes of the infant Jesus, and the coat of many colors. Like rich food, he says, excessively fine dress violates the order of necessity: "It is not that which is more practical which is sought to be worn, but that which is found to be more refined [*non quid utilius, sed quod subtilius*]."[46]

A good part of Bernard's critique in the *Apology* concerns the implied need for harmony or congruence between monastic ethos and its expression in practice. Given the meaning and purpose of monastic life, what practices best express and

---

[44] Mary Carruthers, *The Craft of Thought: Meditation, Rhetoric and the Making of Images, 400–1200* (New York: Cambridge University Press, 1998), 86–87.
[45] Bernard, Apol 22 (SBOp 3:99; Rudolph, *"Things,"* 268).
[46] Bernard, Apol 24 (SBOp 3:95; Rudolph, *"Things,"* 265).

support it? Thus the incongruity between the inner meaning and outer practice of monastic life recurs: "The knight and the monk divide the same bolt of cloth between them for both cowl and cape. No one these days, however high, even if he were a king or an emperor, would appear unsightly in our clothes if only they were prepared and tailored for him in his own way."[47]

While challenging the detractors among the White monks Bernard was prepared to allow that sometimes inner disposition trumped outward practice, he now argues that practice reveals and expresses disposition: "Any shortcoming that appears on the outside undoubtedly proceeds from the treasury of the heart. The empty heart forces on the body the mark of its own emptiness, and exterior excess is an indication of interior emptiness. Soft garments reveal a softness of the soul. The adornment of the body would not be worried about so much if it were not that the soul had been previously neglected, unadorned with virtues."[48] Interior fullness then, by contrast, would find expression in an exterior that is empty and transparent.

The architecture of the Black monks offends against the same ethical and aesthetic principles as their diet and clothing. Bernard calls attention to "the immense heights of their places of prayer, their immoderate lengths, their superfluous widths [*oratoriorum immensas altitudines, immoderatas longitudines, supervacuas latitudines*]." The dimensions are unmeasured (*immensas*) by necessity, out of proportion to the way of life that

---

[47] Bernard, Apol 25 (SBOp 3:102; Rudolph, "Things," 275). *Miles et monachus ex eodem panno partiuntur sibi cucullam et chlamydem. Quivis de saeculo, quantumlibet honoratus, etiam si Rex etiam si Imperator ille fuerit, non tamen nostra horrebit indumenta, si suo sibi modo praeparata fuerint et aptata;* see also Apol 27, where Bernard criticizes abbots for traveling with retinues "sufficient for two bishops": "If you saw them passing by you would say that they were not the spiritual fathers of monasteries, but the lords of castles, not the keepers of souls, but the princes of some region."

[48] Bernard, Apol 26 (SBOp 3:102; Rudolph, "Things," 275).

they ought to express. These (along with *sumptuosas depolitiones, curiosas depictiones*) distract and hinder the devotion of those who pray [*retorquent aspectum, impediunt et affectum*]. The pairing of *aspectum* and *affectus* is common in Cistercian literature, indicating the union of intellect and desire that characterizes prayer in the Spirit. The *aspectum* is literally twisted from its course while the steps of the *affectum* are blocked (*impediunt*). The transparency—the "emptiness" implied above—that ought to characterize monastic art is missing. The one at prayer is unable to move through the images to his goal. Bernard notes in passing of these dimensions and depictions that "to me they somehow represent the ancient rite of the Jews." As the Jews allegedly remained at the level of appearance and were unable to pass through to the reality, so too with those locked in externals.

The meaning and beauty of art works are inseparable from the motives and social contexts from which they emerge. Throughout this portion of *Apology* Bernard argues that avarice is the motive behind the lavish decorations that characterize conventional monasteries; by a kind of mimetic response, the expenditure of vast sums on church adornment elicits donations: "Eyes are fixed on relics covered with gold and purses are opened. The thoroughly beautiful image of some male or female saint is exhibited and that saint is believed to be the more holy the more highly colored the image is. People rush to kiss it, they are invited to donate, and they admire the beautiful more than they venerate the sacred [*magis mirantur pulchra, quam venerantur sacra*]."[49] Thus the value of a work of art for Bernard cannot be divorced from its origin and context, the purpose for which it was made. Sumptuous churches built at

---

[49] Bernard Apol 28 (SBOp 3:105; Rudolph, *Things*, 281). *Auro tectis reliquiis signantur oculi, et loculi aperiuntur. Ostenditur pulcherrima forma Sancti vel Sanctae alicuius, et eo creditur sanctior, quo coloratior. Currunt homines ad osculandum, invitantur ad donandum, et magis mirantur pulchra, quam venerantur sacra.*

the expense of the poor, for instance, fail the test of an aesthetics that is grounded in necessity, an aesthetics that includes the broader social and theological context in which art works have meaning: "The Church is radiant in its walls and destitute in its poor. It dresses its stones in gold and it abandons its children. It serves the eyes of the rich at the expense of the poor. The curious find that which may delight them, but those in need do not find that which should sustain them [*De sumptibus egenorum servitur oculis divitum. Inveniunt curiosi quo delectentur, et non inveniunt miseri qui sustententur*]."[50] Bernard speaks of monks as those who have "left behind all that is precious and beautiful [*pretiosa ac speciosa*] in this world for the sake of Christ," all "material pleasures," and yet this does not mean the renunciation of the aesthetic. He writes as an artist, arguing for one sense of the beautiful over another with both intensity and sensitivity.

Just as Bernard views the figures in Scripture as pathways (*ductus*) leading through themselves to the divine, so he implies that works of visual art ought to be iconic, guiding the viewer to the saint depicted in the image. Just as the devout gaze makes such transparency possible, so avarice objectifies the image and makes it opaque. Bernard complains of the way the images of the saints are depicted on floors, where they are trod and spat on: "Frequently people spit on the countenance of an angel. Often the face of one of the saints is pounded by the heels of those passing by."[51] Instead of an icon's leading the gaze through to the saint depicted in the image, art becomes the tool of avarice, an idol. Images, then, are fundamentally ambiguous. As Bernard writes, "if they are harmful to the shallow and avaricious, they are not to the simple and devout."

---

[50] Bernard, Apol 28 (SBOp 3:105–6; Rudolph, "Things," 281–83). *Fulget ecclesia parietibus, et in pauperibus eget. Suos lapides induit auro, et suos filios nudos deserit. De sumptibus egenorum servitur oculis divitum. Inveniunt curiosi quo delectentur, et non inveniunt miseri qui sustententur.*

[51] Bernard, Apol 28 (SBOp 3:106; Rudolph, "Things," 283).

Despite the subjective element of the viewer's disposition, the meaning and beauty of an image remain inseparable for Bernard from the social context in which it has emerged.

Bernard strategically critiques the excesses of conventional monastic life by calling attention to the incongruity between the austerity of the monastic ideal and the sumptuous art adorning the walls of its cloisters. The hybrid monsters depicted in the capitals and manuscripts of the Black monks become images of the wider disparity between art and life that Bernard condemns: "In short, everywhere so plentiful and astonishing a variety of contradictory forms is seen" that monks are inclined to remain on the brilliant surface instead of "meditating on the law of God," mulling over the more transparent literary figures of Scripture.

## Conclusion

Bernard's *Apology* counters an idolatrous aesthetic born of avarice and characterized by "superfluity" with a monastic poetics sensitive to spiritual beauty and governed by principles of necessity and purpose. By setting his critique of certain abuses in concrete monastic observance, within the horizon of an ecclesial and eschatological vision relayed in essentially aesthetic categories (proportion, diversity in unity, etc.), Bernard grounds his critique of *superfluitates* theologically in art and practice. He is keenly aware of the ambiguous nature of the visible. Exterior beauty, he says, can appear as the expression of an inner reality, but interior beauty can also be revealed, to those with eyes to see, through outward poverty: above all, in the Crucified. Bernard plays on these possibilities of congruence and disparity between appearance and reality throughout the treatise. His artful caricatures are intentional exaggerations, not meant to portray historical fact, and the manner in which they distort yet reveal is one dimension of the way the treatise plays in the space between appearance and reality.

# 7. "Mysticism Turned Inside Out": Julia Kristeva on Bernard of Clairvaux

Henri de Lubac described Bernard as not only the last of the fathers of the church but also "the first of the great moderns."[1] It is principally his attention to the self, experience, and affectivity that marks Bernard as proto-modern. Contemporary thought is marked by critical awareness of how historical, social, and psychological factors impinge on an individual's perception and interpretation. Bernard lacks the critical sense of history and the perspectives opened by the social sciences, but he is sensitive to how the disposition of the will shapes perception, something too often overlooked or explained away in contemporary discourse. For modernity, the problem arises as to whether one can really see through the projection of one's own context to reach something of the world or other people as they are, without reducing the mystery of what is truly unique in another to a more familiar horizon.

The philosopher and critic Julia Kristeva reads Bernard to support her view that ultimately we cannot reach through to the other. She wants to reclaim the physical and imaginative energies invested in "God" conceived as other to bolster the self in a project that seems ultimately solipsistic. When there

---

[1] Henri de Lubac, *Medieval Exegesis, vol. 2: The Four Senses of Scripture*, trans. E. M. Macierowski (Grand Rapids, MI: Eerdmans, 2000), 153. More recently, Emmanuel Falque has remarked Bernard's "étonannte *modernité*" (*Le Livre de L'Expérience: D'Anselme Cantorbéry à Bernard de Clairvaux* [Paris: Les Éditions du Cerf, 2017], 346).

has clearly been so much projection and distortion in the history of the Christian imagination, it is not hard to see how a thinker like Kristeva would conceive the entire tradition in this light. Bernard, however, is remarkably attuned to the way sub-personal influences color the imagination, and he implies a view in which, as part of the incarnation, the divine condescends to work in and through the ambiguities of the images made by human beings, opening them from within. His view allows for the gradual re-appropriation of the projected energies Kristeva also seeks but would consider this maturation as clearing the way for a fuller encounter with the other rather than exposing the other as a fiction.[2] Wrestling with ambiguous images, then, is formative for Bernard, preparing the heart for deeper levels of relationship. Further, Bernard teaches that only the awareness of another's love empowers one to radically reform one's life from within—"Love moves us freely and it makes us free"[3]—and the efficacy of love implies its reality. Jean-Luc Marion develops Bernard's insight that the will as love opens the possibility of contact with the other and that indeed "love itself is knowledge" in terms of contemporary phenomenology.[4]

Julia Kristeva's *Tales of Love* contains a chapter on Bernard that is sensitive to distinctive features of Bernard's work that

---

[2] Carlos Domínguez-Morano has proposed an "impossible synthesis" between religious experience and psychoanalysis in which the two perspectives engage in a perpetual mutual questioning. My aim is not to harmonize Bernard and Kristeva's perspectives or to defend Bernard from suspicion, but rather to show the ways Bernard himself was already subjecting religious images and ideas to a suspicion not altogether unlike Kristeva's while retaining the possibility of actual contact with another. Domínguez-Morano makes a distinction between imaginary versus symbolic levels of engagement reminiscent of Bernard's distinction between carnal and spiritual. See Carlos Domínguez-Morano, *Belief After Freud: Religious Faith through the Crucible of Psychoanalysis*, trans. Francisco Javier Montero (New York: Routledge, 2018), 76, 93.

[3] Bernard, Dil 17 (SBOp 3:134; CF 13B:20).

[4] See Chapter 8.

commentators with a primarily theological or spiritual focus ignore or underappreciate. She is attuned to the way in which elements of Bernard's account of affectivity anticipate the modern unconscious, and she is attracted by his views on self-love. On the other hand, she writes from outside the horizon of faith and glosses over the volitional and moral dimension of human being so central to Bernard's perspective. Like Freud, she holds that the believer's creed expresses subjective fantasy rather than any kind of objective state of affairs.[5] In discussing the treatise *On Loving God*, she fails to address two of its essential ideas, namely, that sin is fundamentally arrogance, arrogating to oneself what is in fact a gift of God, and the related anthropology of the early pages in the treatise, where Bernard understands the attributes that constitute one as a person (dignity, knowledge, and virtue) as gifts deriving from an Other.

Kristeva conceives of believers' God as an ideal projection of their own desire. She sees a God of love such as Christianity introduces, and to which the twelfth-century Cistercian school gives a unique and powerful expression, a God who comes before and grounds the believer's own love, a God who is an unlimited good, as vindicating the voracity, the immoderation of the believer's primal drives. One of the many facets of Bernard's anthropology that emerges in rereading him alongside Kristeva is that for Bernard this modern, psychoanalytic

---

[5] Unlike Freud, however, Arthur Bradley states that Kristeva "argues that religion and psychoanalysis are *both* expressions of a set of psychic illusions or fantasies that are necessary and unavoidable to the development of the subject" (Arthur Bradley, " 'Mystic Atheism': Julia Kristeva's Negative Theology," *Theology and Sexuality* 14, no. 3 [2008]: 282). Ann W. Astell, "Telling Tales of Love: Julia Kristeva and Bernard of Clairvaux," *Christianity and Literature* 50, no. 1 (2000): 129, cites Kristeva as saying, "The representations on which the Credo is based are fantasies, which reveal fundamental desires or traumas but not dogmas." See also David R. Crownfield, "The Sublimation of Narcissism in Christian Love and Faith," in *Body/Text in Julia Kristeva*, ed. David R. Crownfield (Albany: SUNY Press, 1992), 62.

notion of ideality and projection is not wholly alien. For instance, when he speaks in the closing pages of *On Loving God* of the figures of the slave, the merchant, and the son, each conceiving of God in accord with the quality of his desire, Bernard recognizes the way one's state of soul colors perception of the divine.

Although Kristeva speaks of Bernard as "an astute psychologist,"[6] he was in fact more subtle than she recognizes. His account of the four stages of love through which the soul progresses portrays a gradual shift from a centripetal to a centrifugal horizon. The images of slave, merchant, and son correspond: initially, one "is only aware of himself," even, I would suggest, in loving God, so that the God to whom one relates is primarily an image of oneself.[7] The later image, of God as loving Father, holds less projection and more reality; it is a truer, more transparent image. As the soul becomes less centered on itself, its innate self-love unfolding with the grain of its nature, it becomes capable of forming truer images of God, images that mediate more of the reality of which they must be forever partial and imperfect representations. In other words, Bernard is aware of these images as images invested with meaning by human beings but does not see them as for that reason simply fictional.

### Horizons: Kristeva

While she considers religion in terms of wish fulfillment, Kristeva does not, as Freud does, view psychoanalysis as reason shedding light on the vain superstition of religion. For her, there is nothing beneath the mask: psychoanalysis can simply

---

[6] Julia Kristeva, *Tales of Love*, trans. Leon S. Roudiez (New York: Columbia University Press, 1987), 166.

[7] Bernard, Dil 23 (SBOp 3:138; Bernard of Clairvaux, *On Loving God, with an Analytical Commentary by Emero Stiegman*, CF 13B [Kalamazoo, MI: Cistercian Publications, 1995], 25).

help one realize that there is only projection. As Arthur Bradley articulates Kristeva's view of the difference between Christianity and psychoanalysis, "both are seen as fantastic expressions of the subject's desire to gain unity through identification and even fusion with an omnipotent father figure. To be sure, Kristeva remains a self-professed atheist: psychoanalysis helps the analysand to understand this desire for unity, she contends, whereas religion merely dogmatizes and mythologizes it."[8]

Further, Kristeva sees projections as intrinsic to the development of the self and considers that by coming to see them for what they are it becomes possible to regain energies otherwise wasted on illusions. Bradley continues: "Kristeva argues that religion and psychoanalysis are *both* expressions of a set of psychic illusions or fantasies that are necessary and unavoidable to the development of the subject . . . psychoanalysis goes 'beyond' religion because it seeks to relocate fantasy back within the psychic economy that generated it."[9] Clearly this is part of what she finds attractive in the account of the self and of self-love in Bernard's *On Loving God*: the way it privileges the perspective of the desiring subject can be seen as a move in the direction of reclaiming the psychic energy attributed to "God."

Kristeva is fascinated by the way Christian mystics discover an Other within the self as opposed to the external God imagined by a more traditional Christianity. She sees this discovery as an important bridge between a medieval and modern psychoanalytic view.[10] She also distinguishes between religion and

---

[8] Bradley, "Mystic Atheism," 282.
[9] Bradley, "Mystic Atheism," 280.
[10] Though it is clear, says Bradley, that "psychoanalysis is the true successor and replacement of Christianity" ("Mystic Atheism," 281), he goes on somewhat later to say, "There is a problematic sense in which Kristeva sees everything that *transcends* the human subject as still belonging to the subject, in other words, so that subjectivity is always and impossibly placed on *both* sides of the fissure that inaugurates it" (292). In Bernard of course there is a real Other, so the problem does not arise. In his view, as love matures, the

"the sacred"; the former she describes as stifling sexual and narcissistic desires by the formulation of "ego-ideals" like "God," while she speaks of the latter as "the unconscious recognition of an unsustainable eroticism" between "nature and culture, the animal and the verbal, the sensible and the nameable."[11] This sense of a basic antinomy between the body and language shapes her reading of key ideas in Bernard such as self-love and affectivity.

Kristeva's interpretation of Bernard is intrinsically linked to her account of the self. Freud understood love as essentially narcissistic, an inflation of the other based on the autoerotic pleasure of which that other is the vehicle or on the grounds of an idealization of oneself. Kristeva is concerned to understand the narcissistic roots of this dynamic, largely unexplored by Freud, and how they work.[12] In her account, the self is basically triadic, formed from (1) the primordial intuition of something that is an other than its mother, an imaginary "somebody," (2) the mother, and (3) a "collage of sensations" and "a gap," a "nothingness." As David Crownfield explains, "What Kristeva calls the zero degree of subjectivity is my originary imagining of myself as the somebody, an imaginary that takes the form of a sort of rudimentary pattern-replication, or mimicry of the other. The hole, the nothing, is covered over, masked, fictively replaced by this imagined somebody that begins to be myself." The self, he goes on, is "already an imaginary substitution of the image of the other for the gap in being that I am."[13]

In Kristeva's understanding, narcissism involves a rejection of this triadic constitution of the self by siding with either the mother or the imaginary somebody against the other. It is a

---

energies projected onto the beloved are re-appropriated by the self, *and* God is seen more clearly as he is. This is part of what it means when he says of God, "In giving me himself, he gave me back myself" (Dil 15 [SBOp 3:132; CF 13B:18]).

[11] Bradley, "Mystic Atheism," 283.
[12] Crownfield, "The Sublimation of Narcissism," 57.
[13] Crownfield, "The Sublimation of Narcissism," 58.

kind of fearful reduction toward a merely dyadic relation, one that will impede the individual's development and capacity to relate to others. In this view of human love one transfers the imaginary idealization on which one's self is founded to an other and finds in the other's love parental affirmation for one's imaginary being (i.e., the self).[14]

Kristeva interprets the New Testament God of love "as a symbolic representation of the archaic, imaginary father," not the God of Law but "the original, pregenital third party, modeling and reflecting identity as love, affirmation, acceptance. In this image the Christian God marks the clearing of a space for triadic subjectivity."[15]

An essential inference from these briefly summarized views is that Kristeva depicts transference and idealization of an originally imaginary other, a fiction, as constitutive of the human self from its earliest stages. Bernard too assumes an Other to be inscribed, not only, he would say, in a sense of self that has developed but in the very being of the person. The spiritual gift of *dignitas* (freedom, being in the image of God) is something one knows intuitively as derived from an Other. Human beings are not the origin of their own freedom. What is generally defined as knowledge is primally ordered toward this intuition, and virtue looks toward seeking out the One who originates the gift one is, whose image one bears.[16]

---

[14] See Crownfield, "The Sublimation of Narcissism," 59.

[15] Crownfield, "The Sublimation of Narcissism," 59.

[16] Bernard, Dil 3 (SBOp 3:121; CF 13B:5). Mark Burrows locates a crucial epistemological difference between postmodern and medieval approaches in the contemporary abandonment of an ontological ground to the symbolic. He states that medieval readers like Bernard conceived of "the figural world as the *real* world." The reverse of this view is also true, I would suggest, that for Bernard the real world is figural, human being is to begin with in the image. See Burrows, "Hunters, Hounds and Allegorical Readers: The Body of the Text and the Text of the Body in Bernard of Clairvaux's *Sermons on the Song of Songs*," *Studies in Spirituality* 14 (2004): 125.

## Love Makes Us Free

Bernard's *On Loving God* is to some extent apologetic. It argues that Christians and non-Christians ought to love God on the basis of what Bernard claims to be a universal structure of experience, a basic pattern characterizing the self's emergence. For Bernard, patient reading in "the book of our own experience"[17] and the natural unfolding of innate desire lead to God. Underlining Bernard's commitment to the truth of experience, Stiegman speaks of "Bernard's orientation to the concrete problems of his existence and to his demand that reason forever justify itself against intimate personal experience, a larger human knowing."[18] In Bernard's account of life in time, lasting change can only be produced in cooperation with human freedom. Divine love makes freedom fully free: "Charity converts souls because it makes them act willingly" (*Caritas vero convertit animas, quas facit et voluntarias*).[19] Neither the fearful slave who conceives of God as a tyrannical master nor the self-interested merchant who conceives of God as similarly self-interested can bring about deep and lasting conversion. Of such images, Bernard writes, "At times they change one's appearance or deeds; they can never alter one's character."[20] Only belief in and experience of the genuine love of a real other can produce the quality of change witnessed in true conversion.

Bernard in fact argues that rather than acting tyrannically, God awakens a depth of interiority, and a certain distance is gained from the psyche and its images, which now appear to

---

[17] Bernard, SC 3.1 (SBOp 1:14; CF 4:16).

[18] Stiegman, "Analytical Commentary," CF 13B:56. Some (including, from different perspectives, Kristeva and Andrew Louth) discern in Bernard the beginning of the divorce between emotion and rationality associated with Descartes and modernity. See, e.g., Andrew Louth, "Bernard and Affective Mysticism," in *The Influence of Saint Bernard: Anglican Essays*, ed. Benedicta Ward (Oxford: SLG Press, 1976), 3–9.

[19] Bernard, Dil 34 (SBOp 3:149; CF 13B:35).

[20] Bernard, Dil 34 (SBOp 3:149; CF 13B:35).

some extent relative and transparent. Again, divine love moves human beings according to their nature: "Moving us freely, it makes us spontaneous" (*Sponte afficit, spontaneum fecit*).[21] At the same time, Bernard says, the Word that visits the soul can be perceived only by its uniquely profound effects in the soul. Writing of God as the Word, he describes these effects:

> He awakens my slumbering soul; he stirs and soothes and pierces my heart, for before it was hard as stone. . . . It was not by any movement of his that I recognized his coming. . . . Only by the movement of my heart . . . did I perceive his presence; and I knew the power of his might because my faults were put to flight and my human yearnings brought into subjection . . . in the renewal and remaking of the spirit of my mind, that is of my inmost being, I have perceived the excellence of his glorious beauty.[22]

The touch of divine love, Bernard claims, is qualitatively unique. It can change people for the good, make their hidden, even unconscious, faults manifest, and make the psychological realm transparent in a way no other experience can.

## Kristeva on Bernard

Kristeva's reading of Bernard relies on an implicit anthropology. She distinguishes between the sacred and religion, suggesting that the former tends to subvert the latter. So in her chapter on Bernard in *Tales of Love* she reads into Bernard's view a conflict alien to his understanding, speaking of the "subterraneously conflicting nature of incarnational Christianity." In this conflict, as she conceives it, love is the bridge, the hyphen, between nature and meaning, body and ideality,

---

[21] Bernard, Dil 17 (SBOp 3:134; CF 13B:20).
[22] Bernard, SC 74:6 (SBOp 2:243; CF 40:91).

sin and grace.[23] She describes a "wrenching" of body, a "holy violence,"[24] and speaks of "forcing" carnal love to the heights of loving God.[25] The "sacred" involves for her an "unsustainable eroticism" between these poles. While admiring the place of desire and affectivity in Bernard's writings, she sees it in tension with the imposition of "regulating will" and speaks, ironically, of "the vile affect deprived of will."[26] She perceives a certain transcendentalizing of the immanent that she wants to reverse: "Saints and troubadours seem to proclaim, *Ego affectus est*, thus glorifying what, in the light of Reason, will appear to be base irrationality. They impart willpower to their love, enlighten it with reason, tinge it with wisdom, in order to raise it to the dignity of a divine essence. And man, uncertain, passionate, ill, or happy identifies with that affect. For God is love."[27] Or rather, love is god, is apotheothesized. So Bradley describes Kristeva's project as "mysticism turned inside out."[28] Her account of self-love is also arguably "inside out."

Bernard makes it clear in the second part of *On Loving God* that an instinctive love of self, alien to one's original nature but made necessary by the conditions of postlapsarian life, unfolds outward into love of an Other for one's own sake. Astell offers an account of Kristeva's position: "Unable to know and understand himself completely, incapable of recognizing the Other as the illusory product of his own desires, the human subject is and remains Narcissus."[29] At best, then, analysands can recognize that fantasies of a loving God have sexual, bodily origins and suspend disbelief; in the presence of a permissive

---

[23] Kristeva, *Tales of Love*, 166–67.
[24] Kristeva, *Tales of Love*, 159, 165; elsewhere she writes of a "wrenching" of soul for the sake of loving identification with the other (168).
[25] Kristeva, *Tales of Love*, 163–64.
[26] Kristeva, *Tales of Love*, 157.
[27] Kristeva, *Tales of Love*, 154.
[28] Bradley, "Mystic Atheism," 280.
[29] Astell, "Telling Tales," 131.

maternal analyst, they can simply give free play to their unanswerable need for love. Bernard himself recognizes the bodily origins of the human imagination of God and affirms that, like the body itself, instincts and imagination come from God and lead back to him. The love of self for oneself, for instance, is an expression of divine love for human beings in time, a stage that will be outgrown but is no less a gift.

What Kristeva overlooks is that for Bernard ambiguous affect and even deeply disordered unconscious drives are not in any way natural but derive from being born into a network of damaged relationality ("original sin"). However deep-seated destructive tendencies are, Bernard regards them as ultimately extrinsic and alien to the true nature of the human being. Human being in the image of God is ineradicable. As he writes: "So these evils are accidental, and do not result from the good gifts which are natural, but are superimposed on them; they defile but do not wipe them out; they bring confusion upon them but not destruction."[30] Indeed Kristeva's general analysis of Bernard suffers in omitting the *moral* sphere so central to him, his account of sin as arrogance, and his account of freedom as the *dignitas* by which human beings are in the image of God.

This omission comes out in a particular way in Kristeva's interpretation of a passage in which Bernard employs a striking metaphor to describe the situation of the body between spirit and flesh: "Our body finds itself located between the spirit it must serve and the desires of the flesh or the powers of darkness, which wage war on the soul, as a cow might be between the peasant and the thief." In considering this passage Kristeva stresses what she considers Bernard's derogatory image of the body as a cow and apparently overlooks the moral sense Bernard intends: that the body is between its rightful master—a peasant, so one who cares for the animal on behalf of an

---

[30] Bernard, SC 82.5 (SBOp 2:295; CF 40:176).

Other—and one who uses his body selfishly, stealing for himself what is a gift he has on trust.[31]

## Bernard's Anthropology

The opening pages of *On Loving God* provide anthropological underpinnings essential to understanding Bernard's perspective. Responding to the question of why and how God ought to be loved, Bernard supplies two answers: a brief one ("God himself is the reason why he is to be loved") and a more developed reply.[32] For the wise the brief answer suffices. The treatise has from the outset a multiple audience: not only the wise and the less experienced but also Christians and *infideles*.[33] Bernard is concerned to show that non-Christians are bound to love God with their entire being since he is the origin of being.[34] Christians, however, are able to take a shortcut to the perfect love of God, namely Christ, who draws their carnal affections upward by revealing to an unprecedented degree the depths of God's gratuitous love.

In addition to the physical necessities of "bread, sun, and air," Bernard says, God provides all human beings with the "nobler gifts" of dignity (freedom), knowledge, and virtue.[35] By the first we are free, in the image of God. By the second we know both that we are free and that we are not the origin of our freedom, that it is a gift. By the third we seek and adhere to God, the source of these good gifts.[36] Bernard describes the interdependence of these elements, saying that freedom that does not know its origin lacks purchase and direction. Without virtue—ordered affection, right desire—freedom lacks energy

---

[31] Kristeva, *Tales of Love*, 159.
[32] Bernard, Dil 1 (SBOp 3:119; CF 13B:3).
[33] Stiegman, "Analytical Commentary," 68.
[34] Bernard, Dil 6 (SBOp 3:124; CF 13B:8).
[35] Bernard, Dil 2 (SBOp 3:121; CF 13B:5).
[36] See Stiegman's commentary on the choice of the term *virtus*, "Analytical Commentary," CF 13B:95.

and drive. It can become an obstacle, an end in itself:[37] "Who, again, can be wicked enough to think the author of his human dignity, which shines in his soul, is any other than he who says in the book of Genesis, 'Let us make man in our own image and likeness'? Hence God deserves to be loved for his own sake even by the infidel who, *although he is ignorant of Christ, yet knows himself.*"[38] Knowledge of one's origin helps steer affection/desire to its true end, and the quality of desire in turn determines what can be known. The root danger Bernard identifies is that humanity, "not appreciating the gift of reason," and "ignoring his own interior glory, models his conduct on the object of his senses."[39] Worse than appraising oneself as too lowly is the temptation to arrogate to one's self what one knows to be the gift of an Other, "thinking some good is in us of ourselves": "If ignorance makes beasts of us, arrogance makes us like demons";[40] we have "exchanged our glory for the likeness of a calf that eats grass."[41]

Bernard states that God deserves to be loved without measure, but that we are limited by our capacity and unable to love with the same boundless gratuitousness with which God loves us.[42] The degree of likeness to God becomes the measure with which God is loved. For the Christian, Christ crucified becomes in a sense the measure without measure, not only elevating and ordering carnal human affection but modeling and attracting the right use of freedom by the supreme gratu-

---

[37] Bernard, Dil 3–4 (SBOp 3:121–23; CF 13B:5–7).
[38] Bernard, Dil 6 (SBOp 3:124; CF 13B:8) (my emphasis).
[39] Bernard, Dil 4 (SBOp 3:122; CF 13B:6).
[40] Bernard, Dil 4 (SBOp 3:122–23; CF 13B:7).
[41] Investing a beast with reason, and so becoming like it, reverses the recognition of God in human reason, that is, in human knowledge of the divine image within. This in turn is a failure to use reason and freedom as measure.
[42] We can, however, reciprocate by loving freely: "Love is the only one of the motions of the soul . . . in which the creature can respond to its Creator, even if not as an equal, and repay his favor in some similar way" (Bernard, SC 83:4 [SBOp 2:300–301; CF 40:183–85]).

itousness of his love in dying for his enemies.[43] Of divine love, Bernard writes, "moving us freely, it makes us free" (*Sponte afficit, spontaneum fecit*).[44] Further, he says, "When he gave me himself, he gave me back myself."[45] Only the knowledge of being loved sets one free to be oneself to this degree.[46] This is the heart of Bernard's pragmatic argument that the efficacy of what is experienced as being loved by God, the way it sets human being free to be itself most fully, argues against its being simply an illusion.

Divine love empowers human freedom and makes it effective, while by contrast, Bernard writes, "The wicked . . . walk round in circles. . . . They take more pleasure in the appearance of things than in their Creator."[47] He goes on to explain that unless reason guides the senses they cannot attain their end, but rather "run alongside the road." Only desire steered by reason or faith can attain its true goal; otherwise it rebounds on itself. Ironically, those grasping after immediate satisfaction, then, are the ones chasing an illusion, while those for whom created realities have become transparent images of their Creator are able to desire "their true end," a "blessed end."[48] Material goods alone cannot satisfy a rational soul any more than ideas can satisfy the body.[49] Bernard contrasts the circuitous path of

---

[43] Bernard, Dil 7 (SBOp 3:124; CF 13B:9).
[44] Bernard, Dil 17 (SBOp 3:134; CF 13B:20).
[45] Bernard, Dil 15 (SBOp 3:132; CF 13B:18).
[46] In this respect Bernard's anthropology harmonizes with and anticipates aspects of the personalism of theologians like Ratzinger, who writes, "The human person is the event or being of relativity. The more the person's relativity aims totally and directly at its final goal, at transcendence, the more the person is itself" (Joseph Ratzinger, "Concerning the Notion of Person in Theology," *Communio* 17 [Fall 1990]: 452). Bernard describes the soul's mirroring the crucified at Dil 7, where Christ, "pierced by nails, wounded by a lance," is presented alongside the soul of the bride "transfixed" by the "sword of love."
[47] Bernard, Dil 19 (SBOp 3:135; CF 13B:22).
[48] Bernard, Dil 19 (SBOp 3:135; CF 13B:22).
[49] Bernard, Dil 21 (SBOp 3:137; CF 13B:24).

the wicked with the straight way, the "short-cut" of the "shortened and shortening word" taken by the just.[50]

## On Loving Self

An aspect of Bernard's modernity that features in *On Loving God* is the attention he gives to the self and the argument he makes for right self-love. Kristeva likewise articulates the importance of right self-love preceding one's efforts to love others:

> To become capable of loving our neighbor as ourself, we have first of all to heal a wounded narcissism. We must reconstitute narcissistic identity to be able to extend a hand to the other. Thus what is needed is a reassurance or reconstruction of both narcissism, personality, and, of course, the subject for there to be a relation to the other. . . . Love the other as oneself, but by being settled within oneself, by delight in oneself. Thus: heal your inner wounds which, as a result will render you then capable of effective social action, or intervention in the social plane with the other. Therefore, I would argue that we must heal our shattered narcissism before formulating higher objectives.[51]

As Kristeva states, this position is part of her interest in Bernard, who sounds surprisingly modern at times in his account of the self and its rightful place in an economy of love. He cites the

---

[50] Bernard, Dil 19–21 (SBOp 3:135–37; CF 13B:22–24). By going straight for what they think will please them, the wicked caricature the directness of the route taken by the just. One can love only as one is able, so rhetorically, Bernard, who offers both a "shortcut" and a fuller treatment of his theme, speaks of God "in a way no doubt unworthy of him, but according to the gift I have received" (Dil 17).

[51] See Kathleen O'Grady, "An Interview with Julia Kristeva," in *Julia Kristeva 1966–96: Aesthetics, Politics, Ethics*, special issue of *Parallax*, no. 8 (July–September 1998): 5–16.

verse in Ecclesiasticus, "If you are mean to yourself, to whom will you be good?"[52] In a masterful sermon he portrays the need for the soul to see to its own needs first so that it can properly serve others. It must be filled like a reservoir that brims over when full rather than immediately squandering its resources like a canal.[53] Of course, Kristeva's and Bernard's accounts diverge in a number of ways. For Bernard, love of God comes first and sets in order right love for others.[54] With the image of the reservoir, he is describing two kinds of spiritual gifts, those intended for one's own salvation and those meant to build up the common good. Ultimately not only isolated charisms but one's very self is a web of gifts: from and for both an Other and one's fellow creatures. Bernard distinguishes between boasting in the Lord—akin perhaps to loving oneself only for the sake of God—and greedily arrogating to oneself the glory that belongs to another, the basic dynamic of sin.[55] Further implied in Bernard's view is the sense that right self-love is the way to heal this selfish self-love.

It is important to give full weight to this inscription of the Other in the self in Bernard's anthropology: it is a major part of what attracts Kristeva to the Christian mystics. Whereas for Bernard reference to the human being in the image of God describes an ontological reality, Kristeva inverts this understanding in such a way that God is the image of human fantasy. When Bernard writes of God's loving humanity "for himself," Kristeva interprets this as an account of God that simply mirrors and validates the projection of voracious, immoderate, human desire, a force too wild for believers to face openly.[56]

Bernard's treatise charts four degrees in loving God: in the first one loves oneself only for one's own sake, in the second one loves God but for one's own sake, in the third one loves

---

[52] Sir 14:5; Bernard, SC 18:4 (SBOp 1:106; CF 4:135).
[53] Bernard, SC 18.3 (SBOp 1:104; CF 4:134).
[54] Bernard, Dil 25 (SBOp 3:139; CF 13B:27).
[55] Bernard, Dil 3 (SBOp 3:122; CF 13B:6).
[56] Kristeva, *Tales of Love*, 160.

God for God's own sake ("not because he is good to him but because the Lord is good"),[57] and in the fourth one loves oneself only for the sake of God, only because one's self is the place of encounter with so good a God. The discussion of this schema forms the second main section of the text. The third section, originally a letter, is appended to *On Loving God* as complementary. It portrays three stages of growth toward God. In the first one loves like a slave, dominated by fear, and envisions God as a punishing master. In the next, one loves like a merchant, haggling with God out of self-interest. In the last, one loves like a son, fully realizing the Father's goodness and freely responding in kind. There is no one-to-one correspondence between these schemes; they are like overlaid templates interacting in intriguing ways.

In the first of the four degrees the person is "only aware of himself." Bernard makes clear that this love of self is provisional and temporary, a result of the Fall; however instinctive, it is ultimately extrinsic to a self that bears the image of God.[58] This self-love can be read as extending not only to material resources but to psychology as well. Even when a person relates to God at this stage he is relating principally to a projection of himself.[59] So the God who is feared as a tyrant by the slave is largely the flip side of the slave's own fear. The experi-

---

[57] Bernard, Dil 26 (SBOp 3:141; CF13B:28).
[58] Bernard, Dil 23 (SBOp 3:138; CF 13B:25).
[59] That there is some psychological content to one's image of God hardly means that God is altogether a fantasy. Gerald May writes, "While it is true that many 'spiritual' experiences are primarily generated from the psyche (and perhaps almost all of them are in some way mediated by it), I doubt that it helps to become overly preoccupied with arbitrary distinctions between what is 'of the self' and what is 'of God.' The real question, I think, is whether the 'self' aspects of an experience help facilitate or hinder one's growth toward God, or whether they are consonant with or antagonistic towards God's will. To assume that something of the self must inherently be against God is to deny that aspect of ourselves that is made in God's image and to devalue our own intentionality towards God" (*Care of Mind/Care of Spirit: Psychiatric Dimensions of Spiritual Direction* [San Francisco: Harper and Row, 1982], 34).

ence of need and affliction, of calling to God and finding oneself answered, leads the self to realize that loving God is in one's own best interest. The self recognizes an emerging sense that God is a real Other, acting through events, so shifting toward a view of life as dialogical. Faith interpreting experience begins to perceive its transparence. Bernard interprets the body's wants as a kind of speech.[60] Still, in the second stage, the self's love of God is self-interested, like the merchant in the other scheme. In the third stage the self begins to taste the goodness of God himself, and the sense of God's inherent wealth and beauty impels one to love more than material need and its satisfaction.

In the fourth degree of love, only fleetingly experienced in this life, one loves oneself only for God's sake. The movement of the self, for a time necessarily centripetal, has become completely centrifugal. The mind, Bernard writes, "forgets" and "loses" itself: "To lose yourself, as if you no longer existed, to cease completely to experience yourself, is not a human sentiment but a divine experience [*coelestis est conversationis, non humanae affectionis*]."[61] The self is no longer experienced, it disappears from awareness, but continues to exist:

> It is deifying to go through such an experience [*Sic affici, deificari est*]. As a drop of water seems to disappear completely in a big quantity of wine, even assuming the wine's taste and color; just as red, molten iron becomes so much like fire it seems to lose its primary state; just as the air on a sunny day seems transformed into sunshine instead of being lit up; so it is necessary for the saints that all human feelings melt in a mysterious way and flow into the will of God. Otherwise, how will God be all in all if something human survives in man? No doubt, the substance remains though under another form, another glory, another power.[62]

---

[60] Bernard, Dil 26 (SBOp 3:141; CF 13B:28).
[61] Bernard, Dil 27 (SBOp 3:142; CF 13B:29).
[62] Bernard, Dil 28 (SBOp 3:143; CF 13B:30).

In contrast to Bernard's later, better known account, where the soul in the image of God grows in likeness to him, that is, becomes more like itself the more it becomes like God and vice versa, in the letter appended to *On Loving God* Bernard portrays the self as less like itself the more it becomes like God.[63] In the earlier work, Bernard's perspective is more empirical than ontological. The sense seems to be that the self identifies less with itself and more with God; it is "under another power." It is not a question of the replacement of human affectivity with God but the transformation of what is only feeling into an experience of God that realizes and completes beyond imagining the highest possibilities of human nature. Feelings "melt into" the divine will, he says, into harmony, not colonization. In divine love *agape* does not supplant *eros*; rather, what most delights and satisfies God's own desire is to give himself away. So too, to some degree, with the saints, and especially the martyrs, as Bernard discusses at Dil 29. Stiegman articulates Bernard's sense of the harmony between *eros* and *agape*:

> Bernard envisions a love of God in which we human beings respond, not because we wish to please God, but because God pleases us. Although this is not the totality of love, it is the point of view Bernard chooses—not as one intellectual option among several, but as the record of experience. At the same time, this point of view allows him to demonstrate two coordinate ideas: first, that grace works through our very nature to bring us to the perfect love of God (or, seen from the human side, *that loving God is our only possible self-realization*); and second, that God, who is love, is perfectly and unimaginably loveable.[64]

---

[63] For the first, see for instance Bernard, SC 80.1–4; for the second, Dil 32. See also Stiegman, "Analytical Commentary," 62, calling attention to the difference.

[64] Stiegman's "Analytical Commentary" to *On Loving God*, 96 (my emphasis). Kristeva follows Nygren (*Tales of Love*, chap. 4, n. 1). Stiegman underlines a Bernardine sense of the original goodness of *eros*: "Of the two ways of

That human being can only realize itself in reaching out toward the divine other strongly suggests that other's reality.

In the final section of his treatise Bernard explains that while the slave and the merchant "make a law for themselves," the son, by contrast, perceives and lives by the law of love that creates and governs the universe. His trusting love allows him to pierce the cloud of his own fantasies and reach the Other. If he still experiences love by means of images, they have become transparent means through which he intuits the living God. But, Bernard says, the one who wants to be a law to himself will "imitate his Creator in a perverse way and suffer beneath the unbearable burden of his own will."[65] He is forced by fear and drawn by cupidity as opposed to being moved willingly by love. So for Bernard the fear and cupidity of the slave and merchant are not erased or superseded but purified by the love that characterizes the son: fear becomes reverence and cupidity devotion.[66] The two disordered tendencies appear as warped expressions of deeper, more natural possibilities. The process appears as a kind of slant parallel to the four degrees in which selfish self-love becomes boasting in the Lord, delight in being the image of so good a God.[67]

---

looking at concupiscence, the one which places in the foreground an absolute discontinuity between *agape* and *eros* renders any talk of human progress toward God dangerously ambiguous when not wholly meaningless. Concepts of progressive growth can be based only on the other view of the same reality, the one which rests on the equally biblical truth that the *eros* of our fallen nature is not *in itself* sin, but (in its lack of order) the effect of sin" ("Analytical Commentary," 148).

[65] Bernard, Dil 36 (SBOp 3:150; CF 13B:38).

[66] Bernard, Dil 38 (SBOp 3:152; CF 13B:40).

[67] In Bernard, SC 83.4–5 (SBOp 2:300–301; CF 40:183–85), Bernard varies the scheme so that the son is the one akin to the merchant: "Children love their father, but they are thinking of their inheritance." Here he contrasts honor with the love that asks only love and trust. This alternative use of the father figure suggests that while some images are objectively more accurate than others, they do not work magically, and the degree to which they open on truth in a given case always involves the knower's sensibility. One could

## Sermon 50 on the Song of Songs Revisited

In Sermon 50 Bernard revisits and fleshes out themes from *On Loving God*. Here he makes clear that spiritual affection, *eros*, trumps the love in which to some degree we act against our inclination but in accord with reason and the law.[68] For him love guided by the practical needs that arise in a fallen world is a different register from love in the key of spiritual desire; as he says, "Love in action devises its own order."[69] While charity demands that we put aside contemplation to serve one in need, considered in itself, the impulse for delight in God above all else is best. It is from this perspective, within the experience of desire, that Bernard writes in *On Loving God*. But that it is a perspective, and not the full picture, becomes evident in Sermon 50.

Love of others however is not only in tension with and an alternate register to *eros*. Within the key of desire our love for others is shaped by the quality of our love for God. Clearly taking up again the language of the earlier treatise, Bernard writes in SC 50 that when we love ourselves only insofar as we love God, we then love others as we love ourselves, that is, insofar as they love God. Those who do not love God are loved so that they may love him: "As for your neighbor whom you are obliged to love as yourself: if you are to experience

---

have an image of God as father that was almost exclusively one's own projection. Bernard's concern is with love versus fear and which images are more suitable to each state of soul.

[68] Kristeva, *Tales of Love*, 156, renders it "one [affection] issues from the flesh, another *controls* reason, and finally a third brings reason in," where the original reads, *Sed est affectio quam caro gignit; et est quam ratio regit, et est quam condit sapientia*. In Bernard SC 50.4 Bernard speaks of an affection that is born of the flesh, ruled by reason, and conditioned by wisdom. Another English translation (CF 31:32–33) reads, "But there is an affection which the flesh begets, and one which reason controls, and one which wisdom seasons," suggesting three separate affections, where the sense more consonant with Bernard's view seems to be three modes of one affection.

[69] Bernard, SC 50.5 (SBOp 2:81; CF 31:34).

him as he is, you will actually experience him only as you do yourself: he is what you are. You who do not love yourself then, except because you love God, consequently love as yourself all those who similarly love him."[70] The passage suggests the spiritual friendship of those who similarly desire, an interesting addition to the abbreviated treatment of love for others in the treatise, and a contrast to that love of others oriented by dutiful, practical activity. Just as one loves others on the measure of oneself, so God is experienced not in himself but in relation to one's power to enjoy.[71]

It is important to note in this arrangement that the stage of spiritual affectivity superior to "reason" is not an anti-intellectual triumph of emotion. Bernard has in view the most refined spiritual sensitivity, pervaded by wisdom and allowing one to see things "as they are."[72] It is not Feeling but Truth that he invokes at the sermon's close, and the Wisdom that "sets love in order" (SC 50:8).[73]

## Projection

Kristeva explains psychoanalysis as, like Christianity, a "transferential quest for love."[74] Human beings, she says, project onto God the voracity of their own illimitable craving, the *eros* of God merely the projection of human desire.[75] She goes on to write of "the Self as a center that is projected onto others,"[76] and she claims that in Bernard's fourth stage, in which one loves one's self only for the sake of God, Bernard commits a kind of self-deification: "by means of this apparent renunciation, he exorbitantly enlarges love of self to the dimensions of

---

[70] Bernard, SC 50.7 (SBOp 2:82; CF 31:36).
[71] Bernard, SC 50.6 (SBOp 2:82; CF 31:35).
[72] See Bernard, SC 50.6–7 (SBOp 2:81–82; CF 31:35–36).
[73] Song 2:4 at SC 50.8 (SBOp 2:83; CF 31:37).
[74] Crownfield, "The Sublimation," 61.
[75] Kristeva, *Tales of Love*, 161.
[76] Kristeva, *Tales of Love*, 169, 173.

God." Similarly she considers the transformation of affectivity—including self-love—into the highest love of God in terms of self-idealization: "Such a violent apotheosis of love is in the final analysis a violent transformation of carnal love into a jubilatory state of Self idealization through successful identification with the Other,"[77] an Other who is ultimately imaginary for Kristeva—a fiction constitutive of the self at its origins. In Bernard's work—"which save for those who have chosen to live outside of time is only a museum page"—she admires what she perceives as "an exceptional balance between a voracious self and a tyrannical ideal."[78]

Describing how the self mediates knowledge of the divine, Bernard writes, "your self-knowledge will be a step to the knowledge of God; he will become visible to you as his image is being renewed within you."[79] Indeed, as Astell comments, "this humble, transformative facing of oneself and God is at the heart of Cistercian theological aesthetics." She goes on to say, "what one loves depends on what one sees, the *affectus* following the *aspectus*." Innate, carnal love, she suggests, can develop so as to influence the *aspectus* so that it seeks not appearances but "the beauty of what is real."[80]

Kristeva perceives a contradiction in Bernard between passages where he speaks of the fact that because human beings are fallen they must begin with carnal love, and the doctrine that as *imago dei*, human life is originally noble, ordered to God. In fact, in the one case Bernard is speaking methodologically—because one is fallen, in seeking God one must begin from where one is—and ontologically in the other, as created in the image of God and so intrinsically good. Her failure to perceive the reason for this seeming contradiction, to appreciate the two

---

[77] Kristeva, *Tales of Love*, 163.
[78] Kristeva, *Tales of Love*, 169.
[79] SC 36, cited in Ann W. Astell, *Eating Beauty: The Eucharist and the Spiritual Arts of the Middle Ages* (Ithaca: Cornell University Press, 2006), 72.
[80] Astell, *Eating Beauty*, 72, 76.

levels on which the treatise *On Loving God* operates, is significant. Kristeva acknowledges the influence on her thought of an article by Jacques Blanpain, "Langage mystique, expression du désir dans les Sermons sur le Cantique des Cantiques de Bernard de Clairvaux."[81] The article seems to divide the ontological and theological from the world of experience, from the psychological, in a way that is alien to Bernard. While it is true that Bernard writes in *On Loving God* from the perspective of the human person after the Fall, tossed about by the vicissitudes of life and by the person's own conflicting desires, this experiential realm is never separable from the ontological for Bernard. Blanpain notes how concerned Bernard is to show that one's images of God arise from the quality of one's desire,[82] but because the disposition of our being colors our experience at all times, the two spheres cannot ultimately be divided.[83]

Kristeva's scheme is in a sense univocal, failing to move between being and appearance, creation and Creator, as faith, and even reason—that which has encountered the Good as the ground of intelligibility—make possible. On the other hand, psychoanalysis offers a new alternative to faith precisely because it does perceive a certain transparency in experience, another layer beyond the immediate—that of hidden needs and desires coloring knowledge. But the perspective of faith

---

[81] Kristeva, *Tales of Love*, 397, n. 4; Jacques Blanpain, "Langage mystique, expression du desir," *Collectanea Cisterciensa* 36, no. 1 (1974): 45–68.

[82] Blanpain: "Il est frappant de constater que Bernard est très conscient du fait que notre conception de Dieu naît de nos désirs et de nos dispositions et aspirations" ("Langage," 56).

[83] Blanpain is aware of this reality and so brackets the ontological to serve his modern psychological method. Kristeva, however, drops the ontological altogether. Blanpain argues that in *On Loving God*, Bernard presents desire for God as experienced only negatively, as the vanity of lesser desires (49). Even so, it remains the case that the innate, right desire of the person exerts a positive and experienced, if unarticulated, pressure. That is, in loving lesser goods, a person is still trying at some level, without adverting to it, to love God.

does not exclude an awareness of the way unconscious motivations can affect images of God. The view that makes such motivations an ultimate and total source of imagination only creates a new form of opacity. Considered through its analogy with human love, Bernard's view is truer to life than the psychoanalytic perspective.

After an initial phase of infatuation in which lovers partially behold their own bright shadow in the other, the element of oneself in the other wanes, and one comes to appreciate more of the beloved's full and unique reality. Thus the lens of the self grows clearer. But Kristeva depicts the human hope for love as doomed from the outset. The Other in relation to whom one's very identity is formed, and to whom one seeks through life to relate by idealizing other people, is unattainable, a fiction. Further, she insists that the postmodern self finds difficulty in making even the initial transferences of the infatuated lover: "If we have difficulty loving, it is because we have difficulty idealizing—difficulty investing our narcissism in an other who is considered to have immeasurable value, thus guaranteeing our own potentiality for immoderation. And on the contrary, when we succeed in loving, is it not because someone, man or woman or child, or a word, or flower . . . was able to withstand our unflagging power of distrust, hatred and fear of delegating ourselves to an ideal otherness?"[84] For her it is not only love of God that is an illusory projection but human love as well. Psychoanalysis is superior to Christianity for Kristeva in both unmasking and celebrating the transferential dynamics of love. In discourse, in the interaction of analyst and analysand, in which the latter is allowed to speak freely of his or her impossible need for love, she considers that there is at least a certain delight in the freedom of speech, the language of love, to console the self in its plight.

---

[84] Kristeva, *Tales of Love*, 169.

## Body, Feelings, Images

In Bernard's view nature and faith both conflict and cooperate. So he writes that the Word of God with the power of the Spirit can "cook the raw reflections of the carnal man, giving them a spiritual meaning."[85] The "good of nature," he says, emerges from discipline like oil from pounded spices. Virtue is ordered affection. A certain "innate and ready affection" makes the "natural strength of good morals" easier and more attractive.[86] At the same time, faith transcends and can fly in the face of what appears to the senses: "Taste resides in the palate, but wisdom in the heart," and faith "discerns truths unknown to the senses, beyond the range of experience."[87]

Others have argued that Bernard divides affect from rationality in a way that heralds Descartes and the advent of modernity.[88] This view involves both a falsification of Bernard's understanding of *affectus*, reducing it to mere emotion, as Stiegman argues, and a failure to appreciate the degree to which for Bernard faith and wisdom include right reason.[89] Faith, he says, is a "power to understand" that allows "fuller comprehension."[90] The faith that allows the believer to gain distance from the affections, to steer and set them in order, includes reason and provides a shortcut to reaching God. As *On Loving God* demonstrates, the *infideles*, steering by reason, can arrive at the love of God.[91] They pass, with greater difficulty, the same

---

[85] Bernard, SC 22.2 (SBOp 1:130; CF 7:15).

[86] Bernard, SC 23.6–7 (SBOp 1:141–43; CF 7:30–31).

[87] Bernard, SC 85.8 (SBOp 2:312; CF 40:204). "Taste" can also be spiritual taste—*sapientia* from *sapor*, wisdom from taste *for goodness*; hence the need to purify the "palate of the heart" (Bernard, SC 28.8, 9 [SBOp 1:187–88; CF 7:94–96]).

[88] Louth, "Bernard and Affective Mysticism," 1–22.

[89] Stiegman, "Analytical Commentary," 126, esp. n. 322.

[90] Bernard, SC 28.9 (SBOp 1:198; CF 7:95–96).

[91] Bernard's concept of reason here is broader than rationality alone and involves the whole person, in particular virtue, which is directly connected to what humans can know.

threshold, which allows the world of experience to become transparent.

When Bernard argues that a sense of fear before a God "in angry guise"[92] is of greater benefit in the spiritual life than rational knowledge, he has in view, I would argue, that knowledge that is completely abstract, speculative, and prior to faith, a knowledge with no connection to a sense of the living God and more likely to puff up than motivate.[93] The problem with this sort of speculation is precisely that it lacks purchase in the affective life, the deeper springs of the person. By contrast, the *infideles* steered by right reason are involved in a process of ordering affections, growing toward God in a way that involves their whole being.[94]

The ambiguous nature of the body appears in sermons 24 and 25 of *On the Song of Songs*. The former speaks of the body as "made of earthly slime," and its upright stance as "exterior and of little account." Yet it reflects the soul. Its enduring beauty chastises the soul that has grown warped. Bernard portrays the body asking the soul, "Why should the Creator continue to behold the loss of his likeness in you, at the same time that he ceaselessly preserves yours in me?"[95] If Kristeva often stresses the dissimilarity of the spiritual and physical in Bernard, passages like this one suggest rather that the created world remains in a relationship of partial likeness to the spiritual. But even its unlikeness can, to the eyes of faith, point to the spiritual. In Sermon 25, Bernard speaks of the frailty of Paul's body, worn out by labors, as a manifestation of inward

---

[92] Bernard, SC 23.16 (SBOp 1:149; CF 7:40).

[93] Louth, "Bernard and Affective Mysticism," 5, uses the passage to argue that for Bernard emotion trumps rationality.

[94] Bernard, Dil 23–33 (SBOp 3:138–47; CF 13B:25–35). Interestingly, both God the Teacher and God the Judge clearly reflect the soul that encounters them. The one who is fearful sees in him a reverse image, a punishing God (the "guise"), and the one busy with studies sees a God "distracted with cares."

[95] Bernard, SC 24.5–6 (SBOp 1:156–59; CF 7:46–47).

beauty: "Hence this ugliness of Paul is more beautiful than jeweled ornaments, than the raiment of kings."[96] When here and elsewhere Bernard compares inward and outward beauty he does so not simply to disparage the visible exterior. Rather, he implies an aesthetic perspective made possible by the irony of faith. An initial tendency to judge by appearances, to be moved by visible beauty, yields with growth in faith and freedom to a distance from the immediate, an ability to see both moral and spiritual beauty imaged in, for instance, the beautiful form of the body, and implied by outward ugliness.

As Astell points out, Kristeva likens analyst and analysand to "literary artists, who fashion their lives as fictive, novelistic 'works in progress.'" Kristeva opposes Freud's rationalist decoding of religion and proposes psychoanalysis as a parallel but superior imaginative discourse wherein the human person, "consumed by his wishes, produces something similar to the gratification of these wishes." Commenting on the ambivalent character of this psychoanalytic appropriation of imaginative discourse, Astell writes, "In this narcissistic realm of art and imagination, psychoanalysis itself takes refuge, even as its amatory discourse affords its patients a last, admittedly meager, defense against nihilism in the willing suspension of disbelief."[97]

Creativity for Bernard involves a play of human freedom interwoven with its role in the spiritual life.[98] While Kristeva recognizes that Bernard appreciates the reality of something like the unconscious, his project is in fact not to master and colonize the unmeasured wasteland by "regulating will" and the imposition of reason, but to channel what one can of it and to live alongside the uncontrollable fruitfully and well.

---

[96] Bernard, SC 25:6 (SBOp 1:167; CF 7:54).
[97] Astell, "Telling Tales," 130.
[98] In the view of William Lynch, "faith is a form of imagining and experiencing the world" (*Images of Faith: An Exploration of the Ironic Imagination* [Notre Dame, IN: Notre Dame University Press, 1973], 5).

Bernard, as Stiegman notes, admired the fusion of matter and spirit in God's creation of the human person as the supreme model of creativity.[99] Human art seeks to re-create this union, to join symbol and reality, to mirror and give expression to human being, human freedom. Further, Bernard's literary art is in the service of cultivating right desire, allowing his readers to recall and rekindle the spark contained in the moments they have been touched by grace; he seeks to cultivate a taste (*sapor*) for freedom and for the savor of wisdom (*sapientia*). Bernard's literary art is a complement to, or dimension of, spiritual practice, and like spiritual practice it creates distance between the soul and the immediacy of its passions and experience. Rather than a realm of mere fantasy that allows "something like the gratification" of its impossible desires, art can shape right desire and provide an image of human freedom at play that can lead those who encounter it toward the truth of their own best selves.

Bernard's paradoxical expressions regarding the body, affectivity, and images may be designed in part to provoke a crisis and eventual realization in his readers. There is a tension at the root of monastic life, as Leclercq recognized so well, between the desire for God alone and the love of literature (that is, culture, what is best in the sensible order):[100] "There is no ideal synthesis which can be summed up in a speculative formula, as if the solution were of an intellectual order. The conflict cannot be resolved except by a victory which is on a spiritual level." Describing the simplicity of soul in which love for God and the pursuit of art are one, he writes:

---

[99] Emero Stiegman, "A Tradition of Aesthetics in Saint Bernard," in *Bernardus Magister*, ed. John R. Sommerfeldt, CS 135 (Kalamazoo, MI: Cistercian Publications, 1992), 133.

[100] Kristeva chooses to erase the creative tension by dropping God and keeping the auto-erotic *jouissance* of the word, the discourse between analyst and analysand.

> They [the monks] used to like to say that the word monk expresses the unity (*monas*) they realize within themselves. This simplicity of the soul whose sole desire is for God, is apparent in their style. They feel no real conflict between the pursuit of art and the search for God, between rhetoric and the transcendence which is the essence of their vocation, between grammar and the desire for paradise. Rhetoric has become part of them; and without becoming dual personalities, but remaining wholly and uniquely monks, they are able to use it to give expression to their sincerity.[101]

As with these two essentially positive desires, for literature and—on a higher level—for God, so Bernard explains that with uncontrollable unconscious drives and the excess of mystical gifts the soul learns to benefit from whatever happens:

> Indeed you must note the prudence, the great wisdom, the amount of discretion and sense of fittingness generated in the bride by that controlled interplay of lowliness and exaltation according as occasion demands, so that amid the ups and downs of this world her sublime gifts sustain her lowliness lest she succumb in adversity; while her lowliness curbs her exaltation or good fortune will bring it toppling down. These poles of her life act so harmoniously that though of their nature opposites they will work with equal effectiveness for the good of the bride. They subserve her spiritual welfare.[102]

## Conclusion

While they may lead the reader to ask fresh questions of Bernard's writings, often Kristeva's presuppositions concerning

---

[101] Jean Leclercq, *The Love of Learning and the Desire for God: A Study of Monastic Culture*, trans. Catherine Misrahi (New York: Fordham University Press, 1974), 222.

[102] Bernard, SC 27:14 (SBOp 1:191; CF 7:86).

Christian anthropology and the nature of mysticism fundamentally distort her interpretation. Rejecting the possibility of a real Other, Kristeva reads Bernard in a way that is necessarily inside out. She fails to account for the moral dimension of Bernard's perspective, including the important theme of human arrogance's claiming for itself what derives from God. For Bernard, religious and literary imagination interact as distinct and complementary spheres, where for Kristeva psychoanalysis and literature collapse into one another in murky fusion.

Bernard's phenomenological apologetics intuit that psychodynamics play a part in what human beings perceive of God. Why believe that there is an Other beyond experience and not just fantasy? For Bernard, recognition that human beings are not the origin of their own freedom, an intuition that they are fundamentally the gift of an Other, forms part of the response. Further, the unique depth of the experience of mystics and martyrs needs to be given full weight, as well as the degree of lasting change worked in the lives of believers, a change that, Bernard argues, can only derive from the experience of the unconditional love of God. Those who take the risk of trust broaden the field of their perception. The fearful slave sees only himself, where the trusting son may still encounter God. This contact is still by means of an image, "father," but one that has become transparent to reality, and one that the believer is aware of *as* an image. Faith, above all, reveals this transparency of the sensible: body, affectivity, and images. The love of self that is a provisional necessity in a damaged world can circle back on itself, arrogate to itself what it knows to be from God, or open onto love for God. Love of self is already in fact a way, however indirect, of loving him, of obeying the "law of love" that guides the universe. The freedom born of faith allows mature Christians, grounded in the love of God, to grow by means of whatever comes to them. Situated between flesh and spirit, the soul works with grace to set love in order, to remain faithful to and cultivate its deepest desire, so that, consoled by gifts, humbled by adversity, it may "ride above the vicissitudes of good and evil times with the poise of one sustained by values that are eternal, with that enduring unshakeable equanimity of the man of faith who thanks God in every circumstance."[103]

---

[103] Bernard, SC 21.6 (SBOp 1:125; CF 7:8).

# 8. "Love Itself Is Knowledge": Jean-Luc Marion and Bernard of Clairvaux

Where Kristeva sees only vain fantasy in Bernard's account of love, the French philosopher Jean-Luc Marion finds resources for developing a powerful contemporary phenomenology of love. There is a certain kind or quality of knowledge available only to those in love (in an expression of Gregory the Great's that the Cistercians made their own): "Love itself is knowledge" (*Amor ipse notitia est*).[1] Marion develops this insight to express his understanding of the interaction between philosophy and theology. More exactly, he carves a space for what he calls "Christian Philosophy" as mediator between the two, holding that the revelation of love brings to visibility phenomena otherwise invisible, principally, knowledge of the other in his or her irreducible uniqueness.[2] Indeed, Marion calls philosophy back to its practical origins as a way to goodness, a "love of wisdom" that Bernard would have recognized.[3] In an article on Bernard he identifies Bernard's contribution to philosophy as his original understanding of a free choice

---

[1] Gregory the Great, *Forty Gospel Homilies*, trans. David Hurst, CF 123 (Kalamazoo, MI: Cistercian Publications, 1990), 215.

[2] Jean-Luc Marion, "Christian Philosophy and Charity," *Communio* 19 (Fall 1992): 465–73.

[3] Jean-Luc Marion, *The Visible and the Revealed*, trans. Christina M. Geshwandtner et al. (New York: Fordham University Press, 2008), 79.

oriented to love as the chief manner in which human beings are made in the image of God.[4]

In his early work *The Idol and Distance* Marion cites Bernard's view of "carnal" versus spiritual knowledge of Christ to explain his own sense of the iconic and the idolatrous.[5] Both thinkers begin from the crisis of vanity, the threat of existential futility, and view the possibility of loving and being loved as the only source of hope. While Bernard writes on the cusp of the development of systematic metaphysics in the West and Marion in its aftermath, both are wary of what they view as the objectivizing tendency of rationalist thought and prefer an approach from experience. In both his recovery of Christian philosophy and his account of love as the way to know another as other, Marion demonstrates the powerful resources Bernard's writings hold for twenty-first-century thought.

## Marion on "Christian Philosophy"

More than once Marion revisits the early twentieth-century debate concerning "Christian Philosophy." He notes the frequent objection that there cannot be a Christian philosophy any more than a Christian mathematics, and he explains the surprising range and paradoxical reasons for which different thinkers oppose it.[6] He resuscitates Gilson's formula: "Thus I

---

[4] Jean-Luc Marion, "L'image de la liberté," in *Saint Bernard et la Philosophie*, ed. Remi Brague (Paris: Presses Universitaires de France, 1993), 49–72.

[5] Jean-Luc Marion, *The Idol and Distance: Five Studies*, trans. Thomas A. Carlson, Perspectives in Continental Philosophy, No. 17 (New York: Fordham University Press, 2001).

[6] Marion cites one of these paradoxes: "while dialectical theology can only oppose all manner of 'Christian philosophy' in the name of its Pauline heritage, it is this very heritage that supports this tradition of monastic life as being a *philosophia christiana*" (Jean-Luc Marion, "Christian Philosophy and Charity," *Communio* 19 [Fall 1992]: 466–67). Bernard was of course very much a part of this tradition. For a further sketch of the debate see Marion, *The Visible*, 66–69. For more on the tradition of Christian philosophy as a way to union with God, see Marion, *The Visible*, 79.

denominate Christian philosophy *all philosophy which, while distinguishing formally the two orders, considers Christian revelation as an indispensable auxiliary of reason.*" As Marion comments, "Therefore, revelation can never be a substitute for reason. But rather, it suggests to reason how it might rationally approach the themes that reason of its own cannot know."[7]

Marion identifies the risk of Christian philosophy's restricting itself to a Christian interpretation of phenomena otherwise accessible, one option among others, ultimately arbitrary. He proposes taking Gilson's principle in a heuristic rather than an (exclusively) hermeneutic sense.[8] Christ, he says, reveals phenomena that are "absolutely other and new" that make possible the interpretation of commonly held phenomena in a completely new way:[9]

> We propose the following hypothesis: independently of the proper domain of revelation the Christian outlook exercises a radically new hermeneutics vis-à-vis the world only insofar as it sees or facilitates therein the appearance of phenomena that are themselves radically new. The Christian outlook facilitates the resurgence and appearance in the world of phenomena that have up until then remained invisible, on the basis of which a new interpretation of already visible phenomena becomes thenceforth legitimate. What is this new given and this new interpretation? The answer is charity, which gives itself and *only allows itself to be seen by those who love it*.[10]

Christian philosophy, says Marion, beginning from the revelation of God in Christ, looks upon the world through the lens of charity. Through this lens not only acts of love but failures to love, sin as such, become visible, likewise the value of the

---

[7] Marion, "Christian Philosophy," 467, quoting Gilson.
[8] Marion, *The Visible*, 66–79.
[9] Marion, "Christian Philosophy," 468.
[10] Marion, "Christian Philosophy," 469; my emphasis.

weak and destitute, those whom the world overlooks.[11] Only the practice of charity brings this field of knowledge into view, a significant link to the monastic idea of *philosophia christiana*. The love that Christ reveals, in addition to knowledge of mysteries like the Trinity, opens a new perspective on the realities of this world, including the reality of the world as creation, a gift bearing the trace of the One whose goodness diffuses itself.

While this emphasis on a unique quality of knowledge available only to those who love is highly sympathetic to the approach of Bernard, at the same time Marion and his version of Christian philosophy look through the lens of love toward the world and the human person, whereas Bernard appears to direct his gaze more towards God. However, in both cases the humanity of Christ is pivotal. Bernard also emphasizes the need to "set love in order," and the way that loving God "without measure" makes possible a justly measured and, in Marion's language, "iconic" view of creation. Knowing by "union" rather than objectification characterizes the mystical teaching of Bernard; Marion applies this same vocabulary to the knowing of human others. Indeed, he argues that love alone is the only way to know the other in his otherness. As he writes, "To see a person as such, with an individuality that is so irreducible that only love can overtake it—this cannot be done by an outlook that is without charity. The person: behold the new phenomenon which only the outlook of charity can discover."[12] Only love makes it possible to see beyond the idolatrous projections of oneself to reach the other in his or her

---

[11] Marion, "Christian Philosophy," 469. He goes on to say, "Only the outlook of charity, moreover, sees in the poor man the image of God, and can thus render him his humanity and therefore aid him concretely. Whereas, when confronted with the same man, the outlook denuded of love sees nothing more than a small heap of soiled clothes rolled up into a ball on the sidewalk, a thing to be passed by" (472).

[12] Marion, "Christian Philosophy," 471.

mystery. This power of love to reach the other beyond projection characterizes Bernard's presentation of the development of human love for God. Human beings are in the image and likeness of God, who is love.[13] For both Bernard and Marion, in giving himself to a person, the God of love gives that person to himself or herself as lover. Self-knowledge involves an awareness of being loved through and being loved into being a lover.

## Bernard and Philosophy

Bernard is generally thought of as the opponent of Abelard and the tendency toward systemization he represents. Certainly there are rhetorically charged passages in Bernard that could suggest an anti-intellectual tendency. Yet Bernard's own formation was early scholastic, and the two treatises he wrote in a more philosophical line (*On Loving God, On Grace and Free Choice*) show polish and rigor. His starting point is experiential. Emero Stiegman writes aptly of Bernard, "What he and the monastic tradition resisted in philosophers was the conviction that eternal truth could be arrived at apart from an integral experience and purity of heart."[14]

For Bernard, what matters is salvation. Knowledge of self and knowledge of God are essential to this salvation and relativize the value of merely speculative knowledge. The monastery is a *schola*, but a *schola caritatis*. In view of the urgent need for salvation, the engagement of personal affect more powerfully involves the person than a scientific knowledge of theological truths. The need for salvation is bound up experientially with the need to be loved.

---

[13] Marion, "Christian Philosophy," 470.

[14] Bernard of Clairvaux, *On Loving God: With an Analytical Commentary by Emero Stiegman*, CF 13B (Kalamazoo, MI: Cistercian Publications, 1995), 57.

*"Love Itself Is Knowledge": Jean-Luc Marion and Bernard of Clairvaux* 161

Bernard, like Marion, sees the spiritual life beginning with the threat of vanity.[15] In Marion's terms, the question "What's the point?" saps merely intellectual knowledge of its power to satisfy.[16] Commenting on Bernard's version of philosophy, Stiegman writes, "He considers possibilities in relation to nature as *experienced*. To work deductively from a definition of nature, however theologically sound, would beg the only question that mattered in the spiritual life. What is possible, in his view, is what an observed conscience and pattern of behavior, interpreted in the faith, reveals. In this sense his approach is phenomenological."[17] He suggests that Bernard chose "self" and "God" over nature/grace or other theological constructs as the main terms of his treatise *On Loving God* because of their immediacy to consciousness and accessibility beyond the sphere of Christian faith. Implying a sense of God as that than which nothing greater can be desired, Stiegman writes, "If the phenomenon of thought itself suggests to Anselm a concept of God, to Bernard it was the experience of desire that led to such a conceptualization." Noting that Bernard's experiential focus can lead one to overlook the role of reason in his work, Stiegman speaks of "Bernard's orientation to the concrete problems of his existence and to his demand that reason forever justify itself against intimate personal experience, a larger human knowing. In view of this difference from what Bernard considered a rationalist mentality, we may fail to appreciate the strong role of reason in his spirituality."[18]

---

[15] One might read an indication of this in the fact that Bernard alters the traditional (from Origen) order of progression in the spiritual life from Proverbs through Ecclesiastes to the Song of Songs, placing Ecclesiastes first (see SC 1).

[16] Jean-Luc Marion, *The Erotic Phenomenon*, trans. Stephen Lewis (Chicago: The University of Chicago Press, 2007), 16–19.

[17] Stiegman, "Analytical Commentary," 52; a few pages later (56) he acknowledges that it can be anachronistic to speak of Bernard in terms of modern disciplines like phenomenology.

[18] Stiegman, "Analytical Commentary," 56.

Noting the ubiquity in the classical/medieval world of the principle that "one knew as one was," Stiegman comments, "In the Platonism of the Fathers, *intelligentia* was not principally in the domain of abstraction; it was equated with the spiritual. Knowledge of spiritual being had to engage the entire person. Truth was an 'assimilation': one knew as one was, similar to similar . . . when he [a person of that time] says that it is in virtue of the soul's likeness to God that it was *capax dei*, he did not have to demonstrate that; it was a philosophical commonplace. So the very concept of intelligence approached that of love."[19] Arguing for the centrality of knowledge in Bernard, Stiegman helpfully distinguishes fallen reason from full understanding and notes the "temptation . . . to stop in reason, a knowing which is imprisoned within the self." He continues, "What true knowledge attains beyond the self does not come from an *ob-iectum* outside the self; it is from a light proper to the heart. It brings about a union, a *commixio superni luminis et illuminatae mentis*."[20] Marion similarly counterposes objectifying rationality and an erotic reason, that "light proper to the heart" that is the freedom to love, the presence of an Other "nearer to me than I am to myself."

For Bernard *amor ipse notitia est* is more than a metaphor, a mere stand-in for the true (beatific) vision when God will be known in full. Bernard is not simply presenting affective states in cognitive language.[21] Pacifique Delfgaauw, for one, argues compellingly that love is not only the condition of knowledge but its principle and accomplishment:[22] "An ethical life, in other words a concrete life, a life which rules our behaviour not

---

[19] Emero Stiegman, "A Tradition of Aesthetics in Saint Bernard," in *Bernardus Magister: Papers Celebrating the Nonacentenary of the Birth of Bernard of Clairvaux*, ed. John R. Sommerfeldt, CS 135 (Kalamazoo, MI: Cistercian Publications, 1992), 140.

[20] Stiegman, "A Tradition," 143.

[21] As Gilson suggests; see Pacifique Delfgaauw, "La Lumière de la Charité chez Saint Bernard," Coll 18 (1956): 306.

[22] Delfgaauw, "La Lumière," 307.

merely through abstract ideas, but which implies the illumination of a 'real' knowledge, involving the person as a whole. This involvement is realised by our consent, by our adhesion to truth in love, by our *'affectus.'* Love therefore does not merely direct, but also fulfils our knowledge, and integrates it into our life."[23]

The knowledge born of love involves the whole person. Consent is identified here with adherence to the truth in love, *affectus*. Where carnal love encloses people in themselves, spiritual love, love at the level of a union of *wills*, which is possible to a unique degree between God and human beings, opens the way to the highest contemplation.[24]

*On Loving God* deals almost exclusively with human love for God, while Marion's *Erotic Phenomenon* concerns mainly human love for human beings. Bernard does sometimes write of human love, as in this passage from the *Steps of Humility and Love*, where he notes that while the love of a friend may blind one to his faults, love leads to knowledge of other human beings: "The merciful quickly grasp the truth in their neighbors when their heart goes out to them with a love that unites them so closely that they feel the neighbor's good and ill as if it were their own. . . . Their hearts are made more clear-sighted by love. . . . For just as pure truth is seen only by the pure of heart, so also a brother's miseries are truly experienced only by one who has misery in his own heart."[25]

---

[23] "Vie morale, donc concrète, vie qui régit notre comportement non par les seules idées abstraits, mais qui implique la lumière d'une connaissance 'réelle,' engageant toute la personne. Cet engagement se réalise dans notre consentement, notre adhésion à la verité dans l'amour, 'l'*affectus*.' C'est donc l'amour qui non seulement dirige, mais achève notre connaissance et l'insere dans notre vie" (Delfgaauw, "La Lumière," 42).

[24] Delfgaauw, "La Lumière," 69.

[25] Bernard of Clairvaux, "The Steps of Humility and Pride," in *Treatises II*, trans. M. Ambrose Conway, CF 13 (Kalamazoo, MI: Cistercian Publications, 1973), 35.

Bernard's writings aim to educate and kindle desire for God. Marion accents the *"love* of wisdom" in philo-sophia's very name; one must first desire to know before knowing. In his view, certain realities of life fall within a "greater," an "erotic rationality," namely "that which does not limit itself to the world of things nor to the production of objects, but which instead rules our hearts, our individuality, our life and our death, in short, that which defines us deep down in all that concerns us in the final instance."[26] Marion shares with the perspective of *On Loving God* an awareness that "we are, insofar as we come to know ourselves, always already caught within the tonality of an erotic disposition." His articulation of this tonality in terms of "the flesh" is similar to Bernard's understanding of *affectus*. Their projects are distinct insofar as Marion concentrates on outlining a "concept of love" with philosophical rigor. He attempts to rewrite Descartes' *Meditationes* in the key of love, according to the "greater rationality" of love.

Nonetheless there are a number of points where *The Erotic Phenomenon* echoes Bernard's language. Frequently the text speaks of love "without measure."[27] *On Loving God* opens with the statement that God is to be loved for his own sake and "without measure."[28] Both authors speak of the gratuitousness of genuine love, outside all calculation and "economy." One of the most characteristic marks of Bernard's treatise is its treatment of self-love. From an instinctive love of oneself for one's own sake, one arrives, at the summit of the self's development, at a stage where one loves oneself only for God's sake. Marion's analysis of human love culminates in an "inversion of the love of myself into the love even of myself."[29] This love of even

---

[26] Marion, *Erotic Phenomenon*, 4, 5.
[27] E.g., Marion, *Erotic Phenomenon*, 10; according to this view human beings too are to be loved "without measure."
[28] Bernard, Dil 1: *modus, sine modo diligere* (SBOp 3:119; CF 13B:3).
[29] Marion, *Erotic Phenomenon*, 213.

oneself becomes possible through the other's assurance, not that she loves me but that I truly love her, that I am a lover. Bernard has a similar process in view. As he writes of God, "When he gave me himself, he gave me back myself."[30] Self-love maturing into an instinct for self-realization paradoxically reaches fulfillment in gratuitously giving oneself away. One delights and realizes oneself in giving without expecting in return. For both authors the account of love's development involves collapsing a too-rigid distinction between *eros* and *agape*.

### "What Love Knows"

Acknowledging a distinction between charity as theological virtue and love as "the passion of man *in via*," Marion argues that philosophy has imposed its own division, namely that between love as a basically selfish and solipsistic, irrational passion and the intellectual love of the moral law.[31] Considered as passion, he says, "[Love] closes rather than opens access to anyone else." Descartes radicalizes this view of passionate love in such a way that all loves come to be viewed with the same structure: more selfish attractions (e.g., the addict's, the rapist's) appear on a sliding scale with the less selfish (love for God, spouse), "because they all reduce to the same act of will, by which the ego unifies itself with its object, whatever it may be."[32] In this view one cannot love what differs from oneself. As Marion writes, "In the best of all cases, the other (wife, child, prince, or God) merely provides the occasion for a union of will that is irrational (by virtue of passion) and solipsistic (by virtue of the primacy of subjectivity). Love is defined by

---

[30] Bernard, Dil 15 (SBOp 3:132; CF 13B:18).
[31] An understanding that Kristeva, for one, seems to read into Bernard.
[32] Jean-Luc Marion, *Prolegomena to Charity*, trans. Stephen E. Lewis (New York: Fordham University Press, 2002), 156–57.

its ignorance of the other."[33] Contemporary eroticism is characterized by such a solipsism. It fixates on the physical body, apart from its actualization as "flesh": flesh that "can affect itself with (feel) another than itself."[34]

For Marion, the impasse, the impossibility of reaching the other, is reproduced on another level in the concept of intellectual love. Love of rational objects prioritizes mind over will in such a way that it excludes love. Further, love of an abstract ideal, a universal (justice, truth), cannot provide knowledge of a uniquely personal other. Marion views the division of *eros* from *agape* as similar in kind to that marked out by philosophy and holds that "every border traced upon the heart of love, rather than being of service, wounds it definitively." He proposes instead to "think of love itself as a knowledge."

Human beings experience first of all their own affect, Marion says. He explains that for Husserl one can reason from the analogy of one's own experience to infer the reality of the other's "flesh" or affect. However, he points out that this view presumes that the will so envisions the flesh of the other as a real and unique person with his own distinct and unique world of experience. One all too easily and often neglects such a move. In fact, goodwill not only enables one to empathize; it makes the other appear as he is: "The phenomenality of the other does not precede my (good) will with regard to him, but instead is its result . . . in order for the other to appear to me, I must first love him." Beyond this point, for Marion, phenomenology must yield to "a thinking of charity."

Bernard's *On Loving God* speaks of the self as comprising the dignity of free will, the virtue by which one seeks and adheres to one's Creator and the knowledge by which one acknowledges that one's freedom is a gift. The first thing people know is that they are free, and that this is a gift. This understanding is very much akin to Marion's concern for the

---

[33] Marion, *Prologomena*, 157.
[34] Marion, *Prologomena*, 159.

"primacy of love over being."[35] Where the intellect, prone to arrogance, objectifies the gift of its own being, making it into an idol, Marion writes, "I am not, except insofar as I experience love, and experience it as a logic."[36] Further, he concurs that, "for man, his very nature issues from a gift, and testifies to that gift by its very constitution."[37] In writing on Bernard, he singles out the theme of free will's characterizing human being in the image and likeness of God. Free choice is intimately connected to the theme of love's knowledge, since, as Marion writes, "the formal univocality of free will constitutes the unique condition necessary in order to acknowledge charity to be the common denominator of all creatures, among each other as well as with their Creator, for the least act of charity presupposes a free decision of the will."[38]

### *L'image de la liberté*: Marion on Bernard

*Sponte afficit, spontaneum fecit*: of love, Bernard writes that it "moves us freely and makes us free."[39] Indeed only love, as grace, can move human freedom without impinging on or coercing it, can move it according to its own nature, expanding its scope. Freedom, then, falls within the range of those realities to which Christian philosophy as described by Marion can contribute a unique understanding. Only the experience of

---

[35] Marion, *Erotic Phenomenon*, 4.

[36] Marion, *Erotic Phenomenon*, 8.

[37] Jean-Luc Marion, *Questions cartésiennes I: Méthode et métaphysique*, cited in Stephen E. Lewis, "The Lover's Capacity in Jean-Luc Marion's *The Erotic Phenomenon*," *Quæstiones Disputatae* 1, no. 1 (Fall 2010): 236.

[38] "l'univocité formelle de la volonté libre constitue l'unique condition pour reconnaître la charité comme le commun dénominateur de toutes les creatures, tant être elles qu'avec leur Créateur; car le moindre acte de charité suppose une décision libre de la volonté" (Jean-Luc Marion, "L'image de la liberté," in *Saint Bernard et la Philosophie*, ed. Remi Brague [Paris: Presses Universitaires de France, 1993], 57).

[39] Dil 17 (SBOp 3:134; see CF 13B:20).

revealed love opens the perspective onto the nature of human freedom explored by Bernard. In his article *"L'image de la liberté,"* Marion tracks the legacy of Bernard's identification of the *imago dei* with freedom. By variously distorting Bernard's view of freedom, he says, modern philosophers such as Descartes and Kant end up reversing its basic outlook in such a way that human freedom essentially rivals that of God. Instead of being the archetype, God thus becomes no more than a mimetic double. Marion opposes Bernard's theological insight to its metaphysical appropriation in a way that would confirm Bernard's most pessimistic rhetoric about the tendency of speculative thought to objectify the world reductively and arrogate to itself what belongs to God alone.[40]

Marion sets out to study the reception of Bernard's idea that the *imago dei* resides principally in free choice and suggests that it holds possibilities for contemporary appropriation, the outlines of which are suggested in his interpretation of Bernard's treatise. The article has six sections that explore earlier—especially Augustinian—understandings of the *imago dei*, Bernard on free choice, Bernard and image/likeness, and the theological reception of Bernard's idea. The last two sections focus on Bernard's modern/metaphysical legacy in Descartes, then in Kant and Heidegger. Marion sees Bernard as advancing the tradition in two ways: by accenting freedom as the locus of the *imago dei* rather than representative intellect, and by "redoubling" the *imago* (understood as free choice) in *similitudo* (freedom from sin and from misery). Free choice, he argues, is the condition for charity. But the metaphysical appropriation of Bernard's idea loses the connection between love and freedom in such a way that human autonomy is necessarily set in opposition to God. The placement of the *imago*

---

[40] Recently the French philosopher Emmanuel Falque has written on Bernard's view of freedom, taking account of Marion's work: Emmanuel Falque, *Le Livre de L'Expérience: D'Anselme de Cantorbéry à Bernard de Clairvaux* (Paris: Les Éditions du Cerf, 2017), 377–437.

*dei* in radically indeterminate free choice rather than in the static fixity of substance and an objectifying intellect appeals to Marion, for whom love comes before being and ethics precedes ontology.[41]

An especially valuable feature of Marion's analysis is the attention he gives to the place of the self in Bernard's discussion of freedom. He underlines the fact that for Bernard, the self becomes a self by willing. One is always willing in a sense, in Bernard's view: advancing or falling away. Free choice (the image), by which one is given to oneself, demands realization outward, beyond one's current state, and so necessitates likeness, which admits of degree. The self as characterized by freedom is thus invariantly variable, always in motion, becoming other than itself. As Bernard describes this dynamic,

> Created, then, to a certain extent, as our own in freedom of will, we become God's as it were by good will. Moreover he makes the will good, who made it free; and makes it good to this end, that we may be a kind of first fruits of his creatures, because it would have been better for us never to have existed than that we should remain always our own. For those who wished to belong to themselves became indeed like gods, knowing good and evil, but then they were not merely their own, but the devil's. Hence free will makes us our own; bad will, the devil's; and good will, God's.[42]

Marion's exegesis helpfully emphasizes the paradoxical position of the self that must realize the freedom that makes it what

---

[41] Marion has written on Blondel's modern appropriation of the Cistercian idea of love as infinite will (summed up in the expression *Amor siquidem vehemens est voluntas*) as an alternative to the "will to power"; see Jean-Luc Marion, "La Conversion de la Volonté selon L'Action," *Revue Philosophique* no. 1 (1987): 46. Jean Leclercq studied Blondel's reception of Bernard in Jean Leclercq, *Maurice Blondel: Lecteur de Bernard de Clairvaux* (Brussels: Éditions Lessius, 2001).

[42] Gra 18 (SBOp 3:179; CF 19:73–74).

it is by constantly becoming other than it is. The self must move outward towards realization; free choice (*imago*) demands expansion into act, expression as more or less like God. The will cannot remain its own. In a closely interwoven parallel, in *On Loving God* love moves from love of self outward to love of God and resists the law of its own being by turning inward.

Marion's account of the way Descartes twists the tradition of considering the *imago dei* in terms of freedom is helpfully explicated by Stephen E. Lewis: "Descartes, Marion shows, stripped the will of what until then had been its primary dignity—its office of loving God, and thereby knowing God through participation in his incomprehensible infinity—in order to establish an analogical relation between Divine and human freedom, a relation that Descartes secures as part of his quest to lay a foundation or ground for the ego."[43] At issue is the objectification of what is loved. Marion holds that love is not analogous but univocal: God loves in the same way human beings do, but infinitely better. For Bernard, freedom is morally indifferent, open equally to good and evil, not impinged upon in any way by necessity, but love best expresses freedom qua freedom. In *On Loving God* the self-knowledge constitutive of one's being human is principally knowledge of the fact that one is free, and that this freedom is not self-derived but a gift. Throughout the treatise the root temptation is to arrogate to oneself what is a free gift of God, a tendency associated in Bernard's mind with the objectifying tendencies of a speculative thought dangerously cut off from the work of reformation in the school of love.

## The Erotic Phenomenon

Marion's *The Erotic Phenomenon* presents a phenomenology of human love in the form of a rewriting of Descartes' *Meditationes* from within the mind of love. What follows is far from

---

[43] Lewis, "The Lover's Capacity," 226–27.

an adequate survey of the book but simply teases out a few points of contact between certain features of Bernard's account of love and that provided in *The Erotic Phenomenon*. Perhaps the most central of these similarities concerns the encounter with God not as an "object," as in Descartes, but as a reality experienced in and through the human being's own act of love. As Robyn Horner writes, quoting Marion, "'The one who loves does not see God as an object, but recognizes God as the dominant logic of his or her own act of love. . . . In short, God is recognized as and in the very act by which God makes me love.' We find that love is an item of knowledge [*un savoir*] only in the recognition of or acquaintance with [*la connaissance de*] love in the act of loving. In this instance the 'what' and the 'how' of love as knowledge are collapsed."[44] In Bernard, similarly, God is known in and through the realization of one's likeness to the God of love through freely loving, that is, by participation. The discovery of God in one's free act of love recalls the discussion of the *imago dei* as freedom for love. God is known in the act by which he is loved: "Not only is the Bridegroom believed to be on the way, but to be speeding, coming in one's desire. His desire gives rise to yours."[45]

Marion's presentation of the experience of human love begins under the shadow of vanity. The specter of an existential "So what?" relativizes every human project, practical or theoretical, undertaken at the level of a Cartesian manipulation of "objects," and provokes the question, "Am I loved?" For Bernard, similarly, the quest for love originates in and requires a conviction about the futility of "worldly" loves. The would-be lover in this early phase is fearfully preoccupied with being loved in return, in advance even of taking the risk of love, and is thus locked within what Marion describes as "reciprocity."

---

[44] Robyn Horner, "The Weight of Love," in *Counter-Experiences: Reading Jean-Luc Marion*, ed. Kevin Hart (Notre Dame, IN: Notre Dame Press, 2007), 238.
[45] Bernard, SC 57:6 (SBOp 2:123; CF 31:101).

Love, however, can be known only through loving, without guarantee of return. Thus the next step is a radical determination to love first, without certainty of gaining anything. Further along, love culminates in fidelity and the voluntary (spiritual) bond of the "oath." Lovers discover that they can only take the step of loving "first" because at some level they are already loved. In basic outlines this explanation recalls one of Bernard's schemas, presented in Sermon 50 *On the Song of Songs*, in which the lover moves from a self-absorbed affect through a zeal for virtue that yet lacks sweetness to a truly spiritual *affectus* in which loving actions are not forced but easily and willingly performed.

A preoccupation of modern thought has been the problem of how to know others in their uniqueness and mystery without reducing them to the measure of one's own horizon. Marion argues that only love knows another in this way; love knows by affinity and participation, engaging freedom not to master objects but to risk fidelity. For him, only the decision to love allows the other to appear, to be known. The experience of freedom, of oneself as *imago dei*, in Bernard's language, permits recognition of and respect for the other as likewise free. Freedom involves a radical indeterminacy. Knowing the other by affinity at the level of *freedom* means knowing the other as likewise self-determining. As Horner writes, citing Marion,

> Access to the other person is only possible subsequent to my decision to love him or her. Love is a matter of the will first of all. "[T]he phenomenality of the other does not precede my (good) will with regard to him, but instead is its result"; "in order for the other to appear to me, I must first love him." . . . Love is not only a way of seeing, but a will to see in a particular way. Nevertheless, love is not thereby irrational, but allows us "to accede to a knowledge that surpasses our ordinary knowledge."[46]

---

[46] Horner, "The Weight of Love," 239.

For Bernard too the quality of desire affects the nature of the other's appearance. In Sermon 32 *On the Song of Songs*, he says, "He will not reveal himself in this way to every person, even momentarily, but only to the one who is proved to be a worthy bride by intense devotion, vehement desire, and the sweetest affection."[47] In Sermon 1 he writes, "It is vain for anyone who does not love to listen to this song of love, for a cold heart cannot catch fire from its eloquence."[48] In the images of *On Loving God*, the slave driven by fear and the merchant locked in self-interest become laws unto themselves, project their own distorted desire onto God, and block, or at least distort, his appearing. Will and imagination are closely allied. God by contrast lives by the law of charity, and those who adhere to him with love set in order accordingly live in freedom. Marion's language in describing the ego in the early stages of its groping towards love recalls Bernard's account of fear (the slave) and cupidity (the merchant) imagining the Other (God) in their image: "The ego addresses love like a poor man who, with fear in his gut because he is penniless, never imagines he could be dealing with anyone but usurers, each more pitiless and rapacious than the one before him. . . . The ego is quite willing to pay to obtain assurance, but not if someone takes from it more than it will receive. The ego, from the outset, expects from love only a more or less honest exchange, a negotiated *reciprocity*, an acceptable compromise."[49] The same mentality of fearfulness and objectification leads the self to arrogate to itself what are gifts of God. In the terms of *On Loving God* the basic gifts that compose the self are dignity (freedom), knowledge (principally knowledge of this freedom and the fact that it is not self-generated), and virtue (desire).

Marion distinguishes between the ego's attempt to "certify" itself as an object and the assurance that can only come from

---

[47] SC 32.3 (SBOp 1:227; CF 7:135).
[48] SC 79.1 (SBOp 2:272; CF 40:138).
[49] Marion, *Erotic Phenomenon*, 68–69.

another's love: "Certifying my existence myself depends upon my thought, and thus upon me. Receiving assurance against the vanity of my certain existence does not depend upon me but requires that I learn from elsewhere that I am and above all if I have to be. Holding out when faced with vanity, which is to say obtaining the justification to be from elsewhere, which means that I am, not by being (even through myself, even as a privileged being), but insofar as I am loved (and thus chosen from elsewhere)."[50]

## Reciprocity

Both Bernard and Marion describe genuine love as free from self-interest, not a cold deliberate adherence to law devoid of delight, but precisely erotic love. Both thinkers hold true *eros* to be *agapic* and vice versa. As Marion writes, "One must have a good deal of naiveté or blindness, or rather know nothing of the lover and of erotic logic, not to see that *agape* possesses and consumes as much as *eros* gives up and abandons. It is not a matter of two loves, but of two names selected from an infinity of others in order to think and to say the one love."[51] Marion inclines to state things in a provocative, iconoclastic fashion. Thus his view of love as devoid of all reciprocity has been criticized as too extreme.[52] Bernard uses the concept of love at times to cover a wider field. While speaking of love proper he says, in effect, that pure love lacks self-interest; in *On Loving God* he at the same time speaks of instinctual self-interest as

---

[50] Marion, *Erotic Phenomenon*, 23.

[51] Marion, *Erotic Phenomenon*, 221. Falque argues that collapsing *eros* and *agape* in this way risks losing the unique dimensions of *agapic* love and preventing *eros* from being fully assumed and transformed: *Le Livre de L'Expérience*, 350.

[52] See for example Kyle Hubbard, "The Unity of Eros and Agape: On Jean-Luc Marion's Erotic Phenomenon," *Essays in Philosophy* 12, no. 1 (2011): 130–46.

self-*love* and holds that divine love works even in and through this rudimentary selfish affect, unfolding outward. Pure love for Bernard elevates and purifies rather than eradicating the self-interest and fear of the merchant and slave. These do not corrupt love, but love raises them toward itself. He speaks of love as admitting of "degrees." His vocabulary is thus more tolerant than Marion's but perhaps lacks Marion's conceptual precision, whose language allows the idea of love to stand out in sharper relief.

In the second moment of Marion's erotic reduction the lover begins to love without the advance promise of being loved in return. Love becomes a free act, a decision of the will, beyond the instinctive self-protective cringing in which it began. It is a choice to love "first," without a guarantee that one's risk will be rewarded. "Reciprocity" as Marion is using the concept here does not preclude mutuality. Erotic love for him involves an exchange in which each gives the other his or her own flesh, gives what neither has. That will is engaged in taking the risk of loving without return is essential. The will does not seek to manipulate objects as in the Cartesian view, since love is without an object: "Thus it is necessary to reject reciprocity in love, not because it would seem improper, but because in love reciprocity becomes impossible—strictly speaking, without an object. Reciprocity sets the condition of possibility for exchange, but it also attests to the condition of love's impossibility."[53]

Marion's sense of genuine erotic love as providing for the lover, in the act of loving, the assurance it once sought fearfully, his notion of love as sufficient to itself, without "reasons," gels with Bernard's vision: "Love is sufficient for itself; it gives pleasure to itself, and for its own sake. It is its own merit and own reward. Love needs no cause beyond itself, nor does it demand fruits; it is its own purpose. I love because I love; I love that I may love."[54] These qualities make love the perfect

---

[53] Marion, *Erotic Phenomenon*, 70.
[54] Bernard, SC 83.4 (SBOp 2:300–301; CF 40:184).

expression of freedom, in which consists the human likeness to God. Bernard continues: "Love is the only one of the motions of the soul, of its senses and affections, in which the creature can respond to its Creator, even if not as an equal, and repay his favor in some similar way."[55] The language of repayment here should not mislead. Far from indicating an extension of reciprocity into the relationship with God, Bernard is carving out the space of the truly gratuitous and using economic language, as in "repaying," to subvert reciprocity. God reveals himself in free gratuitous love and elicits a response in kind, a free and gratuitous, grateful love. Love, he says, "moves us freely, and it makes us free."[56] Only the experience of such love can prompt one to grow spiritually beyond the bounds of fear and selfishness, can motivate one to change freely, from within. Only such free love can activate human freedom. Gratuity in free response to gratuity is a kind of exchange that undermines the self-interested exchange of economy that is its caricature. Love expressed as freedom is univocal, the one arena in which human beings can respond to God in a similar way.

For God, and for human beings, ultimately "self-realization" is achieved precisely in selfless giving. God's delight is to give himself away without reserve or condition, to love first without the assurance of return, as Bernard elegantly describes: "When God loves, he desires nothing but to be loved, since he loves us for no other reason than to be loved, for he knows that those who love him are blessed in their very love."[57] That is, God desires to be loved because free human beings find true delight only in such love. From the human side, loving God "for his own sake," without reciprocity, becomes the only way to happiness and fulfillment.

---

[55] Bernard, SC 83.4 (SBOp 2:300–301; CF 40:184).
[56] Bernard, Dil 17 (SBOp 3:134; CF 13B:20).
[57] Bernard, SC 83.4 (SBOp 2:301; CF 40:184).

## *Desiderior feror*

In a much earlier article Marion writes that "only those who love see the phenomena of love. Loving becomes a theoretical exigency. . . . Only the person who knows from experience what loving means can perceive love."[58] He gives the example of a beggar on the street who holds value only in the gaze of charity, an example that in other words stresses the *agapic* dimension of love. In the case of erotic love, "falling in love," and healthy sexual attraction the same dynamic obtains, he says. The decision to love without an apparent assurance of being loved in return sets the lover free, allows the phenomenon of the other to appear:

> The lover alone sees something else, a thing that no one other than he sees—that is, what is precisely no longer a thing, but, for the first time, just such an other, unique, individualized, henceforth torn from economy, detached from objectness, unveiled by the initiative of loving, arisen like a phenomenon to that point unseen. The lover, who sees insofar as he loves, discovers a phenomenon that is seen insofar as it is loved (and as much as it is loved).[59]

For Bernard, reaching the degree of love in which one chooses to love God "for his own sake" similarly allows God to be seen more clearly, as the bride sees and not the slave.

Marion writes of the impossibility of "self-love" understood metaphysically. Assurance that one is loved must come from elsewhere, beyond the range and measure of one's own powers: "to love myself, I would have to go beyond myself, in order to respect the measure of love, which has none."[60] Self-love

---

[58] Marion, "Christian Philosophy," 470.
[59] Marion, *Erotic Phenomenon*, 80–81; hearing/faith turns into vision, into experience, as *capax dei* grows.
[60] Marion, *Erotic Phenomenon*, 46.

here is akin to the selfish arrogation to oneself of the gifts that make one who one is, the refusal to acknowledge a giver, which characterizes sin in the account of *On Loving God*. When Bernard writes of self-love he may have in view something like what Marion designates "auto-affection," wherein one feels the world only through feeling oneself feeling. As Marion describes auto-affection, "My flesh surrounds, covers, protects and opens the world—not the reverse. The more my flesh feels, and thus feels itself, the more the world is opened. The interiority of the flesh conditions the exteriority of the world, rather than opposing it, because auto-affection alone makes possible hetero-affection, which grows to its measure."[61] Marion's account of "the flesh" is quite similar to Bernard's *affectus*. In both cases, the quality and clarity of affect serves as lens, a measure, coloring what one loves and so knows. In both accounts a danger occurs when the centripetal force of affect is extended into the realm of the will in such a way that one becomes a law to oneself, outside the law of charity.

*The Erotic Phenomenon*'s description of love arrives at a love "even of myself" just as Bernard's culminates in loving oneself only for God's sake. In both cases, another's love awakens one to his own possibilities as lover. For Bernard, one loves oneself, ultimately, insofar as and because one is capable of loving God: "When he gave me himself, he gave me back myself."[62] The same is true of Marion: "I wind up loving even myself because I have believed, seen, and experienced that I too, even I, could play the lover—make the love to her that she told to me. This time I indeed give myself over to the other, since I indeed receive myself entirely—as lover—from what I receive—her. I love even myself on the word of the other, who says she is my lover. I believe what she tells me more than what I have ever told myself."[63] True self-love then is entirely mediated by the

---

[61] Marion, *Erotic Phenomenon*, 114.
[62] Bernard, Dil 15 (SBOp 3:132; CF 13B:18).
[63] Marion, *Erotic Phenomenon*, 172.

other's love for oneself and in no way an "auto-certification," an arrogation to oneself of the freedom received freely from God.

The language of *measure* features in both Bernard's and Marion's writings on love. For Bernard *measure* has the positive associations of Wisdom 11:20, where God creates all "in order, weight and measure"; at the same time he says that God is to be loved "without measure," that is, without reduction to the dimensions of human selfishness.[64] Love is the one area in which human beings can respond to God as he does to them: gratuitously. The language of a measureless measure, and the danger of reducing the other to one's own limited range, recurs throughout *The Erotic Phenomenon*.[65] It may be that Bernard has a more positive sense of measure than does Marion, for whom the term is often associated with the objectifying, "measuring" gaze of metaphysics. It remains the case for both authors that "auto-affection," the felt sense of self, mediates one's contact with the world in such a way that the quality of one's desire and will shape one's knowledge.[66]

This last point constitutes the main similarity between Bernard and Marion: the quality of one's love affects (and even effects) what is known. Moreover, they agree that "love itself is knowledge." Marion is able to give this insight a strikingly contemporary expression through his appropriation of phenomenology. Love alone allows the other to appear. Love alone knows others in their otherness, knows them as being like oneself, free. The decision to love generates, for Marion, the phenomenality of the other, an accurate perception of the

---

[64] Bernard, Dil 1 (SBOp 3:119; CF 13B:3): *modus, sine modo diligere*.

[65] See e.g., Marion, *Erotic Phenomenon*, 5, 46, 131.

[66] Another similarity is that both Marion and Bernard conceive of desire as *epektasis*: see Lewis, "The Lover's Capacity," 239; McGinn, *The Growth of Mysticism: Gregory the Great through the 12th Century*, Vol. II of *The Presence of God: A History of Western Christian Mysticism* (New York: Crossroad, 1994), 217. This is interesting to consider in connection with the idea of the self as "invariantly variable," always willing.

other's uniqueness. Similarly, for Bernard, the bride who loves freely imagines God with greater accuracy, whereas the slave whose twisted will has become his law is himself, and so projects, a distorted image of God.

## Conclusion

Bernard at times adopts a posture of suspicion toward art, affectivity, images, and the humanity of Jesus, not because these are intrinsically dubious but because of his keen awareness of the ambiguity of desire that mediates and colors whatever one imagines. His sense of the spiritual journey hinges on the transition from carnal to spiritual—terms that describe not objects but modes of desire. Bernard lacks the critical resources of those working in the wake of Freud, but as a deeply intuitive religious and literary genius he sensed the manner in which "unconscious" (powerful carnal, selfish) influences could interfere with how one read both the book of Scripture and the book of one's experience. His writings present a highly nuanced and subtle imaginative field designed to cultivate and liberate spiritual desire.

What we have called Bernard's incarnational poetics entails a view in which God in Christ reveals himself as willing to submit to the distortions and traps of human imagination, working in and through them, to set humanity free. On the cross, Jesus, the image of the invisible God, takes on every disfiguration human beings can project. Because this supreme idol who "became sin" is also the icon of the living God, a path is opened from the *regio dissimilitudinis* to restored likeness. Just as the Israelites were healed by looking upon the bronze serpent, an idol of their collective sin, so human beings gazing on the "black but beautiful" figure of the Crucified can in time find their wounded desire healed and their imaginations redeemed. Bernard speaks of each believer's being likewise "lifted up" like the serpent, so that passing from carnal to spiritual love all creation, every human reality, is recapitulated and made transparent.[67]

While by no means anti-intellectual, Bernard was well aware of how reasoning can be hi-jacked by sub-personal influences, something he no doubt himself underwent in bouts of crusading, persecutory fervor. As an experienced spiritual master, Bernard knew how easily one rationalizes what the body and affectivity communicate, and he aimed to stay attuned and open to those regions that human beings are chronically tempted to ignore. The measure of the human being in the image of God is continually under pressure from what is beyond its control: instincts and passions on the one hand and, on the other, more grace and light than one could ever absorb or integrate. Instead of a futile attempt to colonize and control what lies beyond measure, Bernard models a way of cooperating with the divine in turning all things to good. Just as the artist focused on the good of his work can make use of devastating events beyond his control, using something of their energy to compose a powerful work, so in the life of the spirit a terrible trial or powerful grace, while uncontainable, can yet hone and train one's desire.

Far from being a metaphysical disparagement of the intrinsic value of what falls within the field of the measured, Bernard's frustration with and correspondingly negative statements concerning art, the body, the limits of experience, indicate rather his high estimation of human possibilities in the wake of Christ's ascension. As an artist he keenly senses the limits of his medium before all that he has to communicate—as an ascetic, the frailty of this body compared to the glorious body for which he longs, as a reformer and abbot, his frustration with human failings—precisely because he sees all that one can become. His work aims to expand the measure of what is possible, to enflesh in time more and more of the measureless.

---

[67] Bernard, SC 21.7 (SBOp 1:126; CF 7:9).

The tired stereotype of Bernard as anti-intellectual, like that of his being iconoclastic, derives in part from a failure to appreciate that he is an artist and looks at the world and writes about it from that perspective. Art makes use of the intelligence in a different way from speculative metaphysics, but it is not, for all that, un- or anti-intellectual. In Bernard's case, where so many of his writings comment on Scripture, there is an "exegetical poetics" of great sensitivity at work. His texts interpret while commenting on the process of interpretation. Just as his images mediate between the book of Scripture and the book of the reader's experience, constructing a figural bridge, the same is true of his work in general.[68] Bernard writes sermons—sermons too dense ever to be delivered—and what is the task of the sermon but to mediate between Scripture and the hearer's experience?

At the same time, every work of art tells the story of its making, and the sermons record in code their own genesis, the lack and abundance, the seeking and discovering. The creative process becomes the sculpted analogue for the periods of thirst and satiety that comprise life in the spirit, creativity the expression and mirror of spiritual desire. It is in part because of his sensitivity to the limits of what the measure of art can express that Bernard has been thought an iconoclast. His exegetical poetics aims to "kindle desire, not explain words." While the move beyond measure may be experienced as the erasure of the created, it aims rather at its recapitulation. Bernard's rhetorical art springs from and opens into a boundless silence, and this contemplative aesthetic pervades both his mystical theology and his project of monastic reform.

Alongside 1 Corinthians 3:18, 1 John 3:2, and other texts Bernard associates with mediation, he frequently invokes 1 Corinthians 13:12, "Now we see dimly in a mirror, but then face to face." The mirror represents for him variously Christ the

---

[68] See Bruun, *Parables*, 58.

incarnate Image of the invisible God, ambiguous human desire, and human being *ad imaginem*. Close attention to the different ways Bernard presents the mediation of the divine to human beings can refresh and illuminate numerous central strands of his work: the humanity of Jesus, the nature of affectivity, experience, art, and freedom. It also reinforces the characterization of Bernard as both the last of the fathers, in his saturation in Scripture and Origenist imagination, and, especially in his account of experience and the ambiguity of desire, surprisingly modern.

# APPENDICES

# Appendix 1

## 1 John 3:2; 2 Corinthians 3:18

*Beloved, we are God's children now, and what we will be has not yet appeared; but we know that when he appears we shall be like him, because we shall see him as he is.* (1 John 3:2, ESV)

*And we all, with unveiled face, beholding the glory of the Lord, are being transformed into the same image from one degree of glory to another.* (2 Cor 3:18, ESV)

Chapter 2 discussed the way Bernard employs 1 John 3:2 in Sermon 31 *On the Song of Songs* as a kind of refrain to underscore the tension between God as he is in himself, beyond the measure of words and images, and God as he appears to human beings in time. Not infrequently, in other works Bernard pairs 1 John 3:2 with 2 Cor 3:18, which expresses a related sense of vision. In fact Bernard cites the verse from Paul much more frequently than he does the one from 1 John (thirty-six times, twelve in the *Sermons on the Song of Songs*).[1] Bernard McGinn regards 2 Cor 3:18 as "a favorite" verse of Bernard, the epitome of the "christomimetic process"[2] encapsulated in Bernard's

---

[1] I have chosen to concentrate on those outside SC. There is a brief but worthwhile discussion of Bernard's use of these and other scriptural texts in Pacifique Delfgaauw, "La Lumière de la Charité chez Saint Bernard," Coll 18 (1956): 42–69, 306–20.

[2] Bernard McGinn, *The Growth of Mysticism: Gregory the Great through the 12th Century*, Vol. II of *The Presence of God: A History of Western Christian Mysticism* (New York: Crossroad, 1994), 175, citing SC 62.5.

expression *Transformamur cum conformamur*. ("We are transformed as we are conformed"). True freedom and right desire make possible a more accurate awareness of God: "Therefore, in whatever way you get yourself ready for God, this is the way he will appear to you."

Attending to the various shades of meaning he gives to these verses across a range of contexts lights up multiple facets of his understanding of the way the quality of human desire, and ultimately human being in the image of God, mediate what is known.

## *Sententiae* 3.124

Bernard's *Sententiae* are something like sketches, the skeletal outlines for sermons, and at times their unpolished quality allows the contours of his thought to appear with greater clarity than in the sermons.[3] *Sententiae* 3.124 provides an especially direct treatment of how human beings experience God as they experience themselves (*de Domino sentiunt secundum quod sentiunt de se*). Bernard describes four different types of person (the bad, the worse, the good, the better) and the manner in which their own orientation interferes with or facilitates their sense of God. He here makes a direct connection between this knowledge by way of self and the human being as image and likeness of God. He employs both 1 John 3:2 and 2 Cor 3:18 and describes the divine as unveiled or revealed to those who are unveiled before God.

*Sententiae* 3.124 begins with a favorite verse of the Cistercian writers: "Think about the Lord in goodness and seek him in simplicity of heart" (Wis 1:1). Bernard outlines the four types of person, and of these, the last alone, steered by trust and

---

[3] Bernard, Sent 3.124 (SBOp 6.2:236–39; Bernard of Clairvaux, *The Parables and The Sentences*, trans. Michael Casey and Francis R. Swietek, CF 55 [Kalamazoo, MI: Cistercian Publications, 2000], 433–38).

faith, reaches awareness of God's simplicity: "God must be sought in simplicity—in such simplicity that we recognize him to be utterly simple, neither offended by our sins nor placated by our penance, but simply desiring our repentance." From the human side, simplicity takes the form of not setting a limit of one's own to how far one will obey God, a limit that would only reduce him to human measure. Packed into the complex associative field of simplicity is the idea of seeking one thing. Bernard depicts God as *revelata revelatum*, unveiled to the unveiled.

In the anthropology Bernard sketches here, the animal cannot perceive what is spiritual; the spiritual, however, makes use of the animal, "what is lowly," to perceive what is lowly, and can judge all things.[4] The sensible is transparent in some measure to the spirit. The spiritual person, says Bernard, can only sense (*sentire*) God through itself (*per seipsam*). God is seen in the self both by its ineradicable structure as his image and through its right desire and virtue, which liken it to him. He describes the image as a mirror that both mediates or interrupts direct contact with the divine and makes it at least somewhat visible: "However great the soul may be, she cannot perceive God except through a mysterious reflection in a mirror so long as she remains a pilgrim in this world. Although the mirror can never be eliminated, the mystery can be mitigated to some extent: since the soul is the image and likeness of God, she can—with her face unveiled, if she is not immersed in a dark fog—behold [*speculatur*] the glory of God."[5] Just as the mirror "can never be eliminated," so too *imago dei* in the human person is ineradicable.[6]

---

[4] Bernard, Sent 3.124 (SBOp 6/2:236; CF 55:433), citing 1 Cor 2:14-15.

[5] Bernard, Sent 3.124 (SBOp 6/2:236; CF 55:433).

[6] The mirror that remains also recalls the endurance of the self in mystical union—despite the experience of complete absorption and self-forgetfulness—and the self-love that persists even in heaven; see Dil 12.33.

The mystery (*aenigmate*), by contrast, admits of change and is lessened as the likeness of a person to God increases. If the soul unveils her own face by right thought and desire, she can mirror (*speculatur*) divine glory. The stress or, better, vantage point is different than in the sixth Sermon for the Dedication of a Church (Ded 6), where God is seen as actively presenting and disguising himself. The deponent verb *speculatur* carries well the actively passive sense of the soul's *mirroring* of God. The soul itself is the mirror or image that, depending on its degree of likeness or the degree to which it is veiled, more or less accurately reflects divine glory. Bernard's parenthetical clause "if she is not immersed in a dark fog" is counterposed a little further on to a series of Bernardine images of incarnation: "the word in the flesh, the sun in the cloud, that judgment which is tempered with mercy, the light inside the clay jar."[7] The soul's being transformed in glory is like a light emerging from the cloud of mortal flesh, with the incarnation portrayed as light hiding itself in cloud.

Bernard further articulates the way the soul sees God according to its own degree of realization in terms of how uncovered or shrouded it is before the divine: "It happens that she can see God in the same state with respect to her as that in which she perceives herself: since she is uncovered, she will experience him as uncovered [*revelata revelatum*]. If however the soul is shrouded in fog, whirling about constantly in darkness, she experiences God such as she is herself [*talem eum qualem ipsa est sentit*]: being confused, she will perceive him in confusion. God, therefore, appears holy [*sancto*] to one who is holy, and distorted [*perverso*] to one who is distorted."[8] God appears holy to the holy because the soul itself is the mirror that "speculates" and the sense by means of which God is experienced. As Bernard writes, concisely, "As they are, so they understand God": *Quales isti sunt, talem et Deum sentiunt*. The internal rhymes on *qual* and *tal* as well as on *sunt* and senti*unt*

---

[7] Bernard Sent 3.124 (SBOp 6/2:237; CF 55:435).
[8] Bernard, Sent 3.124 (SBOp 6/2:236; CF 55:433).

underline the likeness between terms, so between being (*sunt*) and knowing (*sentiunt*).

*Sententiae* 3.124 proceeds to a discussion of four types (*genera*) of person, each of which mediates or obscures God in a different way: "Each type experiences God according to the way they think about themselves [*de Domino sentiunt secundum quod sentiunt de se*]."[9] The first type, the bad, are permissive or presumptuous and "sin without fear," imagining that because their sins are of no account to themselves they are of no account to God either: "Because they have no fear, they cannot have any zeal for justice," zeal they are unable to imagine in God. Recalling the double mention of "fog" (*caligine*) above, Bernard describes the bad as "all wrapped up in the darkness wrought by their deep blindness." They project onto God their own negligence: "Having forgotten, through their negligence, the actions they should condemn, they recognize that they are negligent, and so they perceive God as negligent too." This attitude, Bernard continues, characterizes most "worldly people." They are steered by a false confidence, a counterfeit hope. They will eventually hear from God, "Did you really think I would be like you?" (Ps 50:21).[10] So the sinner reverses the course of how things ought to go: instead of becoming like God, he likens God to his own distorted image.

The next type, the worse, are guilty not of presumption but of despair. After heaping up sins, Bernard writes, "they judge themselves for their crimes. The result is that as they approach the sun's rays from out of the thick darkness, they encounter a light so incredibly pure that because of their judgment of themselves they despair of receiving God's forgiveness."[11] Bernard repeats variations of the phrase "judging themselves" to stress the element of willfully cutting oneself off from forgiveness by a false repentance. Bernard elsewhere uses the language of looking at the light directly and being overwhelmed to

---

[9] Bernard, Sent 3.124 (SBOp 6/2:236; CF 55:434).
[10] Bernard, Sent 3.124 (SBOp 6/2:237; CF 55:434).
[11] Bernard, Sent 3.124 (SBOp 6/2:237; CF 55:435).

describe the curious probing of the secular philosopher, who is unprepared for and therefore blinded by the light of divine glory.[12] In both cases this type of person neglects the mystery of the incarnation, the humanity of Jesus, who tempers the light to mortal eyes.

Bernard compares the "worse" to Judas rushing to the noose rather than seeking forgiveness; "they conceive of God as cruel and merciless," just as they are to themselves. Neither the bad nor the worse "think about the Lord in goodness"; rather, "they both think of the Lord as a reflection of their own attitudes" and suffer accordingly, "for it is equally horrible [*detestabile*] to hope without fear and to fear without hope [*sperare sine timore, et timere sine spe*]."[13] Right desire steered by hope makes it possible to "think about the Lord" in a way that reaches beyond the feverish distortions of the passions to make contact with reality. In these passages Bernard clarifies that it is the quality of desire that colors one's image of God, that constitutes one's (un)likeness.

The next type, "the good," fall into anger but relent and forgive and so can imagine a God who forgives, but only as they forgive: first angered and then pardoning, whereas in reality, Bernard says, God is "neither offended nor placated [*nec offenditur, nec placatur*]." He continues, "Such people, then, think about the Lord in goodness, but not in true knowledge or simplicity, because they perceive him as changeable, deeming it proper to multiply his simplicity as a reflection of their own mutability. . . . But God must be sought in simplicity—in such simplicity that we recognize him to be utterly simple, neither offended by our sins nor placated by our penance, but simply desiring our repentance."[14] This group thinks about the Lord in goodness, that is, through the lens of their own relative, human goodness, but not truly or simply. Interest-

---

[12] E.g., SC 8.5.
[13] Bernard, Sent 3.124 (SBOp 6/2:238; CF 55:435–36).
[14] Bernard, Sent 3.124 (SBOp 6/2:238; CF 55:436).

ingly, Bernard considers the mark of a true apprehension of God, unclouded by human passions, to be the capacity to "get up easily even after serious falls" and keep moving.[15] It is simple for God in his simplicity to forgive. Brooding torturous self-recriminations indicate a lack of faith: "Those great souls who abound in prophetic spirit restore themselves at once and immediately say: 'I have sinned; you will cleanse me, and I will shine whiter than snow.'"[16]

This resilience, Bernard continues, is nonetheless only the beginning, for they seek God in simplicity and think about him in goodness but have not yet found him. He identifies a temptation for this type to set a limit of their own to God's work, to give up at a certain point, whereas those whose simplicity is enduring and whose heart is truly "whole" make use of whatever conditions arise to grow closer to God: "The Lord is found by those who walk with him with their whole heart . . . and who look upon each kind of fortune with an unbowed head." The soul becomes like God in his immutability through a firmly stable disposition that is no longer dismayed by misfortune or exalted by consolations but rather cooperates with God in turning all things to good.

In a kind of paraphrase of 1 John 3:2, Bernard writes, "For the Lord will show himself to those who have faith in him. . . . The Lord manifests himself in this world through faith, but in the next through his actual appearance, and there we will be like him."[17] Faith, and the stability it brings, allows a partial movement beyond the limits and distortions of changeable human emotions. Taken by itself, *Sententiae* 3.124 could seem iconoclastic in its evaluation of human emotion and images, because it lacks the different images of God as father, teacher, and bridegroom perceived by the soul in its different states. One could stress "*there* we will be like him," but here we are

---

[15] Bernard, Sent 3.124 (SBOp 6/2:238; CF 55:436).
[16] Bernard, Sent 3.124 (SBOp 6/2:238; CF 55:437).
[17] Bernard, Sent 3.124 (SBOp 6/2:239; CF 55:437–38), citing Wis 1:2.

not. However, just as "a spiritual person can judge the value of everything," a truly spiritual faith allows a distance from experience that makes it transparent and of service in the monastic work of cultivating and maintaining right desire.

## On Grace and Free Choice

In his treatise *On Grace and Free Choice* Bernard employs both 1 John 3:2 and 2 Corinthians 3:18 to elucidate further aspects of how a human being in the *imago dei* mediates contact with the divine. As in *Sententiae* 3.124, he here makes a direct connection between our reform to the likeness and the incarnation of the Word, who is "the figure of the Father's substance." He compares the *imago dei* latent in fallen humanity to the lost coin of the widow in the parable, the coin with the imprint of the image covered with dust that must be retrieved from the *regio dissimilitudinis*. Wisdom—understood here as both Christ and the widow—having conformed herself to human weakness, will then make humanity "conformable to herself—on that day, namely, when the words of Scripture would be fulfilled: 'We know that when he appears we shall be like him, for we shall see him as he is.' "[18]

As Bernard himself has noted, along with subsequent commentators, the account of image/likeness in this treatise is somewhat different from that found in his *Sermons on the Song of Songs* in the way it accents free will and, less directly than there, includes the idea of human being *in* the Image.[19] The incarnation retains a central position in this work, however, and Bernard makes it clear that it is only through the entry of

---

[18] Bernard, Gra 10.1 (SBOp 3:173: Bernard of Clairvaux, *Treatises III*, trans. Conrad Greenia, CF 19 [Kalamazoo, MI: Cistercian Publications, 1977], 88), citing Heb 1:3; 1 John 3:2.

[19] Bernard says that the two accounts are complementary (SC 81.11; see McGinn, *Growth*, 168–74). If he conveys the idea less directly in *Grace and Free Will* than in the Sermons, the idea is still there: Christ is "the very form" (Gra 10.33), as later he is the Image itself.

the Form itself into deformity that the reform of humanity could begin. He connects the Word through whom the universe was made to the activity of human virtue: "That very form came, therefore, to which free choice was to be conformed, because in order that it might regain its original form, it had to be reformed from that out of which it had been formed. Now, wisdom is the form, and conformation means that the image fulfills in the body what form does in the world." He goes on to eloquently describe the creative work of Wisdom, which combines strength and gentleness and is unforced by "any inner compulsion." This same creative freedom, he says, is expressed "no less gently than mightily," in the "prompt and ready will" of a "cheerful giver."[20]

Bernard understands the verse from 1 John here clearly as the culmination of a trajectory that begins with human creation in the image of God, is recapitulated and given new force and possibility with the incarnation of the Image, and progresses through a life of moral reform as conformation (*conformare—transformare*). This process is characterized by growth in freedom and creativity, a likening to the power, ease, and freedom that marks divine Wisdom.[21] Interestingly, "con-formation" here means that a human being (the image) acts in the world, in the body, incarnating itself as divine wisdom or form does in the world. In the *way* the image incarnates itself, powerfully but gently, it is likened to the form, that is, wisdom, but by its outward action too it makes a likeness of itself, and so indirectly of the form of wisdom. Human activity can be an image of the image—as in Ded 6, where Bernard implies "the walls"

---

[20] Bernard, Gra 10.33, 34 (SBOp 3:189–90; CF 19:89, 90).

[21] The thrust of this forward eschatological momentum is one reason that Bernard does not stop to tarry long over the earlier stages of devotion to the humanity of Jesus; a person is not intended just to stir emotions by reflecting on Jesus' mortal humanity but to express zeal for justice in this life; not only is Christ an outward exemplar, but a person must now shape himself or herself in conformity to the life of the risen one within, now.

and by implication the practices of monastic life as representations of the self.

The incarnate form educates desire in this simultaneous strength-gentleness, force-ease, Bernard says, until it is "conformed and transformed into the same image from glory to glory, as by the Spirit of the Lord. But if by the Spirit of the Lord, then hardly by free choice."[22] While he places the accent here differently than in Ded 6, where he emphasizes God's activity, and one must strive for a balance of force and gentleness, both conformity and transformation, though realities in which we participate, are free gifts from God and beyond the power of human beings if left to themselves.

### De Consideratione 5.27–30

Bernard's epistolary treatise to Pope Eugene III also repeatedly uses 1 John 3:2 and the associated cluster of ideas. Here he makes a distinction between God "as he is" and the limited understanding human beings form of him. Referring to a formulation of God's fourfold attributes (the "length, width, height, and depth" [Eph 3:18] of eternity, charity, majesty, and wisdom respectively), Bernard states, "The one God has been described for our understanding, not as he actually is [*pro captu nostro, non pro suo statu*]. Divisions exist in our understanding, not in God. There are various names, many paths [*voces diversae, semitae multae*], but one thing is signified by the names, one is sought by the paths."[23] Bernard's emphasis here is somewhat more conceptual than figurative; different ideas more than images of God (father, bridegroom, etc.) are in play, though the dynamic is the same. That God has been described with the limits of our understanding in view (*pro captu nostro*), not in his own state (*non pro suo statu*), sets up the first direct allu-

---

[22] Bernard, Gra 10.35 (SBOp 3:190; CF 19:90).

[23] Bernard, Csi 5.27–30 (SBOp 3:489–92; Bernard of Clairvaux, *Five Books on Consideration: Advice to a Pope*, trans. John D. Anderson and Elizabeth T. Kennan, CF 37 [Kalamazoo, MI: Cistercian Publications, 1976], 173–78).

sion in this work to 1 John 3:2: "When we see him face to face we shall see him *as he is*." In this life by contrast God is seen "in a glass darkly."[24]

The "seeing him as he is" of 1 John is a vision "face to face." This fact may not seem very surprising, yet in the context, mention of the face suggests a warmth and intimacy lacking in the conceptual schemes (the fourfold attributes) available in this life. Whereas at present "the fragile gaze" is turned back on itself, unable to penetrate the glory of God's face, in heaven it will be able to pass through into a far more direct encounter with the divine: "At that time the fragile gaze of our souls [*fragilis acies mentis nostrae*], however assiduously applied, will in no way return or break down [*resiliet desilietve*] into its own multiplicity. It will draw more together, unite, and conform itself to God's unity, so one will answer the other face to face. Indeed, 'we will be like him because we will see him as he is.'"[25] The gaze of the mind will thus no longer rebound on itself but will at last find purchase and full conformity with the oneness of God.

Bernard goes on to imagine the four "dimensions" of God as a "four-horse chariot" required by the mind in its weakness and calls Paul, who spoke of the length, width, height, and depth of God, "the charioteer." Interestingly Bernard states that "[God] is the reason for this vehicle." For him concepts and scriptural expressions are vehicles, not ends in themselves, concessions to the human mind in its limits: "Not content with a curiosity for knowledge, we should long for fruition with all our care. Fruition is not in knowledge [*cognitione*] but in comprehension [*comprehensione*]. Indeed, as someone says, 'It is a sin for him who knows what is good and does not do it.' And Paul in another place says, 'Thus run so you may comprehend.'"[26] Bernard distinguishes "comprehension" from mere

---

[24] 1 Cor 13:12, a verse Bernard often uses in connection with the mediating role of the *imago dei*.

[25] Bernard, Csi 5.27 (SBOp 3:490; CF 37:174).

[26] Bernard, Csi 5.27 (SBOp 3:490; CF 37:175), citing Jas 4:17; 1 Cor 9:24.

intellectual curiosity by underlining its aim of savoring, enjoying what it knows. The moral status of the knower conditions the quality of his knowledge. "Thus *run* so you may *comprehend*," he writes; that is, act in a way that will purify the heart and so allow understanding.

Further developing the connection between virtue and knowledge, Bernard says of the fourfold attributes, "It is not disputation but sanctity that comprehends them [*non ea disputatio comprehendit sed sanctitas*]. . . . The saints, then, comprehend. Do you ask how? If you are a saint, you have comprehended and you know; if you are not, be one and you will know through your own experience [*experimento scies*]."[27] The point is not anti-intellectualism. To know God's oneness by affinity means to know him with the entirety, the integrity of one's own being in the image. Bernard identifies fear as the appropriate response to "height and depth" (majesty and wisdom), love to "width and length" (charity and eternity): "God is eternity, God is love: length without extension, breadth without broadness. In both cases he equally exceeds local and temporal constraints, but by the liberty of his nature, not because of the mass of substance. He is unmeasured [*immensus*] in this way, who has made all things to measure [*mensura*]; and though unmeasured, yet this is the measure of his unmeasuredness."[28] God is not the biggest Being among beings, too immense to fit inside the universe, but of a different order, a different quality of freedom altogether. Some of the ambiguity in Bernard with regard to what falls within "measure" (human experience, representation) can surely be traced to the fact that God, the supreme good, is without measure, and yet all that exists (in measure) has been created by him and is therefore good. M. B. Pranger carefully distinguishes Bernard's language here from the apophatic approach of Dionysius: "It is safe to

---

[27] Bernard, Csi 5.30 (SBOp 3:492; CF 37:177).

[28] Translation by M. B. Pranger, *Bernard of Clairvaux and the Shape of Monastic Thought: Broken Dreams* (Leiden: Brill, 1994), 248.

assume that this free divinity, not being the result of either negation or super-affirmation, maintains its geometrical form: it really is length and breadth, however subtle and however close perhaps to invisibility. Further, not being measured by man and not admitting extension, it stays in touch with the measure it has created to measure."[29] There remains a form in God to which human beings in the image can be conformed and transformed.

## Other Texts

A passage in the sermons *On Conversion* employs 1 John 3:2 (along with 1 Cor 13:12 and the vision "face to face") by way of commenting on Matthew 5:8, "Blessed are the pure of heart, for they shall see God." Bernard states that seeing God is our "assurance" (*confirmatio*), for "We are now God's children. It does not yet appear what we shall be, but we know that when he appears we shall be like him, for we shall see him as he is." The vision of God can be obscured from within or from without, whether what stirs distorted desire arises from the promptings of the flesh or the lure of worldly goods. Sin "dims, blurs, and screens" the light: "It is a hateful blotch which deprives us of this vision, and a damnable negligence which makes us meanwhile neglect to cleanse our eye. Just as our bodily sight is blurred by some inner fluid or some outer speck of dust, so spiritual insight is impeded either by the lust of our own flesh or by worldly curiosity and ambition. . . . In both instances, however, it is sin that dims and blurs the eye, and that alone screens the light from the eye, and God from man."[30] Vision in this life then remains partial, and "we see in a mirror dimly, but in the future we shall see face to face," Bernard adds, once

---

[29] Pranger, *Bernard of Clairvaux*, 248–49.
[30] Bernard, Conv 30 (SBOp 4:107; Bernard of Clairvaux, *Sermons on Conversion*, trans. Marie-Bernard Saïd, CF 25 [Kalamazoo, MI: Cistercian Publications, 1981], 67); compare SC 31.2.

"our face shall have been cleansed of all smut and he shall present it to himself resplendent, without spot or wrinkle."[31]

In the Lenten sermons *Qui habitat*, Bernard again blends this last verse (Eph 5:27) into the discussion. When they have been made like to God by peace, virtue, and serenity, he tells his readers, "You will be able to see the serenity and the fullness of majesty, for you will see him as he is." The passage continues: "Or perhaps once he is filled with all that glory himself, the completely delighted dweller of a completely delightful world shall spy outside the salvation God has wrought and see all about him the whole earth filled with his majesty."[32] Here the one seeing God "as he is" sees with new eyes the work of salvation, the creation transfigured.[33] Once again likeness to God transforms the appearance of created reality.

Elsewhere Bernard employs 1 John 3:2 with yet another variation, one that sheds light on his understanding of the role of Christ's humanity: "You will be like him when you see him as he is; be like him now, seeing him for what he became for your sake. For if you do not refuse a likeness in his humility, you will certainly be granted a likeness in his splendor."[34] Thus conformity to the incarnate Christ in his poverty leads to transformation into his risen humanity and beyond, to the vision of his divinity.

Bernard's fourth sermon *For the Feast of All Saints* similarly underlines the role of Jesus' humanity. Bernard interprets the verse "Where the body is, there the vultures will gather" (Luke 17:37) as referring to the mystical altar of the Body of Christ. Where the saints now rest in the shade of the risen humanity,

---

[31] Bernard, Conv 30 (SBOp 4:107; CF 25:68), citing Eph 5:27 and 1 Cor 13:12.

[32] Bernard, QH 17.6 (SBOp 4:491; CF 25:260).

[33] He is commenting on the verse "I will show him my salvation" (Ps 91:16), and it is a striking effect: the purified gaze, saturated in the vision of God, looking out on creation.

[34] Bernard, 1 Nov 1.2 (SBOp 5:305; Bernard of Clairvaux, *Sermons for the Autumn Season*, trans. Irene Edmonds, CF 54 [Collegeville, MN: Cistercian Publications, 2016], 102).

they will at last be raised upon it as an altar. Bernard's high regard for the humanity of Jesus is apparent. In this interim time the saints rest in joy under the human nature of Christ, a thing that the angels themselves long to look upon, until the time comes when they no longer lie beneath the altar but are raised above the altar."[35] Souls are raised "above" it, "By vision and contemplation, not by authority! For the Son, as he promised, will show us himself, not in the form of a servant, but in the form of God." Souls will behold the divinity of the Son along with the other persons of the Trinity.[36] With this context in place Bernard cites 1 John 3:2 in full, suggesting that it is the fullest vision of the triune God, "as he is" that the verse suggests. Does the "we shall be like him" then refer to a likeness to the Trinity? It is possible to read the passage this way. At the same time, the soul being described is still upon, lifted up onto, and supported by the risen humanity, the altar of the Body of Jesus; this relation (sharing in the risen humanity) could be the likeness that allows vision of the Trinity, God, as he is.

Through a collage of verses including Matthew 5:8 and 1 Corinthians 13:12, Bernard develops an account of three modes in which God is seen: in creation, in oneself, "as he is." One can gain some sense of the first two in this life, while the latter is reserved for heaven. Of the vision of God as he is in himself, Bernard writes, "It is the peace of God that surpasses all understanding. How much more does it surpass our power of speech? [*quae exsuperat omnem intellectum, quanto magis omnem sermonem nostrum?*] To experience it is given to no one, nor may any try to express it." Measure encloses what is beyond measure as the husk protects the grain of wheat, he says: The visions of God in creation and in the self are "like the husk surrounding a grain of wheat, while this truly great knowledge of beatitude is the kernel of the wheat, the fat of the grain with

---

[35] Bernard, OS 4.2 (SBOp 5:35b; CF 54:161).
[36] *St. Bernard's Sermons for the Seasons and Principal Feasts of the Year*, trans. Ailbe J. Luddy (Westminster, MD: The Carroll Press, 1950), 3:374.

which Jerusalem, the holy city, is nourished."[37] Bernard reiterates this scheme of three modes while adding a fourth dimension by means of Luke 6:38: " 'Full measure,' says the Lord, 'pressed down, shaken together, and running over shall they pour into your lap.' Full measure in the whole of creation, pressed down in the inmost part of our humanity, shaken together in the outer part, and running over in God himself. Here is the sum of happiness, here the towering glory, here the overflowing of blessedness."[38] Bernard spends the rest of the sermon unpacking this passage. With a view to the themes we have been pursuing, we can note here the identification of "measure" with the created order (here *plenam* with God). The vision of God in oneself is a *compression*, a kind of recapitulation in a higher order of that in creation, but the exterior is not excluded. The body is taken up, shaken together with these other modes at its resurrection. The vision of God "as he is" overflows all "measure."

In a similar vein elsewhere Bernard writes that currently the glory of God is "in" the soul; in heaven it will be revealed: "Even now the glory is in us, but then it shall be revealed. For 'now we are children of God, but what we shall be has not yet been revealed.' " Framing this use of 1 John 3:2, he describes the soul as no mere spectator from the sidelines, but intimately bound up with the revelation of God: "For we shall not just stand there as idle and empty-handed spectators, nor shall that glory be revealed to us from beyond, but from within us. For we shall see God face to face. That is, not outside us, because the glory shall be within us, so that God shall be all in all. Certainly all the earth shall be filled with that glory, so how

---

[37] Bernard, OS 4.3 (SBOp 5:357–58; CF 54:166).
[38] Bernard, OS 4.3 (SBOp 5:357–58; CF 54:163): *"Mensuram," ait Dominus, "plenam, et confertam, et coagitatam, et supereffluentem dabunt in sinus vestros." Plenam in universitate creaturarum, confertam in interiori homine nostro, coagitatam in exteriori, supereffluentem in Deo ipso. Ibi cumulus felicitatis, ibi supereminens gloria, ibi effluens beatitudo.*

much more shall it fill the human soul!"[39] In the beatific vision the interior measure of the *imago dei* and the material measure of creation are both full to overflowing with the radiance of divine glory.

Both 1 John 3:2 and 2 Corinthians 3:18 refer primarily to the vision of God in heaven, though the same dynamic of mediation and unveiling characterizes the awareness of God possible in this life. After explaining that God's mercy will sometimes dispel the cloud that blocks the passage of prayer so that one may contemplate the glory of the Lord "with unveiled face" (2 Cor 3:18), Bernard goes on to state that one's face is only "unveiled" in relation to the body, which remains in a greater state of darkness. The veil consists in the reflections (*speculatoriis*) and shadows (*umbratilibus*) of images (*imaginibus*): "However, let us not take 'revealed face to face' too literally, since we still 'see through a glass darkly,' and we are held in a bodily prison; 'revealed,' he says in fact, partially through the body's gloom."[40] In Bernard's account of both the beatific vision and the mystical experience that foreshadows it, the veil of the mortal body is not dissolved altogether but filled to overflowing with the light of glory.

---

[39] Bernard, Div 1.4 (SBOp 6/1:73; Bernard of Clairvaux, *Monastic Sermons*, trans. Daniel Griggs, CF 68 [Collegeville, MN: Cistercian Publications, 2016], 7): *Non enim astabimus quasi inanes et vacui spectatores, nec gloria illa quasi extrinsecus revelabitur nobis, sed in nobis. Videbimus enim Deum facie ad faciem, sed non extra nos, quia in nobis erit, utique omnia in omnibus. Nimirum plena erit gloria illa etiam omnis terra; quanto magis anima ipsa replebitur.*

[40] Bernard, Div 41.11 (SBOp 6/1:252; CF 68:223). *Non autem ita proprie "revelata facie" accipiamus, cum videamus adhuc per speculum et in aenigmate, et carcerali corpore teneamur; "revelata" vero dicit, quantum ad caliginem corporum.*

# Appendix 2

Bernard's short sermon *In Dedicatione Ecclesiae VI* and Sermon 31 *On the Song of Songs* both focus on God's self-presentation to differently disposed human beings and on modes of activity by which human beings are likened to God and so increasingly able to accurately perceive him. Whereas in Sermon 31 Bernard presents human beings as coming to be like God by cooperating with him in turning all things to good, sharing something of divine stability in the midst of change, in the shorter sermon he places the focus on God as Lord of the garden, who actively and creatively cares for those in the household of faith. He characterizes him as *operans et servans*, and he shows the monks who likewise cultivate the garden of the heart by repentance as becoming like the Lord of the garden by a comparable ethos of care, so improving their ability to see him. Towards the end of the sermon he speaks of Christ as the second Adam, tilling the soil in the Paradise of the church, and states that Christ's "delight is to be with the children of men" (Prov 8:31). The passage in Proverbs from which the phrase comes depicts Wisdom as a co-creator with God, at play everywhere on the earth. That image gives something of the flavor of how Bernard imagines the monk's cooperative work of the heart in the garden of the cloister.

At little more than a page in length, Sermon 6 for the Dedication of a church (Ded) sheds light on the distinction Bernard wants to make between the one unchanging God and the multiplicity of his appearances, adding a distinctive twist to the idea that one's state of soul colors what one knows of God.[1] Bernard accents God the "Lord" and the manner in which he actively presents himself under different aspects to both the just and the unjust.[2]

The sermon begins with the verse from Genesis as its heading: *In loco isto vere Dominus est*—the awestruck exclamation of Jacob on awakening from his dream at Bethel (Gen 28:16)—followed by a brief, complex gesture in which Bernard applies the text to the monastic feast of the abbey church's dedication, but even more to the dedication of the monks themselves, whom, Bernard claims, the feast more properly celebrates. This movement at once resituates the verse in the present and sets up the consecrated buildings as an image of both the monastic community and the individual self. God is in *isto loco*, the place of the self in the sense that it is only through the movements of the human heart, through the mirror of human being in the Image, that one experiences God.

In one sentence, then, Bernard brings a whole field of representation into play: the buildings, and by implication monastic liturgy and ritual, as well as the whole realm of Old Testament figures, become fair game as images of the self, of the "image in the Image." The first mention of God connects him with *care*, a theme that reemerges near the sermon's end. Does God care about the mere walls of a building? "It is human beings, not walls, who say, 'His care is for us.'"[3] The sermon contains a miniature echo of the hierarchy of three visions described in SC 31: the vision of God in creation through reason, the visions granted to the patriarchs, and the more intimate experience of God made available with the coming of

---

[1] For a brief but valuable discussion, see Mette B. Bruun, *Parables: Bernard of Clairvaux's Mapping of Spiritual Topography* (Leiden: Brill, 2007), 258–63.

[2] "Actively" as opposed to Bernard's more usual emphasis on one's state of soul limiting one's vision.

[3] *Non parietes dicunt, sed homines: Ipsi enim cura est nobis* (Bernard, Ded 6.1 [SBOp 5:396; CF 54:210]).

Christ.[4] Jacob's knowledge of God present in all places is akin to the first level of vision; his dream-vision to the second. Comparing the place of Jacob's vision ("How terrible is this place!" Gen 28:17) to the site of the monastery on the feast of its dedication, Bernard exclaims, "How frightful is this place! . . . For we have not received the spirit of this world but the Spirit that is from God, that we may know what God has given us" (1 Cor 2:12).[5] That the place is more holy because we have received the Spirit underlines the sense that the self is itself the place, the *isto loco* where God dwells—or, rather, where the "Lord" is ("*Vere* Dominus *est in loco isto*"), as Bernard emphasizes. The monastic community then, as the place of the Spirit, is like the third vision, the intimacy between bride and groom.

Midway through the sermon, noting that God is not present in one place more than another, Bernard qualifies that while God is present everywhere, he is present in different ways: "He may show himself as present there in some other way that is particularly his own—though not because he himself is different, but because each one distinguishes different things. He is, therefore, in every place, embracing all things and disposing all things but in far different ways. To the wicked he is present but hiding, to the elect he is both acting and watching."[6]

The choice of verbs here (specifically *praestans, dissimulans, operans,* and *servans*) is somewhat unusual. In an earlier translation Ailbe Luddy has *benefitting* for *praestans*.[7] While this is one sense of the word, it is hard to see what it would mean here. Loosely it perhaps connects to the idea stated a little later that God makes his rain fall on the just and unjust alike. It could

---

[4] Bernard, SC 31.3–5 (SBOp 1:221–22; CF 7:126–28).

[5] Bernard, Ded 6.1 (SBOp 5:397; CF 54:210).

[6] Bernard, Ded 6.2 (SBOp 5:397; CF 54:211) (*praesentem se exhibeat, non quidem ipse diversus, sed diversa distinguens. Est ergo in omni loco, omnia universaliter continens omniaque disponens, sed longe tamen aliter atque aliter. Apud malos homines est praestans atque dissimulans, apud electos homines operans et servans*).

[7] Ailbe J. Luddy, *St. Bernard's Sermons for the Seasons and Principal Feasts of the Year*, vol. 2 (Westminster, MD: The Carroll Press, 1950), 431.

also have the sense of "exceeding": that God exceeds the capacity of the unjust to receive him as he is. It seems more likely, though, that Bernard is pairing *praestans* with *dissimulans*.[8] *Praestans* can mean "to make good a promise," the opposite of dissimulation, but the best sense is perhaps "presenting, making present." To the unjust, Bernard seems to say, God is at once presenting and disguising himself. This reading would fit the surrounding play on *praesentem*, suggesting that God is present in one way but presents himself in many, depending on the receiver.[9] *Dissimulans* calls to mind the *dissimilitudine* between God and the unjust soul as a distorting factor. Yet, strikingly, the accent here is placed squarely on God's actively disguising himself. Just as to the just God is actively working and serving, to the unjust he is actively presenting and disguising himself at once, as though by a distorted countenance, the only one they can receive, to shock them toward change. It is as though God were to condescend to be misperceived, to enter the figural "land of unlikeness" of the unjust, to reach sinners.

The one God, *non quidem ipse diversus*, makes his rain fall on just and unjust alike: "where dissimulation exists among the wicked, the truth is not present. So, if one can say so, with the wicked he is in hiding, with the righteous in truth."[10] While Bernard speaks as though God is different vis-à-vis the just and the unjust, *si dicere licet* (and *quodammodo*) acknowledges that this difference is only a way of speaking. God presents his presence differently. With those who are unlike him by their injustice, he is unlike himself, as if the truth were not. With the unlike he is in disguise; with the like, that is, the just, he is in truth. The unjust are unlike themselves, because their true

---

[8] That is, rather than the pair being opposite *operans/servans*.
[9] Oddly, the sermon ends with the occlusion of the temporal present, which dissolves into erasing the past by penance and longing forwards.
[10] Bernard, Ded 6.2 (SBOp 5:397; CF 54:211): *sed ubi malorum interim dissimulatio est, quodammodo veritas non est. Itaque, si dicere licet, apud impios est in dissimulatione, apud iustos in veritate.*

being is in the image of God, and so they perceive a God unlike himself. The text continues, "*apud angelos in felicitate, apud inferos in feritate sua*": to the infernal he appears in his savagery, with the repeated sound of *fer* emphasizing the likeness in unlikeness of God and sinners.

Continuing to play on these syllables, Bernard asks if *feritate* sounds (*sonat*) too harsh, and then teases sound and sense into *furorem*: "For where he makes it rain on the just and the unjust, he is our father and the father of mercies, hoping for people to repent. When he condemns the stiff-necked, he is judge . . . where he takes rest, he is spouse."[11] So he paints a kind of compressed miniature of previously seen figures: father, judge, spouse. He uses *is* in effect to mean "appears," to say that God is a father, judge, and spouse when in fact there is no change in his being or way of acting toward humanity, only changes in how he is perceived, some of these images being more true to the reality than others. He gives his sentence the structure, "Where he *does* this he *is* that, though it remains the case that *non quidem ipse diversus*."

In this passage Bernard also introduces the theme of *paenitentiam*, that which the father of mercies awaits (*exspectans*). The just perceive God as *Dominus*, the lord of the garden,[12] he says, as the second Adam in the *paradisus claustralis*, in the garden of the church/soul/monastic community, when they, like him, are actively working the soil. When they watch (*serviamus*) in Spirit and truth they are able to perceive the God who is *operans et servans*. As elsewhere in Bernard, active conformity leads to spiritual transformation.[13] That God appears

---

[11] Ded 6.2 (SBOp 5:397; CF 54:211): *Ubi enim pluit super iustos et iniustos, pater est, et pater misericordiarum, exspectans homines ad paenitentiam. Ubi damnat obstinatos, iudex est. . . . Ubi cubat, sponsus est.*

[12] In Bernard's *On Loving God* human beings are like God insofar as they are lords of creation.

[13] Bernard McGinn, *The Growth of Mysticism: Gregory the Great through the12th Century*, vol. II of *The Presence of God: A History of Western Christian Mysticism* (New York: Crossroad, 1999), 175.

in and through his activity is a deeply biblical idea. Here he appears through his activity in the monastery. It is his activity as Lord that constitutes and sustains the community. Only if the monks themselves watch (*serviamus*) in the same Spirit will they as the just perceive the Lord as Lord, in truth, as opposed to those who hear the word but do not do (*facitis*) it.[14] A certain ethos of care is required of the monks for them to appreciate the Lord's care for them. The allusion to Proverbs 8:31 evokes an element of delight and creative play in the monk's activity, coinciding with the penitential associations of tilling the soil.

This ethos of care takes shape above all in tending the garden of the heart. The monk ought to stand with reverence (*reverentia stare*) in the place where God is *operans et servans* by repenting his past life and expecting the next (*paenitentes et exspectantes*). In this sense the monk is both the garden and the co-gardener, tilling the soil by repentance and right desire. The Lordship of God is revealed in his generative action (*operans, servans, custodieret*); human dignity likewise corresponds to the work of the heart, that is, penance and desire: "We have come to this place, here we stand fast" (*Ad hoc venimus, in hoc positi sumus*). The present, the "today" of the feast being celebrated, consists in a creative tension that continually sifts the past and strains forward to the future.

---

[14] Bernard, Ded 6.3 (SBOp 5:398; CF 54:211).

# Appendix 3

Bernard tests what will become his artful critique of art in the *Apology* in two letters related to its inception. He mentions that because a Brother Oger (Apol 30) is eager to depart Clairvaux with the text of the *Apology*, he must cut short his discourse (*sermonem brevio*). Oger, a learned canon regular of Mont-Saint-Elois whom Bernard admired, may have been the first to request the treatise, and he was involved in its revision.[1] Bernard's decision to cut short the *Apology* comes after his most profuse and detailed description, that of the monstrous "variety of contradictory forms" decorating the cloisters of Cluny. His rhetoric in general is characterized by an alternation between compressed miniatures and extensive digression. In two similarly structured letters to Oger, Bernard appears to ramble before explicitly calling attention to this rambling and abbreviating his discourse. Letter 92 probably contains Bernard's refusal to take up the work that would later become the *Apology* and his reasons for declining.

Bernard begins both letters (92 and 93) with a reference to past correspondence and to the brevity of his current replies. Next he draws attention to the work involved in the composition and exchange of letters, underlining the artificiality of the medium. After a mini-teaching, in the first letter on silence, in the second on love, both letters stop short abruptly (*Quid ego*

---

[1] Conrad Rudolph, *The "Things of Greater Importance": Bernard of Clairvaux's Apologia and the Medieval Attitude Toward Art* (Philadelphia: University of Philadelphia Press, 1990), 179–80.

*facio?*) and point to the absurdity of using many words to speak of silence. *Quid ego facio?* calls attention both to Bernard's digressing and to his act of abbreviation. The letters both conclude with a mention of Guerric of Igny, a mutual friend, and a brief treatment of practical matters (illness, the exchange of manuscripts).

In letter 92 Bernard begins by setting a measure to speech. He says that he is replying to a long note with a short one, and, observing that it is Lent, he appeals to the measure of liturgical time and the words of Ecclesiastes 3:1, 7: "All things have their season: there is a time for speaking and a time for keeping silence." It is possible to read Bernard's option for silence in this letter in relation to both the letter and Oger's appeal for a treatise against the Cluniacs.[2] By underlining the work involved in composition, Bernard calls attention to rest, the leisure it contains. By complaining about the lack of silence that characterizes the busy-ness of composition and by underlining the measured quality of written discourse, he suggests a realm beyond measure—that is, love—opening out from within. The measured speech of artfully composed letters, he implies, is a poor substitute for presence and conversation, and yet the letter does make Bernard present in a way; it stands in as his envoy.

Bernard begs off from both the exchange of letters with Oger and (perhaps) the writing of the *Apology* on the grounds that he lacks time, that writing it would go against the grain of his monastic life, and that he lacks the requisite ability, measuring and limiting his literary art by these three excuses. As though suddenly aware that he is rambling about the value of concision, Bernard abruptly interrupts himself: "But what am I doing? I wonder you do not laugh. For, while appearing to condemn strongly much speaking, I still continue to pour out words, and in recommending silence to thwart silence by my

---

[2] In Ep 92.2 when Bernard refers to "the sort of work you want me to do," he probably refers to the *Apology*.

verbosity."[3] Bernard advocates and evokes silence not with silence but by means of a measured, artful speech that by underlining its own artificiality opens onto the unmeasured space of love (presence).

Letter 93 likewise highlights the limitations of artificial language ("verses, phrases, and quotations") to express all that is within the writer's heart: "I feel sure you express less than you feel; and you would not be wrong if you believed the same thing of me. When your letter was delivered into my hands, you were already in my heart. While I write this letter you are present to me, as I am sure I shall be present to you when you read it."[4] Bernard contrasts the work of writing and exchanging letters with the work of meditating on the law of love, a work that brings rest: "The more we rest from doing this, the less rested we become; the more we apply ourselves to it, the more repose we derive from it." Anticipating the approach of the *Apology*, the letters use artful writing to criticize artful writing. They underline their own made and measured qualities as a way to invoke what is beyond measure, the direct communication of spiritual love.

---

[3] Bernard, Ep 92.3 (SBOp 7:236): *Sed quid ego facio? Mirum si non rides, quod ego, qui multiloquium tantopere damnare videor, in tam multa verba tam loquaciter iam progredior, et, dum cupio tibi commendare silentium, contra silentium per multiloquium pugnat.*

[4] Bernard, Ep 93.1 (SBOp 7:237).

# Bibliography

## Primary Sources

Augustine of Hippo. *De doctrina christiana*. Ed. and trans. R. P. H. Green. Oxford Early Christian Texts. Oxford: Clarendon Press, 1996.

———. *De Trinitate*, Libri I–XII. Ed. W. J. Mountain. Series Latina Libri XV. Turnhout: Brepols, 1968.

———. *The Trinity (De Trinitate)*. Trans. Edmund Hill. New York: New City Press, 1991.

Bernard of Clairvaux. *Apologia*. Trans. in Conrad Rudolph, *The "Things of Greater Importance": Bernard of Clairvaux's Apologia and the Medieval Attitude Toward Art*. Philadelphia: University of Pennsylvania Press, 1990. 232–87.

———. *Five Books on Consideration: Advice to a Pope*. Trans. John D. Anderson and Elizabeth T. Kennan. CF 37. Kalamazoo, MI: Cistercian Publications, 1976.

———. *Monastic Sermons*. Trans. Daniel Griggs. CF 68. Collegeville, MN: Cistercian Publications, 2016.

———. *On Loving God, with an Analytical Commentary by Emero Stiegman*. CF 13B. Kalamazoo, MI: Cistercian Publications, 1995.

———. *On the Song of Songs I*. Trans. Kilian Walsh. CF 4. Kalamazoo, MI: Cistercian Publications, 1971.

———. *On the Song of Songs II*. Trans. Kilian Walsh. CF 7. Kalamazoo, MI: Cistercian Publications, 1976.

———. *On the Song of Songs III*. Trans. Kilian Walsh and Irene M. Edmonds. CF 31. Kalamazoo, MI: Cistercian Publications, 1979.

———. *On the Song of Songs IV*. Trans. Irene M. Edmonds. CF 40. Kalamazoo, MI: Cistercian Publications, 1980.

———. *The Parables and The Sentences*. Trans. Michael Casey and Francis R. Swietek. CF 55. Kalamazoo, MI: Cistercian Publications, 2000.

———. *St. Bernard's Sermons for the Seasons and Principal Feasts of the Year*. Trans. Ailbe J. Luddy. 3 vols. Westminster, MD: The Carroll Press, 1950.

———. *Sancti Bernardi Opera*. Ed. Jean Leclercq, C. H. Talbot, and H. M. Rochais. 8 vols. Rome: Editiones Cistercienses, 1957–1977.

———. *Sermons for the Autumn Season*. Trans. Irene M. Edmonds. CF 54. Collegeville, MN: Cistercian Publications, 2016.

———. *Sermons for the Summer Season*. Trans. Beverly Kienzle. CF 52. Kalamazoo, MI: Cistercian Publications, 1991.

———. *Sermons on Conversion*. Trans. Marie-Bernard Saïd. CF 25. Kalamazoo, MI: Cistercian Publications, 1981.

———. *Treatises III*. Trans. Conrad Greenia. CF 19. Kalamazoo, MI: Cistercian Publications, 1977.

## Secondary Sources

Anderson, Luke. "The Appeal to Reason in Saint Bernard's *De diligendo Deo*." In *The Chimaera of His Age: Studies on Bernard of Clairvaux*, edited by E. Rozanne Elder and John R. Sommerfeldt. Studies in Medieval Cistercian History 5. CS 63. Kalamazoo, MI: Cistercian Publications, 1980. 132–39.

———. *The Image and Likeness of God in Bernard of Clairvaux's Free Choice and Grace: Reflections both Philosophical and Theological*. Bloomington: Author House, 2005.

———. "The Rhetorical Epistemology in Saint Bernard's *Super Cantica*." In *Bernardus Magister: Papers Celebrating the Nonacentenary of the Birth of Bernard of Clairvaux*, edited by John R. Sommerfeldt. CS 135. Kalamazoo, MI: Cistercian Publications, 1992. 95–128.

———. "Wisdom and Eloquence in St. Bernard's *In dedicatione ecclesiae sermo primus*." In *Erudition at God's Service: Studies in Medieval Cistercian History, XI*, edited by John R. Sommerfeldt. CS 98. Kalamazoo, MI: Cistercian Publications, 1987. 117–32.

Astell, Ann W. *Eating Beauty: The Eucharist and the Spiritual Arts of the Middle Ages*. Ithaca: Cornell University Press, 2006.

———. "Telling Tales of Love: Julia Kristeva and Bernard of Clairvaux." *Christianity and Literature* 50, no. 1 (Autumn 2000): 125–47.

Bell, David N. *The Image and Likeness: The Augustinian Spirituality of William of Saint Thierry*. CS 78. Kalamazoo, MI: Cistercian Publications, 1984.

Blanpain, Jacques. "Langage mystique, expression du désir, dans les Sermons sur le Cantique de Bernard de Clairvaux." *Collectanea cisterciensia* 36, no. 1 (1974): 45–68.

Boismard, M. E. "La Connaissance dans L'Alliance Nouvelle d'après la Première Lettre de saint Jean." *Revue Biblique* 56 (1949): 365–91.

Boquet, Damien. "Le libre arbitre comme image de Dieu: l'anthropologie voluntariste de Bernard de Clairvaux." *Collectanea Cisterciensia* 65 (2003): 179–92.

———. *L'ordre de l'affect au Moyen Âge: Autour de l'anthropologie d'Aelred de Rievaulx*. Caen, France: Crahm, 2005.

Bradley, Arthur. " 'Mystic Atheism': Julia Kristeva's Negative Theology." *Theology and Sexuality* 14, no. 3 (2008): 279–92.

Brague, Rémi, ed. *Saint Bernard et la Philosophie*. Paris: Presses Universitaires de France, 1993.

Bredero, Adriaan H. *Bernard of Clairvaux: Between Cult and History*. Grand Rapids: Eerdmans, 1996.

Bresard, Luc. "Bernard et Origène commentent le Cantique." *Collectanea Cisterciensia* 44 (1982): 111–30, 182–209, 293–308.

Bruun, Mette B. *Parables: Bernard of Clairvaux's Mapping of Spiritual Topography*. Leiden: Brill, 2007.

Burrows, Mark. "Foundations for an Erotic Christology: Bernard of Clairvaux on Jesus as 'tender lover.' " *Anglican Theological Review* 80 (1998): 477–93.

———. "Hunters, Hounds and Allegorical Readers: The Body of the Text and the Text of the Body in Bernard of Clairvaux's *Sermons on the Song of Songs*." *Studies in Spirituality* 14 (2004): 113–37.

Carruthers, Mary. *The Craft of Thought: Meditation, Rhetoric and the Making of Images, 400–1200*. New York: Cambridge University Press, 1998.

———. *The Experience of Beauty in the Middle Ages*. Oxford: Oxford University Press, 2013.

Casey, Michael. *Athirst for God: Spiritual Desire in Bernard of Clairvaux's Sermons on the Song of Songs*. CS 77. Kalamazoo, MI: Cistercian Publications, 1998.

———. "Bernard of Clairvaux: The Face Behind the Persona." CSQ 27, no. 2 (1997): 133–51.

———. "In Pursuit of Ecstasy: Reflections on Bernard of Clairvaux's *De diligendo Deo*." *Monastic Studies* 16 (Christmas 1985): 139–56.

Coleman, Janet. "Cistercian 'Blanched' Memory and St. Bernard: The Associative, Textual Memory and the Purified Past." In *Ancient and Medieval Memories: Studies in the Reconstruction of the Past*. Cambridge, UK: Cambridge University Press, 1992. 169–91.

Constable, Giles. "Aelred of Rievaulx and the Nun of Watton: An Episode in the Early History of the Gilbertine Order." In *Medieval Women*, edited by Derek Baker. Oxford: Blackwell, 1978. 205–26.

Crouzel, Henri. *Origen: The Life and Thought of the First Great Theologian*. Trans. A. S. Worrall. San Francisco: Harper and Row, 1989.

———. *Théologie de l'image de Dieu chez Origène*. Aubier: Éditions Montaigne, 1956.

Crownfield, David, "The Sublimation of Narcissism in Christian Faith and Love." In *Body/Text in Julia Kristeva: Religion, Women, and Psychoanalysis*, edited by David Crownfield. Albany, NY: State University of New York Press, 1992. 57–66.

Danielou, Jean. "Saint Bernard et les Pères Grecs." In *Saint Bernard Théologien: Actes du Congrès de Dijon 15–19 Septembre, Analecta SOC* 9 (1953): 46–55.

Déchanet, Jean-Marie. "La Christologie de S. Bernard." In *Saint Bernard Théologien: Actes du Congrès de Dijon 15–19 Septembre, Analecta SOC* 9 (1953): 78–91.

Delfgaauw, Pacificus. "La Lumière de la Charité chez Saint Bernard." *Collectanea Cisterciensia* 18 (1956): 42–69, 306–20.

———. *Saint Bernard: Maitre de l'Amour Divin*. Paris: FAC-éditions, 1994.

Dietz, Elias. "Aelred on the Humanity of Christ: A Theology in Images." *CSQ* 45, no. 3 (2010): 269–78.

Dimier, Anselme. "Les Amusements Poétiques de Saint Bernard." *Collectanea Cisterciensia* 11 (1949): 53–55.

Dominguez-Morano, Carlos. *Belief After Freud: Religious Faith through the Crucible of Psychoanalysis*. Trans. Francisco Javier Montero. New York: Routledge, 2018.

Dupont, Jacques. "Le Chrétien, Miroir de la Gloire Divine d'après II Cor., III. 18." *Revue Biblique* 56, no. 3 (1949): 392–411.

Dutton, Marsha L. "Eat, Drink and Be Merry: The Eucharistic Spirituality of the Cistercian Fathers." In *Erudition at God's Service: Studies in Medieval Cistercian History, XI*, edited by John R. Sommerfeldt. CS 98. Kalamazoo, MI: Cistercian Publications, 1987. 1–31.

———. "The Face and Feet of God: The Humanity of Christ in Bernard of Clairvaux and Aelred of Rievaulx." In *Bernardus Magister: Papers Celebrating the Nonacentenary of the Birth of Bernard of Clairvaux*, edited by John R. Sommerfeldt. CS 135. Kalamazoo, MI: Cistercian Publications, 1992. 203–23.

———. "Intimacy and Imitation: The Humanity of Christ in Cistercian Spirituality." In *Erudition at God's Service: Studies in Medieval Cistercian History, XI*, edited by John R. Sommerfeldt. CS 98. Kalamazoo, MI: Cistercian Publications, 1987. 33–69.

Evans, G. R. *Bernard of Clairvaux*. Oxford: Oxford University Press, 2000.

Falque, Emmanuel. *Le Livre de l'expérience: D'Anselme de Cantorbéry à Bernard de Clairvaux*. Paris: Les Éditions du Cerf, 2017.

Farkasfalvy, Denis. "The Role of the Bible in Saint Bernard's Spirituality." *Analecta SOC* 25 (1969): 3–13.

———. "St. Bernard's Interpretation of the Psalms in His Sermons *Super Cantica*." In *Erudition at God's Service: Studies in Medieval Cistercian History, XI*, edited by John R. Sommerfeldt. CS 98. Kalamazoo, MI: Cistercian Publications, 1987. 109–16.

Freeman, Elizabeth. "Nuns in the Public Sphere: Aelred of Rievaulx's *De Sanctimoniali de Wattun* and the Gendering of Authority." *Comitatus* 27 (1997): 55–80.

Gilson, Étienne. *The Mystical Theology of St. Bernard*. Trans. A. H. C. Downes. London: Sheed and Ward, 1940.

Häring, N. H. "The Case of Gilbert de la Porrée, Bishop of Poitiers (1142–1154)." *Mediaeval Studies* 13 (1951): 1–40.

Hart, Kevin, ed. *Counter-Experiences: Reading Jean-Luc Marion*. Notre Dame, IN: University of Notre Dame Press, 2007.

Hecke, Lode van. *Le Désir dans l'Expérience Religieuse: L'Homme Réunifié. Relecture de Saint Bernard*. Paris: Les Éditions du Cerf, 1990.

Horner, Robyn. "The Weight of Love." In *Counter-Experiences: Reading Jean-Luc Marion*, edited by Kevin Hart. Notre Dame: IN: University of Notre Dame Press, 2007.

Hubbard, Kyle. "The Unity of Eros and Agape: On Jean-Luc Marion's Erotic Phenomenon." *Essays in Philosophy* 12, no. 1 (2011): 130–46.

Hufgard, Kilian. *Bernard of Clairvaux's Broad Impact on Medieval Culture*. Mediaeval Studies, Vol. 13. Lewiston: Edwin Mellen, 2001.

———. *Saint Bernard of Clairvaux: A Theory of Art Formulated from His Writings and Illustrated in Twelfth-Century Works of Art*. Mediaeval Studies, Vol. 2. Lampeter: The Edwin Mellen Press, 1989.

Keener, Craig. "Transformation through Divine Vision in 1 John 3:2-6." *Faith and Mission* 23, no. 1 (2005): 13–22.

Kelly, Oliver, ed. *The Portable Kristeva*. New York: Columbia University Press, 1997.

Kereszty, Roch. "Relationship between Anthropology and Christology: St. Bernard, a Teacher for our Age." *Analecta Cisterciensia* 46 (1990): 271–99.

Krahmer, Shawn Madison. "Interpreting the Letters of Bernard of Clairvaux to Ermengarde, Countess of Brittany: The Twelfth-Century Context and Language of Friendship." *CSQ* 27, no. 3 (1992): 217–50.

Kristeva, Julia. *Tales of Love*. Trans. Leon S. Roudiez. New York: Columbia University Press, 1987.

La Corte, Daniel M. "Flawed Portrayals of Bernard of Clairvaux's Attitude Towards Art." *CSQ* 29, no. 4 (1994): 451–69.

Leclercq, Jean. "From the Tender Heart of Christ to His Glorified Body." *Word and Spirit: A Monastic Review* 12 (1990): 80–91.

———. "L'écrivain." In *Bernard de Clairvaux: Histoires, Mentalités, Spiritualité: Colloque de Lyon-Dijon, 5-9 juin 1990*. Ed. Dominique Bertrand et al. Sources Chrétiennes 380. Paris: Les Éditions du Cerf, 1992.

———. *The Love of Learning and the Desire for God: A Study of Monastic Culture*. Trans. Catharine Misrahi. New York: Fordham University Press, 1974.

———. *Maurice Blondel: Lecteur de Bernard de Clairvaux*. Brussels: Editions Lessius, 2001.

———. "The Mystery of the Ascension in the Sermons of Saint Bernard." *CSQ* 25, no. 1 (1990): 9–16.

———. *Recueil d'études sur St. Bernard et ses ecrits*, Vol. 3. Rome: Edizioni di Storia e Letteratura, 1969.

———. "Saint Bernard et Origène d'après un manuscrit de Madrid." *Revue Benedictine* 59 (1949): 183–95.

Lewis, Stephen E. "The Lover's Capacity in Jean-Luc Marion's *The Erotic Phenomenon*." *Questiones Disputatæ* 1, no. 1 (Fall 2010): 226–44.

Louth, Andrew. "Bernard and Affective Mysticism." In *The Influence of Saint Bernard: Anglican Essays*, edited by Benedicta Ward. Oxford: SLG Press, 1976. 3–9.

Marion, Jean-Luc. "Christian Philosophy and Charity," *Communio* 19 (Fall 1992): 465–73.

———. *The Crossing of the Visible*. Trans. James K. A. Smith. Stanford: Stanford University Press, 2004.

———. *The Erotic Phenomenon*. Trans. Stephen Lewis. Chicago: The University of Chicago Press, 2007.

———. *The Idol and Distance: Five Studies*. Trans. Thomas A. Carlson. Perspectives in Continental Philosophy, No. 17. New York: Fordham University Press, 2001.

———. "La Conversion de la Volonté selon *l'action*." *Revue Philosophique*, No.1 (1987): 33–46.

———. *Prologomena to Charity*. Trans. Stephen E. Lewis. New York: Fordham University Press, 2002.

———. "Resting, Moving, Loving: The Access to the Self according to Saint Augustine." *The Journal of Religion* 91, no. 1 (January 2011): 24–42.

———. *The Visible and the Revealed*. Trans. Christina M. Geshwandtner et al. New York: Fordham University Press, 2008.

McDonnell, Kilian. "Spirit and Experience in Bernard of Clairvaux." *Theological Studies* 58 (1997): 3–18.

McGinn, Bernard. *The Growth of Mysticism: Gregory the Great through the 12th Century*. Vol. II of *The Presence of God: A History of Western Christian Mysticism*. New York: Crossroad, 1994.

———. "Resurrection and Ascension in the Christology of the Early Cistercians." *Cîteaux: Commentarii Cistercienses* 30 (1979): 5–22.

Melczer, Elisabeth, and Eileen Soldwedel. "Monastic Goals in the Aesthetics of Saint Bernard." In *Studies in Cistercian Art and Architecture*, Vol. 1, edited by Meredith P. Lillich. CS 66. Kalamazoo, MI: Cistercian Publications, 1982. 31–44.

Mohrman, Christine. "Observations sur la langue et le style de saint Bernard." SBOp 2. Rome: Editiones Cistercienses, 1958. ix–xxxiii.

———. "The Style of Saint Bernard." *Berryville Cistercian Studies* II, Part I. Berryville, VA, 1961. 1–20.

Mommaers, Paul. *The Riddle of Christian Mystical Experience: The Role of the Humanity of Jesus*. Louvain Theological and Pastoral Monographs, No. 29. Louvain: Peeters Press, 2003.

Morris, Anne. "The Trinity in Bernard's Sermons on the Song of Songs." CSQ 30, no. 1 (1995): 35–50.

Morrow, Derek. "The Love 'Without Being' that Opens (to) Distance Part One: Exploring the Givenness of the Erotic Phenomenon with J-L. Marion." *Heythrop Journal* 46 (2005): 281–98.

———. "The Love 'Without Being' that Opens (to) Distance Part Two: From the Icon of Distance to the Distance of the Icon in Marion's Phenomenology of Love." *Heythrop Journal* 46 (2005): 493–511.

Murray, Paul. "The Word into Words: "Grace and Truth in St. Bernard of Clairvaux." *Communio* 28 (Spring 2001): 3–25.

O'Grady, Kathleen. "An Interview with Julia Kristeva." In *Julia Kristeva 1966–96: Aesthetics, Politics, Ethics*. Special issue of *Parallax*, no. 8 (July–September 1998): 5–16.

Pranger, M. B. *The Artificiality of Christianity: Essays of the Poetics of Monasticism*. Redwoods City: Stanford University Press, 2003.

———. *Bernard of Clairvaux and the Shape of Monastic Thought: Broken Dreams*. Leiden: Brill, 1994.

———. "Bernard the Writer." In *A Companion to Bernard of Clairvaux*, edited by Brian Patrick MacGuire. Brill's Companions to the Christian Tradition, vol. 25. Leiden: Brill, 2011. 220–48.

———. "The Persona of the Preacher in Bernard of Clairvaux." *Medieval Sermon Studies* 51 (2007): 33–40.

Reilly, Dianne J. "Bernard of Clairvaux and Christian Art." In *A Companion to Bernard of Clairvaux*, edited by Brian Patrick MacGuire. Brill's Companions to the Christian Tradition, vol. 25. Leiden: Brill, 2011. 279–304.

Renna, Thomas. "St. Bernard and the Pagan Classics: An Historical View." In *The Chimaera of His Age: Studies on Bernard of Clairvaux*, edited by E. Rozanne Elder and John R. Sommerfeldt. Studies in Medieval Cistercian History 5. CS 63. Kalamazoo, MI: Cistercian Publications, 1980. 122–31.

Rigolot, Irénée. "Bernard de Clairvaux, Lecteur d'Augustin." *Collectanea Cisterciensia* 54 (1992): 132–44.

Rudolph, Conrad. *The "Things of Greater Importance": Bernard of Clairvaux's Apologia and the Medieval Attitude Toward Art*. Philadelphia: University of Philadelphia Press, 1990.

Ryan, Patrick. "*Sensus Amoris*: The Sense of Love in Two Texts of William of Saint Thierry." CSQ 40, no. 2 (2005): 163–72.

*Saint Bernard Théologien: Actes du Congrès de Dijon 15–19 Septembre*. Analecta SOC 9 (1953).

Saint-Germain, Christian. "The Intimate and Its Metaphors: Two Love Letters from Saint Bernard to Ermengarde." CSQ 27, no. 3 (1992): 209–16.

Schindler, D. S. *Plato's Critique of Impure Reason: On Goodness and Truth in the Republic*. Washington, DC: Catholic University Press, 2008.

Smith, Richard Upsher, Jr. "Saint Bernard's Anthropology: Traditional and Systematic." CSQ 46, no. 4 (2011): 415–28.

Sommerfeldt, John R. "The Epistemological Value of Mysticism in the Thought of Bernard of Clairvaux." In *Studies in Medieval Culture*, edited by John R. Sommerfeldt. Kalamazoo, MI: Western Michigan University Press, 1964. 48–64.

Stiegman, Emero. "The Aesthetics of Authenticity." In *Studies in Cistercian Art and Architecture*, vol. 2, edited by Meredith Parsons Lillich. CS 69. Kalamazoo, MI: Cistercian, 1984. 1–9.

———. "An Analytical Commentary." In Bernard of Clairvaux, *On Loving God: An Analytical Commentary*. CF 13B. Kalamazoo, MI: Cistercian Publications, 1995. 43–195.

———. "Humanism in Bernard of Clairvaux: Beyond Literary Culture." In *The Chimaera of His Age: Studies on Bernard of Clairvaux*, edited by E. Rozanne Elder and John R. Sommerfeldt. Studies in Medieval Cistercian History 5. CS 63. Kalamazoo, MI: Cistercian Publications, 1980. 23–38.

———. "The Language of Asceticism in Bernard of Clairvaux's Sermones Super Cantica Canticorum." PhD dissertation, Fordham University. Ann Arbor: University Microfilms, 1973.

———. "A Tradition of Aesthetics in Bernard of Clairvaux." In *Bernardus Magister: Papers Celebrating the Nonacentenary of the Birth of Bernard of Clairvaux*, edited by John Sommerfeldt. CS 135. Spencer, MA: Cistercian Publications, 1992. 129–47.

Stock, Brian. *The Implications of Literacy: Written Language and Models of Interpretation in the Eleventh and Twelfth Centuries*. Princeton: Princeton University Press, 1983.

Studzinski, Raymond. *Reading to Live: The Evolving Practice of Lectio Divina*. CS 231. Collegeville, MN: Cistercian Publications, 2009.

Turner, Denys. *Eros and Allegory: Medieval Exegesis of the Song of Songs*. CS 156. Kalamazoo, MI: Cistercian Publications, 1995.

Van Kirk, Natalie B. "Finding One's Way Through the Maze of Language: Rhetorical Usages that Add Meaning in Saint Bernard's Style(s)." CSQ 42, no. 1 (2007): 11–35.

Verbaal, Wim. "*Bernardus Philosophus*." *Revista Portuguesa de Filosofia* 60, no. 3 (2004): 567–86.

Ward, Graham, ed. *The Postmodern God: A Theological Reader*. Oxford, UK: Blackwell, 1997.

Wharff, Jonah. "Aelred of Rievaulx on Envy and Gratitude." CSQ 43, no. 1 (2008): 1–15.

Zona, James W. " 'Set Love in Order in Me': *Eros*-Knowing in Origen and *Desiderium*-Knowing in Saint Bernard." CSQ 34, no. 2 (1999): 157–82.

# Scripture Index

References are cited by page number.

| Gen | | Wis | | 1 Cor | |
|---|---|---|---|---|---|
| 28:16 | 205 | 1:1 | 188 | 2:12 | 206 |
| 28:17 | 206 | 1:2 | 193 | 3:18 | 182 |
| | | 11:20 | 179 | 4:5 | 113 |
| Deut | | | | 5:16 | 85 |
| 6:5 | 76 | Sir | | 13:12 | 32, 182 |
| | | 14:5 | 139 | 15:19 | 105 |
| | | | | 15:46 | 114 |
| 2 Kgs | | Isa | | | |
| 4:3 | 48 | 9:2 | 34 | 2 Cor | |
| 4:6 | 48 | 49:15 | 86 | 3:18 | 27 |
| | | | | 5:16 | 36 |
| Job | | Lam | | | |
| 24:21 | 115 | 4:20 | 32–34, 56 | Gal | |
| | | | | 2:20 | 74 |
| | | Matt | | 5:16 | 70 |
| Prov | | 11:27 | 11 | | |
| 8:31 | 204, 209 | | | Eph | |
| | | Mark | | 4:10 | 45 |
| Eccl | | 8:31-32 | 76 | | |
| 3:1 | 211 | | | Phil | |
| 3:7 | 211 | Luke | | 2:7 | 49 |
| | | 1:35 | 34 | | |
| Song | | John | | Col | |
| 1:4 | 83 | 16:13 | 46 | 2:9 | 40 |
| 1:6 | 25 | 19:23 | 45 | | |
| 2:2 | 33 | | | 1 John | |
| 2:3 | 33, 34 | Rom | | 2:15-16 | 73 |
| 2:4 | 78, 112 | 8:28 | 72 | 3:2 | 25, 26, 28, 32, 182 |

# Author Index

Authors listed here are those most frequently discussed or cited, with the page numbers on which they appear. Bernard is not included, but his works are indexed in the Subject Index under "Bernard of Clairvaux, Works." Paul also appears in the Subject Index.

Abelard, 160
Aelred of Rievaulx, 3, 61, 65–67
Anderson, Luke, 6
Anselm, 161
Astell, Ann W., 133, 146, 151
Augustine, 7–11, 17
  Augustinian, 15, 19, 64, 168

Blanpain, Jacques, 1, 147
Blondel, Maurice, 5, 169
Boethius, 17
Boquet, Damien, 68
Bradley, Arthur, 126, 128, 129, 133
Bresard, Luc, 56
Bruun, Mette B., 30, 182, 205
Burrows, Mark, 130

Carruthers, Mary, 23, 54, 118, 119
Cassian, John, 1, 53
Crouzel, Henri, 55, 58–59
Crownfield, David R., 126, 129, 130, 145

Danielou, Jean, 21, 56
Déchanet, Jean-Marie, 56, 63

Delfgaauw, Pacifique, 162, 163, 187
Descartes, 131, 149, 164, 165, 168, 170, 171
Dietz, Elias, 67, 68
Domínguez-Morano, Carlos, 125
Dutton, Marsha L., 61, 62, 64–67

Falque, Emmanuel, 5, 124, 168, 174
Freud, Sigmund, 126, 127, 129, 151, 180

Galen, 110
Gilbert of Poitiers, 15, 17
Gilson, Étienne, 44, 99, 157
Giussani, Luigi, 111
Gregory of Nyssa, 59
Gregory the Great, 57, 156
Guerric of Igny, 211

Häring, N. H., 17
Heidegger, Martin, 168
Horner, Robyn, 171, 172
Hubbard, Kyle, 174
Hufgard, Kilian, 101–4
Husserl, Edmund, 166

Kant, Immanuel, 168
Kereszty, Roch, 45
Kristeva, Julia, 124–55, *passim*; 156, 165

Leclercq, Jean, 10, 44, 56, 100, 101, 107, 152, 153, 169
Lewis, Stephen E., 167, 170, 179
Louth, Andrew, 131, 149, 150
Lubac, Henri de, 4, 5, 124
Luddy, Ailbe, 58, 201, 206
Lynch, William, 105, 151

Marion, Jean-Luc, 49, 50, 60, 66, 95, 125, 156–83 *passim*
May, Gerald, 140
McDonnell, Kilian, 7
McGinn, Bernard, 38, 67, 179, 187, 194, 208
Melczer, Elisabeth, 99
Mohrmann, Christine, 20, 21
Mommaers, Paul, 40–44
Morris, Anne, 14

Nygren, Anders, 142

Origen, 1, 4, 21, 33, 34, 36, 55–61, 161, 183

Plato, 1, 2
Pranger, M. B., 30, 90, 91, 99, 102, 108, 198, 199

Ratzinger, Joseph, 137
Reilly, Dianne J., 100
Rudolph, Conrad, 100–122 *passim*, 210
Ruusbroec, Jan, 41

Sartre, Jean-Paul, 41
Schindler, D. S., 2, 3
Soldwedel, Eileen, 99
Stiegman, Emero, 52, 65, 98, 99, 110, 113, 114, 117, 118, 131, 135, 142, 149, 152, 160–62

Van Kirk, Natalie B., 54, 55
Verbaal, Wim, 83

William of Saint-Thierry, 3, 103, 104, 109

Zona, James W., 56

# Subject Index

Items are identified by the page or page numbers on which they appear.

Adam, 76, 103, 204, 208
Aesthetic(s) (adj., n.), 65, 92, 93,
 98–101, 104, 107, 110, 113,
 115–17, 120, 122, 123, 146,
 151, 182
Affect (n.), 79, 133, 134, 149, 160,
 166, 172, 175, 178
Affection(s), 18, 29, 38, 47, 48,
 50, 52, 58, 62, 69, 73, 74,
 76–78, 80, 83, 87, 89, 90,
 103, 136, 144, 149, 150, 173,
 176
 Auto-affection, 178, 179
 Carnal, 73, 90, 96, 98, 136
 Ordered, 135, 149
 Spiritual, 96, 98, 144
Affective(ly), 38, 42, 46, 48, 67,
 79, 81, 90, 150, 162
Affectivity, 2, 3, 5, 6, 19, 84, 92,
 124, 126, 129, 133, 142, 145,
 146, 152, 154, 180, 181, 183
 Spiritual, 61
*Affectus*, 31, 43, 45, 46, 58, 75,
 78–80, 88, 121, 133, 144–46,
 149, 163, 164, 172, 178
*Agape*, 70, 79, 142, 143, 165, 166,
 174
 *Agapic*, 177

Ambiguity, 20, 89, 93, 109, 114,
 180, 183, 198
Anthropology, 126, 132, 135,
 137, 139, 154
*Apologia, Apology, see* Bernard of
 Clairvaux, Works
Appearance(s), 14, 20, 25, 32, 33,
 71, 93, 107, 113, 114, 118,
 121, 131, 137, 146, 151, 158,
 173, 193, 200, 204
 And being; and reality, 62, 84,
 89, 90, 100, 105–7, 109, 110,
 113, 121, 123, 146, 147, 200;
 *see also* Being; Reality,
 Realities
Architecture, 53, 98, 102, 117,
 120
Arrogance, 108, 109, 126, 134,
 136, 154, 167
Art(s), 2, 3, 90–92, 95, 96, 98–
 104, 106, 107, 109, 110, 114,
 116, 121–23, 151–53, 180–83,
 210
 Literary, 100, 104, 152, 211
 Monastic, 100, 102, 121
 Of living, 65
 Of memory, 118
 Visual, 111, 116, 118, 122

227

Artful(ly), 34, 91, 99, 104, 123, 210–12
Artificial, Artificiality, 99–102, 210, 212
Artist(s), 95, 99, 101, 110, 112, 122, 151, 181, 182
Ascension, 39, 43–46, 48–51, 54–56, 60, 62, 63, 69, 73, 74, 76, 78, 181
    Feast of the, 44
Asceticism, 102, 109
Attachment(s), 3, 38, 42, 47–49, 61, 66, 73
Attributes, 12, 16, 17, 19, 126, 197, 198
    Of God; divine, 7–9, 12, 13, 15–17, 19, 20, 196
    Of the soul, 17–19

Bands, swaddling, *see* Clothing, Clothes
Beatific, *see* Vision, beatific
Beauty, the beautiful, 20, 25, 67, 98, 99, 103, 105–9, 117, 121–23, 132, 141, 146, 150–51
    Black but beautiful, 83–97 *passim*
    Of the church, 110–13
    Spiritual beauty, 123, *see also* Black but beautiful
Being (n.), 4, 10, 11, 16, 19, 26–29, 62, 107, 112, 130, 134, 135, 143, 147, 150, 162, 167, 169, 170; *see also* Appearance
    Of God, 8, 9, 16
Benedictine(s), Black monks, 98, 100, 104, 105, 107, 109, 111–14, 119, 120, 123

Bernard of Clairvaux, Works
    *Apologia ad Guillelmum abbatem* (*Apology*; Apol), 45, 98–123 *passim*, 210–12
    *De Diligendo Deo* (*On Loving God*; Dil), 57, 71, 75, 78, 80, 102, 118, 125–29, 131, 133, 135–43, 147, 149, 150, 160, 161, 163, 164, 166, 170, 173, 174, 176, 178, 179, 208
    *De gratia et libero arbitrio* (*Grace and Free Choice*; Gra), 160, 194, 196
    Epistles (Ep[p]), 103, 109, 210–12
    *Liber de gradibus humilitatis et superbiæ* (*Steps of Humility and Love*; Hum), 163
    Sermo in ascensione Domini (Asc), 44–49 *passim*, 51–54, 82
    Sermo in dedicatione ecclesiæ (Ded), 204
    Sermo in Nativitate B. Mariae (Nat BVM), 108
    Sermo in Pentecost (Pent), 48
    Sermones diversis (*Monastic Sermons*; Div), 71, 73, 74, 76, 79–81
    *Sermones super Cantica Canticorum* (*Sermons on the Song of Songs*; SC), 2–4, 10–19, 21, 22, 24–38, 42, 57, 71–73, 75–81, 83–97 *passim*, 131, 132, 134, 136, 139, 142–46, 149–51, 153, 155, 161, 171–73, 175, 176, 181, 187, 192, 194, 205, 206
Black monks, *see* Benedictine(s)
Blanpain, Jacques, 1, 147

## Subject Index

Body/Bodies, 1, 14, 27, 32, 49, 52, 53, 57, 60, 63, 64, 76, 80, 81, 88, 89, 92, 94, 110–12, 115, 117, 118, 120, 129, 132–35, 137, 141, 149–52, 154, 166, 179, 181, 195, 202, 203
   Body of Christ/of Jesus, 200, 201
   Christ's risen body, 23, 66
Bride, 12, 13, 14, 25, 28, 30, 31, 33, 34, 36, 37, 80, 83, 84, 88, 90, 92, 93, 97, 137, 153, 173, 177, 180, 206
Bridegroom, 8, 14, 18, 25, 30, 31, 33, 41, 113, 171, 193, 196, 206

Carnal, 39, 49, 87, 51, 58, 71, 149, 180; *see also* Affection(s), carnal; Love, carnal
   And spiritual, 3, 6, 61–97 *passim*, 98, 157, 180
Charity, 28, 43, 70, 79, 86, 112, 131, 144, 158, 159, 165–68, 173, 177, 178, 196, 198; *see also Schola caritatis*; Wine of
Christian, *see* Philosophy
Christianity, 126, 128, 132, 145, 148
Church, 17, 45, 93, 111, 112
Cistercian(s), White monks, 3, 23, 104, 105, 107, 111, 121, 156
Clothes, Clothing, 108, 112, 119, 120, 159
   Coat of many colors, 110, 112, 119
   Swaddling clothes, swaddling bands, 107–9, 112, 119
Cluny, Cluniacs, 116, 210, 211

Concupiscence, 78, 115, 143
Contemplation, 43, 44, 58, 59, 75, 86, 87, 144, 163, 201; *see also* Desire, contemplative
Creation, 2–4, 7, 9, 13, 28, 30, 44, 72, 76, 96, 105, 147, 152, 159, 181, 195, 200–3, 205, 208
Cross, 39, 50, 51, 74–76, 81, 82, 93, 94, 105, 106, 108, 111, 180
Crucified (n., adj., v.), 59, 60, 64, 69, 71, 88, 92–95, 97, 123, 136, 137, 180
Cupidity, 143, 173
Curtains of Solomon, 83, 89–91, 97

Delight, 82, 98, 106, 144, 174, 176, 204, 209
Desire(s), 2, 4, 8, 13, 18, 19, 22, 24, 26, 29–31, 33, 38, 39, 43, 47, 49, 50, 53, 59, 60, 64, 65, 70, 93–95, 97, 98, 103, 115–18, 121, 126–29, 131, 133, 134, 136, 137, 139, 144, 145, 147, 152–54, 161, 171, 173, 179–83, 188, 196, 199, 209
   Bridegroom's, 171
   Contemplative, 90
   For contemplation, 86
   For God, 79, 147, 152, 153, 164
   For heaven, 40
   God's, 142
   Right, 4, 5, 8, 16, 26, 50, 78, 94, 135, 147, 152, 188–90, 192, 194, 209
   Spiritual, 117, 144, 180, 182
*Dignitas*, 130, 134
Dignity, 135, 173, 209

Disciples, 45–52, 68, 69, 74, 76, 78
Diversity, 110–13, 118
  Divinity, 17, 49, 65, 66, 199, 200
  In unity, 111, 113, 116, 123
  Of Christ/Jesus/the Son, 23, 24, 35, 51, 59, 65, 66, 201
  Unity and/in, 110–13
*Ductus*, 23, 35, 54, 55, 58, 122

Easter, 39, 45, 57
Ecclesial, 100, 110–12, 115, 123
Ecstasy, 35, 41, 43, 55, 63, 75, 80
Ego, 165, 170, 173
Elijah, 46, 47
Emotion(s), 131, 145, 149, 150, 193, 195
Emptiness, 62, 121
  Interior/Spiritual, 48, 53, 120
*Epektasis*, 59, 60
Epistemology, 5, 6
*Eros*, 70, 79, 142–45, 165, 166, 174
Eroticism, 129, 133, 166
Eschatological, 100, 111, 113, 115, 123, 195
Eucharist, 21, 22, 32, 34, 40, 56, 60
Evil, 134, 169, 170
Excess, *Excessus*, 43, 98–100, 107, 115, 120, 123, 153
Experience(s), 2, 4, 5, 7, 8, 10–12, 14, 18–21, 23, 31, 33, 35, 36, 39, 41, 42, 44, 53, 65, 75, 77, 83, 87, 88, 92, 96–98, 101, 103, 113, 124, 125, 131, 140–42, 144, 147, 149, 150, 152, 154, 157, 160, 161, 166, 167, 171, 172, 176, 177, 180, 181–83

Mystical, 11, 12, 25, 35, 40, 42, 43, 55, 63; *see also* Mystic(s), Mystical
Eye(s), 11, 27, 33, 35, 73, 95, 107

Face, 3, 27, 32, 36, 39, 50, 56, 76, 87, 189, 190, 197, 200, 203
  To face, 32, 66, 89, 182, 197, 199, 202, 203; *see also* Vision(s), of God
Faith, 4, 7, 8, 18, 19, 21–24, 32–36, 45, 48, 51, 52, 59, 62, 64, 66, 68, 69, 72, 83, 84, 86–88, 94–96, 100, 101, 105, 108, 126, 137, 141, 147, 149–51, 154, 155, 161, 177, 189, 193, 194, 204
Fall, the; Adam's, 61, 103, 140, 147
  Fallen world, 34, 144
Father, 14, 18, 39, 49, 50, 154, 208; *see also* Son
  And Son, 11–13
  Figure, 128, 143
Fear, 30, 140, 143, 144, 148, 150, 173, 175, 176, 191, 192, 198
Figure(s), scriptural, 7, 20, 33, 39, 122, 123, 205
Flesh, 14, 20–22, 32, 34, 36, 46, 47, 52, 53–55, 58, 59, 61–64, 66–71, 73, 77–82, 85, 87, 88, 94, 97, 108, 134, 144, 154, 164, 166, 175, 178, 190, 199; *see also* Spirit
Food(s), 2, 22, 53, 105, 108, 114–19
  Spiritual, 117
Foreshadow, 62, 108, 203
Free choice; free will, 41, 156, 166–70, 194–96

*Subject Index* 231

Freedom, 5, 6, 53, 57, 72, 74, 75, 81, 95, 96, 130, 131, 134–37, 148, 151, 152, 154, 162, 166–73, 176, 179, 183, 188, 195, 198
Friendship, 41, 87, 88
  Spiritual, 145

Garden, 204, 208, 209
Garment(s), 65, 66, 120
  Seamless, 45, 56, 62, 111
Gerard, 28, 83, 84, 86–91
Gift(s), 16, 27, 30, 33, 52, 71, 82, 90, 93, 97, 111–13, 130, 134–36, 138, 139, 153–55, 159, 166, 167, 173, 178, 196
  Of God, 63, 126, 170
  Of the Spirit, 45, 46, 77
Glory, 32, 33, 51, 57, 59, 60, 62, 84, 85, 89–91, 97, 96, 109, 111, 136, 139, 141, 187, 189, 190, 192, 196, 197, 200
  Divine, 190, 192, 203
  Light of, 35, 37, 43, 45, 64, 92, 203
  Of God, 19, 24, 189, 202
  Temporal, 35, 106
God,
  As bridegroom, 8, 14, 18, 30, 31, 38, 41, 193, 196
  As judge, 30, 41, 150, 208
  As love, 85, 133, 142, 160, 198
  As spouse, 208
  As teacher, 8, 10, 14, 18, 30, 41, 150, 193
  Greatness of, 9
  In Christ, 158, 180
  Presence of, 26, 29, 84, 132, 162, 207
Goodness, 156, 159, 188, 192, 193

Grace, 3, 6, 9, 22, 30, 32, 49, 63, 80, 83, 97, 133, 142, 152, 154, 161, 167, 181
Greatness, 10, 15–17; *see also* God, greatness of
Grief, 83, 87–91, 93, 98; *see also* Sorrow
Groom, *see* Bridegroom

Harp(s), 106, 107, 114
Heaven, 5, 6, 10, 11, 28, 32, 40, 43, 45–47, 58, 60, 66, 68, 79, 86, 93, 94, 106, 113, 115, 189, 197, 201–3
  Heavenly, 43, 52, 84, 88, 92
  Third, 36
  Vision of, 25, 95
Heavens, 45, 112
Holy Spirit, *see* Spirit
Humanity, 2, 9, 20, 43, 44, 58, 89, 108, 136, 139, 159, 180, 194, 195, 202, 208
  Of Jesus, 2, 3, 6, 20, 21, 23, 24, 32, 34–36, 38–43, 47, 50, 51, 53, 54, 56–66, 72, 73, 76, 78, 80, 180, 183, 192, 195, 200, 201
Humility, 13, 37, 76, 91, 106, 108, 109, 114, 200
Hypocrisy, 106, 107, 109, 111, 113
Hypocrite(s), 106, 107, 109, 112, 115

Icon, 3, 50, 60, 122, 180
Iconic, Iconicity, 54, 58, 59, 66, 71, 96, 122, 157, 159
Iconoclasm, 2
Iconoclast, Iconoclastic, 118, 174, 182, 193
Idol(s), 3, 38, 40, 50, 60, 71, 94, 122, 167, 180

Idolatrous, 3, 38, 123, 157, 159
Image(s), *passim*
  Ad imaginem; In the Image
    (of God), 3, 7–20 *passim*, 28,
    41, 44, 55–57, 72, 75, 122,
    130, 134, 135, 139, 142, 146,
    157, 160, 167, 181, 183, 188,
    194, 195, 198, 199, 205, 208
  *Imago, Imago dei*, 7–20 *passim*,
    28, 41, 57, 96, 146, 168, 170–
    72, 189, 194, 197, 203
Imagination, 1, 8, 35, 38, 56, 59,
  60, 62, 63, 101, 103, 108, 109,
  125, 134, 148, 151, 154, 173,
  180, 183
Incarnation, 2, 7, 13, 21, 23, 24,
  32, 34, 36, 38, 50, 54, 55, 59,
  62, 67, 73, 82, 86, 108, 110,
  112, 190, 192, 194
Incarnational, 39, 83, 88, 108,
  132; *see also* Poetics
*Infideles*, 135, 149, 150
Intellect, 31, 121, 167–69
Irrational(ity), 133, 165, 172

Jacob, 93, 205, 206
Jesus, Crucified, 59, 60, 69, 71,
    88, 92–95, 97, 123, 136, 137,
    180; *see also* Passion, of
    Jesus
  Divine nature, 39, 54, 57, 66
  Human nature, 7, 13, 14,
    16, 38, 51, 54, 57, 62, 64,
    66, 201
  Ministry, 36, 38, 39, 45, 51,
    53, 63
  Resurrection, 50, 69, 96
Judge, 30, 31, 41, 150, 208
Judgment, eschatological/Final,
  113, 190
Just, the, 138, 205–8

Kedar, *see* Tents of
King, 22
Kiss, 11–14
Knowledge, 1, 12, 13, 26, 35, 36,
    42, 46, 51, 57–59, 69, 104, 126,
    130, 135–37, 147, 150, 156,
    159–63, 166, 167, 170–73, 179,
    188, 192, 197, 198, 201
  Love as/Love itself is, 4, 6,
    12, 42, 125, 156, 166, 167, 171,
    179
  Of Christ, 157
  Of God, 46, 65, 146, 160, 206
  Of self/Self-knowledge, 25, 31,
    41, 114, 146, 160, 170

Language, 1, 4, 7–11, 16, 18–20,
    34, 71, 80, 87, 115, 118, 129,
    144, 148, 162, 175, 176, 179,
    191, 212
  Bernard's, 164, 172, 198
Law(s), 103, 130, 143, 144, 165,
    170, 173, 174, 178, 180
  Of Charity/Love, 143, 154,
    173, 178, 212
  Of God, 123
Letters, *see* Bernard, Works of,
  Ep(p)
Light, 11–13, 15, 24, 27, 33, 35–37,
    39, 43, 45, 53, 64, 85, 86, 89,
    92, 93, 98, 106, 112, 113, 133,
    162, 181, 190–92, 199, 203;
    *see also* Glory
Likeness, 2, 6, 7, 11, 13, 15, 16,
    21, 22, 27, 33, 41, 44, 57, 80,
    150, 168, 169, 180, 190, 192,
    194, 195, 200, 201, 208
  Of God, 167, 188, 189
  To/With God, 5, 16, 18, 19, 23,
    28, 41, 72, 81, 96, 136, 142,
    160, 162, 171, 176, 190, 200

Literature, 152–54
  Christian, 121
  Patristic, 39
Liturgy, 102, 205
Logos, 31, 58
Longing, 5, 15, 16, 43, 62, 82, 91, 94
Love, 4, 6, 11–13, 32, 39, 40–43, 48, 50, 58, 60, 61, 65, 67, 69–81, 84–88, 95–97, 103, 111–15, 117, 125, 129–34, 137–39, 142–46, 148, 154, 156–60, 162–79, 198, 210–12; *see also Agape; Eros; Knowlege; God; Self*
  Carnal, 38, 39, 42, 48–50, 59, 61–82 *passim*, 133, 146, 163
  Degrees/Modes/Stages of, 73, 77, 78, 80, 127, 141, 145
  Divine, 28, 82, 85, 131, 132, 134, 137, 142, 175
  Erotic, 80, 86, 87, 174, 175, 177
  For/Of God, 135, 139, 141, 144, 146, 149, 152, 154, 160, 165, 270
  For Jesus/Jesus' humanity, 50, 52, 66, 67, 77, 78
  Human, 48, 130, 163, 170
  Of Christ, 39, 76
  Of God, 61, 65, 71, 126, 130, 135, 139, 141, 142, 146, 148, 149, 154, 170, 171, 178
  Of self/Self-love, 70, 71, 126–29, 133, 134, 138–41, 143, 144, 146, 154, 164, 170, 177, 178, 189
  Of wisdom, 156, 164
  School of, 170; *see also Schola caritatis*
  Spiritual, 39, 50, 59, 61–82 *passim*, 85, 163, 181, 212
  Wine of, 73, 74, 80, 81

Lust, 73, 199
  For glory, 84, 91

Martyr(s), 73, 75, 80, 81, 115, 142, 154
Martyrdom, 35, 61, 73, 75, 76, 79–81, 111
Mary (the Virgin), 24, 34, 53
Measure, 34, 35, 40, 44, 45, 50, 55, 59, 60, 81, 84, 87, 92, 96, 97, 102, 105, 108, 111, 115, 117, 136, 145, 159, 164, 172, 177–79, 181, 182, 187, 189, 198, 199, 201–3, 211, 212
  Measureless, 179, 181; *see also* Unmeasured
Mediation, 2, 6, 20, 33, 40, 56, 58, 64, 183, 203
  Of images, 40, 58, 64
Meditation, 41, 42, 45, 55, 63, 65, 66, 72, 74, 80, 212
  *Meditationes* of Descartes, 164, 170
Merchant, 127, 131, 140, 141, 143, 173, 175
Mercy, 85, 190, 203
Metaphor(s), Metaphorical(ly), 7, 9–11, 18, 28, 33, 65, 112, 134, 162
  For God, 41
Metaphysics, 4, 157, 179, 182
Mind(s), 24, 31, 35, 36, 45, 47, 48, 51, 55, 72–79, 96, 118, 132, 141, 166, 197
  Mind of love, 170
Mirror, 16, 24, 32, 33, 37, 57, 63, 79, 89, 182, 189, 190, 199, 205
Modernity, 5, 124, 131, 138, 149

Monastery, 160, 206, 209
Monastic, 1, 53, 59, 98–100, 102, 104, 108, 110–12, 114, 115, 117, 119, 121, 123, 159, 160, 182, 194, 205
  Community, 205, 206, 208
  Life, 55, 99, 100, 102, 106–8, 113, 115, 119, 123, 157, 196, 211
  Rule, 114
Monk(s), 2, 46, 53, 55, 64, 81, 98, 101, 102, 105, 106, 112, 115, 117–20, 122, 123, 153, 204, 205, 209; *see also* Benedictines, Cistercians
Mother, 10, 52, 129
Mutuality, 25, 27, 175
Mysteries, 32, 36, 39, 45, 56, 62, 84, 159
Mystic(s), Mystical, 3, 14, 19–21, 31, 33, 41–43, 61, 63, 66, 75, 96, 128, 133, 139, 153, 154, 159, 189, 200
  Experience, 11, 12, 19–21, 25, 40, 42, 43, 63, 203
  Theology, 182
  Visitation, 28–30
Mysticism, 14, 53, 57, 154
  Trinitarian, 14

Narcissism, 129, 138, 148
Nature(s), 7, 13, 18, 19, 43, 49, 51, 66, 79, 85, 93, 97, 102, 103, 108, 110, 116, 123, 127, 129, 132–34, 142, 149, 153, 161, 167, 198
  Divine, 9, 14, 39, 51, 54, 57, 66
  Fallen, 143
  Human, 7, 13, 14, 16, 38, 51, 54, 57, 62, 64–66, 142, 201

Necessity, 89, 99, 102, 104, 116, 117, 119, 120, 122, 123, 154, 170
Necessities, physical, 135
Needs, 70, 71, 75, 80, 102, 117, 139, 144, 147
New Testament, 30, 36, 39, 40, 56, 64, 130; *see also* Scripture

Objectification, 159, 170, 173
Oger, 104, 109, 210, 211
Old Testament, 30, 39, 56, 205; *see also* Scripture
Ontology, 169
Ontological(ly), 11, 15, 24, 27, 36, 41, 44, 55, 99, 130, 139, 142, 146, 147
Original sin; *see* Sin
Other, the / an, 5, 94, 95, 124, 125, 128–31, 133–36, 138, 139, 141, 143, 146, 148, 154, 156, 157, 159, 160, 162, 165, 166, 172, 173, 175, 177–80
  Divine, the, 6, 143
Otherness, 5, 6, 62, 148, 159, 179

*Paenitentia*, 208
Pagan(s) (adj., n.), 13, 30, 39, 56
Pain(s), 80, 81, 85, 87, 88
Passion(s) (human), 52, 73, 90, 103, 152, 165, 181, 192, 193
  Of Jesus, 69, 70, 73, 74, 78, 80, 106
Patriarchs, 29, 205
Paul, 14, 36, 40, 67, 72, 150, 151, 187, 197
Pauline, 52, 70
Pedagogy, Divine, 22, 26, 58, 59, 109
  Of desire, 50
  Of the heart, 78

Penance, 189, 192, 207, 209
Perception, 2, 5, 24, 43, 53, 93, 124, 154, 179
  Of God/the divine, 18, 59, 127, 208
Peter, 69, 74, 76
Phenomenological, 154, 161
Phenomenology, 125, 156, 161, 166, 170, 179
Philosopher(s), 2, 3, 13, 25, 28, 37, 84, 89, 91, 124, 156, 168, 192
Philosophy, 156, 159–61, 165, 166
  Christian, 156–59, 167
Plato, 1, 2
Platonism, 162
Poetics, 4, 15, 49, 53, 59, 62, 108, 113, 182
  Incarnational, 83, 98, 180
  Monastic, 99, 100, 102, 111, 115, 123
Postmodern, 130, 148
Poverty, 53, 72, 106, 109, 123, 200
Prayer, 39, 42, 43, 71, 82, 91, 120, 121, 203
Pride, 37, 108, 109, 114, 119
Projection(s), 5, 42, 62, 93, 124–28, 139, 140, 144, 145, 148, 159, 160
Prophet(s), 25, 28
Prophetic, 54
Psychoanalysis, 125–28, 145, 147, 148, 151, 154
Psychological, 5, 41, 124, 132, 140, 147
Psychologist, 127
Psychology, 140

Rational(ly), 3, 77, 84, 137, 150, 158, 166
Rationalism, 91

Rationalist, 151, 157, 161
Rationality, 131, 149, 150, 162, 164
Rationalize, 181
Reality, realities, 2, 4, 5, 21, 24, 28, 32, 35, 36, 49, 51, 56, 59, 69, 72, 84, 89, 90, 96, 98, 100, 101, 105–7, 109, 110, 113, 121, 123, 125, 127, 139, 143, 147, 148, 151, 152, 154, 159, 166, 171, 181, 192, 200, 208; see also Appearance
Realization, 40, 70, 76, 152, 169–71, 190
  Self-, 27, 142, 164, 176
Reason, 13, 30, 31, 67, 77, 127, 131, 133, 136, 137, 144, 145, 147, 149–51, 158, 161, 162, 205
Reciprocity, 26, 28, 171, 173–76; see also Unity
Reform, 194, 195
  Monastic, 98, 99, 104, 182
Religion, 126–28, 132, 151
Repentance, 189, 191, 192, 204, 209
Representation(s), 32, 126, 127, 130, 196, 198, 205
Resemblance, 15, 26, 30
Resurrection, 39, 52
  Christ's, 50, 69, 96
Revelation(s), 2, 13, 18, 21, 27, 63, 86, 101, 156, 158, 202
  God's self-, 59, 105
Rhetoric, 39, 64, 102, 108, 117, 119, 151, 168, 210
  Divine, 4, 23
Rhetorical(ly), 1, 6, 22–24, 51, 54, 87, 88, 90, 91, 99, 107, 109, 111, 117, 138, 160
Rhetorician, 23, 26, 91

Righteous, 91, 207
  Self-, 106, 114
Righteousness, 15, 16, 113
  Self-, 98, 107, 114

Sacred, the, 90, 121, 129, 132, 133
Salvation, 64, 65, 139, 160, 200
*Sapientia*, 144, 149, 152; *see also* Wisdom
*Sapor*, 149, 152; *see also* Taste
Satire, 98, 100, 101, 103, 104, 107, 111
*Schola caritatis*, 160; *see also* Love, school of
Scripture(s), 2, 3, 7, 10, 18, 20, 22, 23, 33, 39, 50, 51, 56, 90, 103, 122, 123, 180, 182, 183, 194; *see also* New Testament; Old Testament
Seeing, 26–28, 172, 197, 199, 200
Seeker(s), 31, 59, 60, 97
Self, 5, 6, 13, 26, 27, 33, 46, 62, 69, 71, 113, 124, 128–31, 133, 134, 136, 138–42, 145, 146, 148, 161, 162, 166, 169, 170, 172, 173, 179, 188, 189, 193, 196, 201, 205, 206
  Development of, 128, 164
  Self-forgetful(ness), 35, 43, 80, 189
  Self-indulgent, 115, 119
  Self-interest(ed), 75, 131, 140, 141, 173–76
  Self-knowledge, 25, 31, 41, 114, 146, 160, 170
  Self-love, 70, 126–29, 133, 134, 138–40, 143, 146, 154, 164, 165, 170, 175, 177, 178, 189
  Self-realization, 27, 142, 165, 176
  Self-revelation, 59, 105, 204
  Self-righteous(ness), 98, 106, 107, 114
Selfish(ly), 71, 135, 139, 143, 165, 175, 178, 180
Selfishness, 176, 179
Selfless, 176
Senses, 24, 29, 35, 94, 96, 136, 137, 149, 176
Shadow(s), 20–37 *passim*, 39, 56, 60, 91, 148, 171, 203
Shadowy, 24, 33
*Sicuti est*, 10, 24–28, 32, 62, 72
Silence, 29, 115, 182, 210–12
Simplicity, 16, 103, 117, 152, 153, 189, 192, 193
  God's, 189, 192, 193
Sin(s), 52, 58, 63, 76, 88, 93, 126, 133, 134, 139, 143, 158, 168, 178, 180, 189, 191, 192, 197, 199
  Original, 134
Sinful, 57, 93
Sinner(s), 191, 207, 208
Slave, 127, 131, 140, 143, 154, 173, 175, 177, 180
Socratism, Christian, 114
Son, 10–14, 16, 18, 20, 23, 39, 49, 50, 54, 66, 112, 127, 140, 143, 154, 201; *see also* Father
  Of God, 7, 9, 62, 65, 69
Song of Songs, 2, 21, 22, 112; *see also* Bernard, Works
Sorrow, sorrowful, 20, 74, 83, 91, 92; *see also* Grief
Soul(s), 3, 10, 11, 14–22, 24–31, 33, 35, 36, 42, 48, 52, 58, 62, 63, 72, 73, 76, 77, 80, 81, 88, 89, 96, 97, 110, 115–17, 120, 127, 131–34, 136, 137, 139, 142, 150, 152–54, 162, 176,

Subject Index  237

189, 190, 193, 197, 201–3, 207, 208
State of, 30, 114, 127, 144, 205
Speech, 20, 71, 109, 115, 141, 148, 201, 211, 212
Spirit, 4, 12–14, 27, 28, 32, 35, 36, 39, 47, 52, 56, 58, 62–64, 66–70, 72, 73, 76, 77, 79–81, 88, 96, 110, 112, 115, 132, 134, 152, 154, 181, 182, 189, 206–9
  Holy Spirit, 9, 10, 12–14, 18, 34, 38, 45–48, 52, 53, 55, 63, 66, 70, 76, 77, 121, 149, 196
  Of this world, 206
  Prophetic, 193
  Unity of, 74
States (of life, of the soul, etc.), 30, 36, 62, 110, 113, 114, 127, 144, 193, 205
Suffer, 51, 74, 80, 83, 85, 93, 143, 192
Suffering(s), 65, 85, 88, 106
Sun, 2, 3, 11, 27, 33, 45, 112, 135, 191
  Of Justice, 27
  Of Righteousness, 113
Superfluity, Superfluities, 102, 103, 115, 118, 123
Swaddling clothes, *see* Clothing, clothes

Taste(s) (n., v.), 3, 26, 34, 37, 63, 117, 118, 141, 149, 152; *see also* Sapor
Teacher, 8, 10, 14, 18, 30, 31, 41, 150, 193
Tents of Kedar, 83, 89, 90, 92
Theology, 6, 21, 24, 39, 43, 57, 156, 157, 182

Thought, 2, 5, 6, 21, 124, 147, 157, 161, 168, 170, 172, 174, 188, 190
Transcendence, 62, 137, 153
Transformation, 38, 45, 59, 77, 78, 95, 109, 142, 146, 196, 200, 208
Transparency, 7, 121, 122, 147, 154
Trinity, 9, 10, 12, 14, 15, 17, 19, 39, 86, 159, 201
Triunity, 8
Truth, 1, 4, 8, 12, 15, 16, 21, 32, 33, 35, 46, 59, 77, 79, 87, 88, 92, 131, 143, 145, 152, 160, 162, 163, 166, 207–9
Truths, 8, 149, 160
Type(s), scriptural, 21, 22, 39

Ugliness, 93, 94, 105–7, 111, 151
Ugly, 84, 94, 96, 107
Unconscious (adj., n.), 115, 126, 129, 132, 134, 148, 151, 153, 180
Understanding, 2, 6, 15, 20, 35, 41, 48, 55, 56, 68, 84, 101, 111, 117, 129, 135, 139, 149, 156, 162, 164, 166–68, 196, 198, 200, 201
  Christian, 30
  Human, 10, 45–48, 51, 55, 69
  Spritual, 47, 49
Union, 14, 24, 41, 50, 57, 58, 74, 75, 82, 121, 152, 162, 163, 165
  Hypostatic, 8
  Mystical, 189
  With God, 6, 41, 82, 85, 157
  With the Spirit, 52
Unity, 12, 13, 28, 43, 47, 65, 74, 99, 110–13, 116, 123, 128, 153, 197; *see also* Diversity; Reciprocity; Spirit

Unjust, the, 205–8
Unlikeness, 11, 150, 208
  Land of, 63, 207
Unmeasured, 102, 106, 120, 151, 198, 212; *see also* Measure; Measureless
Unmeasuredness, 198

Vanity, 147, 157, 161, 171, 174
Virtue(s), 3–6, 34, 37, 46, 61, 65, 74, 78, 79, 97, 104, 115, 120, 126, 130, 135, 149, 165, 166, 172, 173, 189, 195, 198, 200
Vision(s), 11, 19, 25–31, 33, 35, 37, 39, 44, 51, 55, 58, 66, 86, 89, 95, 99, 100, 111, 114, 123, 162, 175, 177, 187, 199, 200, 201, 203, 205, 206; *see also* Face, to face
  Beatific, 162, 203
  Of God, 10, 26, 28, 30, 35, 197, 199, 200–203, 205
  Of heaven, 25, 60, 95

White monks, *see* Cistercian(s)
Wicked, the, 10, 34, 137, 138, 206, 207
Will(s), 13, 26, 31, 41, 42, 47, 48, 55, 67, 124, 125, 133, 140–43, 151, 163, 165–67, 169, 170, 172, 173, 175, 180, 194, 195; *see also* Free choice, Free will
  Act of, 165
Wine, 75, 80, 116, 141
  Of charity/love, 73, 74, 80–82
Wisdom, 12, 15, 16, 30, 31, 73, 74, 76, 77, 79, 91, 92, 97, 105, 112, 133, 144, 145, 149, 152, 153, 156, 164, 194–96, 198, 204; *see also* Sapientia
Word (the incarnate), 2, 4, 5, 10, 11, 13–17, 19, 20, 22, 23, 25, 26, 29–32, 52, 54, 56–60, 73, 75–77, 81, 82, 86, 89, 108, 112, 132, 149, 190, 194, 195
Writer(s), 3, 41, 54, 55, 188, 212
Writing(s), 23, 39, 41, 104, 109, 132, 179, 180, 211, 212
  Bernard's, 5, 41, 43, 44, 117, 133, 153, 157, 164, 180, 182

Zeal, 46, 53, 79, 86, 191
  For justice, 191, 195
  For virtue, 3, 45, 61, 63, 78, 172

www.ingramcontent.com/pod-product-compliance
Lightning Source LLC
Chambersburg PA
CBHW030438300426
44112CB00009B/1062